Unless one has gone through adversity and come out again into the sunlight, there is no way to describe the desolation of the soul such times can generate . . .

What good comes from such times of trial? The sweetest gift is the restoration of faith and that is what this book is about. It is a personal statement of faith that needs to be shared with others who find themselves in a similar situation. Its message is this: so long as the inner light be lit, the darkness cannot overcome it.

∼

About the Author

Dolores Ashcroft-Nowicki is one of the most respected and experienced esoteric practitioners currently at work in the British Isles. She teaches to packed seminars worldwide. Her most recent publication is *Magical Use of Thought Forms*, with J. H. Brennan (Llewellyn, 2001). See her website (dolores.ashcroft-nowicki.com) or the SOL website (servantsofthelight.org) for current information.

ILLUMINATIONS

MYSTICAL MEDITATIONS ON THE HEBREW ALPHABET

THE
HEALING
OF
THE SOUL

DOLORES ASHCROFT-NOWICKI

2003
Llewellyn Publications
St. Paul, Minnesota 55164-0383, U.S.A.

FIRST EDITION
First Printing, 2003

Book design by Rebecca Zins
Chapter opener illustration ©Dover Medieval Illustrations
Cover background and gold leafing images ©PhotoDisc
Cover design by Lisa Novak
Editing by Jane Hilken and Rebecca Zins
Interior illustrations by Llewellyn Art Department
Mudra illustrations on pages 132 and 133 by Kevin R. Brown

Library of Congress Cataloging-in-Publication Data
Ashcroft-Nowicki, Dolores.
   Illuminations : mystical meditations on the Hebrew alphabet : the healing of the soul / Dolores Ashcroft-Nowicki.—1st ed.
      p. cm.
   ISBN 0-7387-0186-6
   1. Cabala.   2. Hebrew language—Alphabet—Miscellanea.   I. Title.

BF1623.C2A84 2003
135'.47–dc21   2003040082

Llewellyn Publications
A Division of Llewellyn Worldwide, Ltd.
P.O. Box 64383, Dept. 0-7387-0186-6
St. Paul, MN 55164-0383, U.S.A.
www.llewellyn.com

Printed in the United States of America

Acknowledgments

My heartfelt thanks go to:

Alma Stephens, who was an endless supply of help and advice.

Dr. Stanley Cohen, for his encouragement and for making me feel that I was doing something worthwhile. I will always be indebted to you.

Nancy Mostad at Llewellyn, who knew exactly why this had been written, and who had been there, and found her way out of the dark tunnel. Bless you, Nancy.

Colin Wilson, for permission to use the quotation from *Frankenstein's Castle*, and for writing some of the most interesting books in the last fifty years. Thank you, Colin, and please keep writing.

Herbie and Jackie Brennan, dear, staunch friends of many years, who always listen patiently when I ring up to moan about things . . . which is frequently.

Michael, my husband, who not only keeps the office running like clockwork but cooks wonderful meals and stands behind me like a large Polish rock when I need support.

My children, Tamara and Carl, who put up with people constantly asking them, "Is your mother the one who writes those strange books?" . . . and still love me.

Rabbi Michael L. Munk, whose book *The Wisdom in the Hebrew Alphabet* was my constant companion for eight months. I have never met you, Rabbi, but you have my deepest respect.

The Aleph-Beth, the letters, who began it all by revealing themselves to me that day, and dancing for me.

~

To those who have never ceased to believe in the truth,
and to my Inner Companion who walks with me constantly.

Contents

Foreword by Stanley Cohen . . . ix

Foreword by Gareth Knight . . . x

Preface . . . xi

Introduction . . . xiii

Pronunciation of the Hebrew Letters and Sephiroth . . . xxi

〜 THE LETTERS 〜

Aleph . . . 1

Beth . . . 15

Gimel . . . 29

Daleth . . . 43

Heh . . . 57

Vav . . . 71

Zayin . . . 83

Cheth . . . 97

Teth . . . 113

Yod . . . 127

Kaph . . . 141

Lamed . . . 155

Mem . . . 169

Nun . . . 183

Samech . . . 195

Ayin . . . 211

Peh . . . 227

Tzaddi . . . 245

Qoph . . . 259

Resh . . . 273

Shin . . . 287

Tau . . . 299

Wheel of the Letters and Their Correspondences . . . 318

Epilogue . . . 320

Paths on the Tree of Life . . . 321

Tarot Cards on the Tree of Life . . . 322

Appendix: The Work of Wisdom and Understanding
by Salomo Baal-Shem . . . 323

Further Reading . . . 331

Index . . . 332

Foreword

There is a tradition of meditation and self-awareness in many Western religions that is often forgotten. Science has been so successful that we prefer its objective logic to the subjective magic of an emotional or spiritual experience as a way of discovering truth.

But now many scientists realize that their theories depend on the laws of physics, which themselves needed to be brought into existence at some stage. In branches of science like medicine, ethical problems arise which underline the fact that science can tell us "how" but not "why." We do not know Who made the rules, nor why He made them.

In this book, Dolores Ashcroft-Nowicki shows us how to open our minds to meditation and self-awareness using the letters of the Hebrew alphabet. In Jewish Cabbalistic tradition these letters existed before the universe was created and contain all the spiritual power of that creation. Dolores believes that each one of us has an inner source of knowledge from which we can learn about G-d. Her work is to be applauded as it is crucial to our humanity that we understand His ways from within ourselves. I hope that this book enables each reader to become more aware of those eternal fundamental truths that lie within his or her innermost being.

STANLEY COHEN

Foreword

Dolores Ashcroft-Nowicki has probably done more than any other teacher in her generation to bring the practical elements of the secret wisdom to so large a number of students spread over so wide a geographical area over so long a period of time. She is a pioneer of what might be called the "esoteric workshop" movement and has traveled the world tirelessly, bringing to her students a rare depth of knowledge and experience, to say nothing of an example of dedicated commitment.

The book you have before you is perhaps the most important piece of writing that she has done. It goes back to the first principles in Qabalistic studies, concentrating on the symbolism of the Hebrew alphabet, which is fundamental to most Western esotericism, Jewish or gentile. In the beginning was the Word, and it is the use and development of language that marks the spiritual distinction between humankind and the animal kingdom. The fundamental building blocks of written language, and particularly the language of the sacred books, provide an ancient key upon which centuries of meditation have been spent. It was Dion Fortune's contention that such accumulated wisdom could be tapped by whoever set about it in the right way. Dolores, in this book, provides ample guidance on finding that right way.

She has had to dig deep within herself to provide the material for this book, and she also casts her net wide, giving instruction in meditation, visualization exercises, and simple ritual performance by the lone student. This may not be the Qabalism of the library guru or of the ivory tower esotericist, but it is a sleeves-rolled-up, no-nonsense approach to practical occult development that at the same time maintains the essential sense of reverence to the divine power that the alphabet of the secret wisdom represents.

One warning: it will be hard work! But if the way to the Mount of Illumination be a hard and long one, at least with the help of Dolores' book, that way has been made plain.

GARETH KNIGHT

Preface

Unless one has gone through the utter darkness of trial and adversity and come out into the sunlight once more, there is no way to describe the desolation of the soul such times can generate. Some people go through it many times during their lifetime and still manage to keep smiling.

The cause is often one of perception, for when fate puts one into a position others perceive as being powerful, it can and often does invite jealousy, adverse criticism, and often, outright hatred. W. E. Butler, my late and much-loved teacher, once told me that power often goes to those who do not seek it. I have experienced it myself and have seen it happen to people I admire and respect and I've seen the pain it brings them. It can be likened to being the lead goose in a skein flying south. The point bird deflects the buffeting wind from its fellows so they may fly more easily. However, there the similarity ends for while the lead goose is relieved by those on either side on a regular basis, a human leader more often than not has to go the whole distance. This is a fact that those who aggressively seek power do not anticipate or fully understand, and will inevitably come to regret when the wheel turns full circle, as it always does.

When the dark night of the soul falls upon you, what can you do? Nothing; it must be endured and its lesson learned. Slowly and painfully, everything is taken from you—knowledge, faith, and strength, both physical and spiritual; all are gone. Friends you thought you would never lose desert you one by one; those who stay are treasures to be cherished. Though you may not know or believe it, you are never entirely alone at such times. There are always a few whose love never wavers, and there is the Inner Guardian who walks beside you, unseen and unfelt but ever present. You, as a spiritual being, never quite reach the end of either strength or faith, though it may feel like it. Often you think you have reached the end of the darkness only to find yourself plunged back into it again and again.

Such events can happen when the unseen levels are changing and your soul is reaching out for a higher plane, though the human personality may scream against the cost. Only when the spiritual warrior has been tempered by fire and water, time after time, does the darkness gradually lift. Faith and hope return and the whole experience manifests as increased knowledge and wisdom. Then you have to piece it together.

You begin to understand the gift of love given to you by those who supported you through the trial. Your faith is stronger and deeper for the testing. But you now face the tasks of manifesting the lessons learned, and one of these is to forgive. To forgive unconditionally is harder than enduring the dark night itself. It is a task that often takes the rest of one's lifetime to achieve, if at all.

What good comes from such times of trial? The sweetest gift is the restoration of faith and that is what this book is about. It is a personal statement of faith that needs to be shared with others who find themselves in a similar situation. The message is this: so long as the inner light be lit, the darkness cannot overcome it.

"Blessed are ye when men shall revile you and persecute you and shall say all manner of things against you falsely, for my sake. Rejoice and be exceeding glad for great is your reward in heaven: for so persecuted they the prophets which were before you."

MATTHEW 5:11–12

Introduction

I am not a Hebrew scholar; I do not speak or read Hebrew. So why do I have the temerity to write a book like this? Because I have spent over thirty years of my life working with the Qabalah and the Western Mystery Tradition, and the Aleph-Beth has become a living part of that life. I feel its presence around me every day, especially in times of great stress. I have tried to approach the subject with due respect for a religion that is not my own. I have not touched upon the variations of the letters but simply used the basic forms with which I myself am familiar. Similarly, I have kept away from the various assignments of letters and Tarot cards and kept solely to those with which I am accustomed to working. If you disagree with me, I suggest you switch things around to suit yourself. I know there are other applications of both, but to deal with all of them would have meant running to two volumes!

In light of these shortcomings I apologize in advance to those whose knowledge and expertise is far greater than mine. My only excuse is that the Aleph-Beth called to me and I answered.

It may seem strange to those who know little of the Mysteries that one born and baptized a Christian (albeit a very unorthodox one) should lean so heavily on the symbols of another faith. However, is it another faith? It has been said that all roads lead to God, or by whatever name you use to call upon your deity. Only on Earth are beliefs divided. Jesus lived and died a Jew. He was *never* a Christian; that term came into use after his death, and was probably introduced by Paul. Jesus practiced the religion into which he was born. Granted, he did not teach it in the way of his time but he was *still a Jew*. In that case, I will take what I need from any source, so long as it is of the Light.

This book is born of experience that I want to share. I have no time for the "mine all mine" grip on knowledge. What I have learned and found useful, I teach in workshops and in books. If others can benefit from it, good; if they can't use it now, they may do so later. Either way, knowledge should be shared, not kept for a favored few. I have often said that teachers are rungs on the ladder of knowledge;

they are there to help a student reach the fullest ability in their chosen field. The symbol of a ladder does not mean teachers are there to treat as a mundane tool— far from it; if a student needs a lesson, the rung can give way, taking them down a peg or two! However, for a worthy student, the rung can be a support. Figuratively, a good teacher is the understanding virtue of Binah. A good student is a pearl of great price. Both are hard to come by.

The Beginning

Let me begin by stating the obvious. In religious circles, it has always been assumed that matter was created by the One from its own substance. (Please note I will not be drawn into the God versus Goddess argument. I regard God as an all-gender being.) However, it seems to me as a purely personal theory that it would make more sense to suppose that not one but two primal entities sought each other out from opposite ends of space and came together in a cosmic mating. The result of this was a cosmic conception, a child equaling matter, an event resulting in a melding of all three. This would explain the three-in-one idea we see occurring in many religions around the world. Perhaps the spectacle of two galaxies colliding, as photographed by the Hubble telescope, is a miniature version of this event, the first of the "as above, so below" examples. Nothing in the universe is inanimate; it is part of a living whole. Whatever was, has been, or will be created in the future comes from this primal triune entity.

This book includes the twenty-two letters of the Aleph-Beth, for it is held by wiser men and women than I that each letter is the living energy pattern of a being of grace and power. Each letter holds, controls, and can dispense a certain type of power. The core of this power can be found in a study of the shape, placement, and inner meaning of the letter itself. There are many variations both in spelling and pronunciation, so I decided to stay with one form to avoid confusion.

This is not a book about the finer points of Hebrew, but how one person found comfort and strength in a set of ancient, powerful, and symbolic forms. These forms are primal, powerful, and highly spiritual forces that enabled the One to implement its ideas.

We are told "In the beginning was the Word"; this implies there must already have been letters that formed the Word itself. Furthermore, before the utterance of the Word must come the indrawn breath to empower it. If this is so, or even if it is not, we have twenty-two very different powers to call on in times of need, powers that will answer when called and assist where possible.

A few years ago, I went through a time of great stress when I felt I could no longer cope with what was going on in my life. I felt powerless to deal with things on a physical level so I turned to the spiritual, as we all do at such times. At first it seemed that no help would be offered; then one day I began to draw the familiar shapes of the Aleph-Beth over and over with the help of a Jewish primer, a child's Aleph-Beth book. In doing so I discovered many things; one was that there are really just a few basic shapes that are used and presented in different combinations. Sometimes a curved shape is straightened (*poshut*); sometimes the tail is curved (*kofoofa*). Most but not all of the forms of the Aleph-Beth are constructed from combinations of the Yod ׳, the Vav ׀, the Zayin ׀, and the Daleth ׳. For instance, the Aleph א is composed of two Yods placed on either side of a Vav with its foot pointing to the right. Time spent with each letter soon shows you how the letters are combinations of these basic shapes.

As you become familiar with the shapes, the idea can be taken deeper into Western Tradition and different combinations will lead you into deeper realizations. For instance, the Yod, Daleth, and Vav can then become the father, son, and holy spirit. In imagery, this becomes the hand, the door, and the nail. We can take the hand as the creative instrument of the father. The door, as the human woman, was opened by the divine hand, enabling the son (the nail) to manifest on the physical level. The nail is the intent that holds the upper and lower levels together and in doing so becomes an integral (third) part of the whole. Esoterically it is the crook and the flail over the Djed or spine of Osiris.

At the time I had these thoughts, they led to a meditation in which the Aleph became a scarlet vortex from which protruded two smaller vortices. This in turn became an image of Job listening to the voice of the One speaking from within the whirlwind. As I was feeling very like Job at the time, it seemed an apt image. Then the whirlwind engulfed me and for several minutes I was very disoriented. During the next twenty minutes or so, the strength and reassurance I had asked for in the prayer was "created" (the only word that fits the feeling) within the heart and solar plexus simultaneously. I felt renewed and replenished, physically and spiritually.

The feeling lasted for several days, then slowly diminished but has never entirely left me.

Inspired and encouraged, I began to explore other letters and found that each had a different kind of strength to share with me. Slowly and surely, I was led back to the path I thought I had lost. Closer contact with each letter resolved itself into a cross between a prayer and an invocation until I had twenty-two signposts illuminating the way for my sorely tried spirit to find its way back home.

For the first time I understood that adversity can sometimes be a blessing in disguise, directing one's attention to a certain area that needs to grow and expand through the trials that one faces. When I began to write this book, preparing to share the prayers that are the core and the heart of it, the power built up even though the circumstances that brought about their creation are now different. I have never lost contact with the powers of the Aleph-Beth since I began to work with them on a regular basis.

When they manifest in a meditation, they bring with them an overwhelming feeling of love and support. This sense of being surrounded by an invisible yet palpable strength is the gift of the beings that constitute the living power of the Aleph-Beth. This is not to be seen or experienced as something sweet and sugary, but as an injection of strength, will, and the ability to endure. These influences are nothing like the sentimental angels so beloved of the Victorian era. They are powerful primal presences that carry out their tasks with total obedience to the One.

On pages 318–319, you will find a wheel chart with the Hebrew letters, their images, numbers, and values that can be used as an aid to visualization. However, before using this book as a spiritual journey, you need to spend time looking at the combinations of shapes that form the actual letters.

I suggest you copy the whole Aleph-Beth to keep as a reference. Draw on scraps of paper with a black felt tip to get the feel and flow of the letters. Do these two or three times, then you will have a basic grasp of the shape and form of the letters and their component parts. The best way to do this is to use a child's Hebrew lettering book. It is similar to Chinese calligraphy.

When you feel confident with the shape, draw a permanent set in black felt pen on thick white paper in a size that is quickly and easily recognized. Then you are ready for the first exercise. For this you will need a blindfold. For best results in visualization, a close-fitting blindfold provides a background for internal vision.

You also need quiet and privacy. Music can help to set the mind free in meditation; Baroque music played softly at the threshold of hearing can be soothing and encourages the building of memory tracks, though some prefer quiet.

Visualize as many of the Hebrew letters as you can remember. Against the darkness of the inner screen, see them in brilliant colors. Make them move or turn slowly on their axis. Look for their component parts and see how they are put together to form a greater whole. Select one letter and dismiss the others—Aleph is an easy choice for this experiment because its shape suggests a butterfly. Imagine an Aleph made up of many layers on top of each other. Each layer is an Aleph in a different color. Peel away the top Aleph (as if it was a Post-It note) and let it float away like a butterfly. Do this three or four times. Each copy of the Aleph is a new color, and soon you are surrounded by a flight of floating letters. Watch them flutter around you. Using your imagination like this will help you to "fix" the shape in your memory.

Choose a second letter—for example, Yod, for it is easy to remember and to draw. Repeat the instructions and the astral photocopies of the basic letter until it becomes a flock of Yods, but you will see the original letter remains unchanged. Continue this exercise using two letters each day until you have gone through the whole Aleph-Beth. This will help you to memorize them and make them easy to recall. They can be used in meditations as mobile images, as companions or guardians in pathworkings, or as carriers of prayers, petitions, and thanks to the One.

These presences are catalysts; they cause changes in you while remaining themselves, something that is true of all Godforms or primal creations. After a while you will find that although your visual perception of the letters remains the same, the *feel* of them becomes so spiritual that you will begin to experience the power they generate on a very personal level.

After some weeks of working with them, they will begin to reveal as much of their true form as the human mind can deal with. Beings of power and light cannot easily be understood with the limited human understanding at our disposal. Note I do not describe them as angels. They are not angels; they are something else, something far older and more powerful. They are possibly of a similar nature to the *Chaioth Ha Kadesh* or the Four Holy Creatures.

When you have completed your building of the Aleph-Beth, your next task is to quietly contemplate the letters and allow them to communicate with you, something that can often change your whole life. Communication may not happen right away, but in a few days or weeks you will begin to get information from them; not much and often obtuse, but it will come. Simply sit down, build up the image of the letter, and try to see, feel, or accept it as a being; think of it as an alien life form, if that makes it easier. After all, that is basically what it is. Its reality lies elsewhere. It is simply "visiting" with us.

Always bless and courteously dismiss these beings at the end of each meditation and before returning to your own level. Be meticulous in your closing down and always record any results you may have had. This may seem a simple, even childish, exercise, but you will be surprised by the results. Remember, simplicity is the virtue of Kether, the crown of the Tree of Life. Now you have reached a point when you can begin to work with the letters in a more personal way. The two or three weeks of preparation you have already gone through will have attuned your spiritual senses to a slightly finer, higher level.

Without preparation, you will only be able to touch the lower levels of the work and that will not bring the results you hope for. You either go into this work fully or you leave it alone. The desire for speed, and the urge to rush through the necessary preparation for a high-level spiritual experience, is one of the main reasons for the failure of some students to achieve anything of real spiritual value.

The Intent of This Book

The title of the book explains it all. From now on, everything you do, experience, or undergo is designed to illuminate your spiritual self and bring about the meaning of the letter Heh within you. The image given for this letter is that of a window. The real image is that of incoming light, or enlightenment in its truest form.

Each chapter begins with the prayer of the letter. It is an invocation to the power of that letter. It takes into account meanings and images as well as the feelings and emotions that were uppermost in my heart and mind at the time of writing. It speaks of the power and strength to be found within the form and grace of the being that was there in the beginning, and is behind the ritual meaning of that letter.

Read the prayer several times, aloud. Record your voice speaking the prayer and listen to the inflection and tone of your voice. Make several recordings; try to make each one different in meaning and understanding. Commit the prayer to memory to make it as perfect as possible. After the prayer, there is a summary of the letter with ideas, images, advice, and information designed to help you deepen your realizations in the meditations. As you go deeper into the world of the letters, you will find personal images rising from the subconscious, bringing valuable insights with them. All this will enrich your spirit, your mind, your physical life, and your environment.

The letters are a living part of the original Word of Creation. Because of this, they are inextricably linked with the ongoing evolution of this universe. The whole point and meaning of their existence is to create, to teach, and to empower, so working with them cannot help but bring their powers into your life. It is as simple as that. When you work with glue, your fingers stick together; when you paint, you get paint over you; when you dig in the garden, you get earth under your fingernails. When you work with the letters of the creative Word, you get more creative, often to the point of re-creating yourself! After the summary there are meditations and these lead to a specially written pathworking. When you have worked through the book, you will begin to feel the need to create your own inner workings. From this the next step is working slowly toward teaching others; however, this takes time. Some people think the reading of a few books and the attending of a few workshops bestows the right to teach others all the things you do not know yourself!

Go through the Aleph-Beth slowly. If you are an experienced practitioner of the Mysteries (five years or more), a letter a week is fine. If you have little experience or need to give more time to them, one every ten days is better. Once through the entire Aleph-Beth, review your notes and diary records. (Yes, you must keep records, how else can you judge your progress?) At the end of your work, put it aside for a few months, then do it all again, taking two letters a week. The second time around is when the power really starts to flow.

After the pathworkings are psalms and poems; some are taken from the Old Testament and were chosen to fit with the letter and its inner meaning, others are paraphrased from them. The poems are mostly taken from the *Oxford Book of Mystical Verse*. Read them carefully. Each psalm, like the prayers given in this book, is a hymn of praise, a request for help, or a thanksgiving for help received. They hold within them the sonic and visual powers of an ancient tradition, far older than the pyramids, as old in fact as the Word that created them.

The psalmists were aware of the power of music and words linked to visualization. So try to visualize the events and pictures painted by the psalmist as if they were happening before you. Do the same with the poems. Look for links between the psalm and the prayer and enhance your daily meditations with them. Finally comes a solo ritual connecting them together. The aim is to forge a link between you as a human being and the inheritor of the Point of God Within. Moreover, as you move from one area to the next, you will feel the living power contained within each letter of the Aleph-Beth growing within you.

I cannot promise the work will be easy; something that is worth having can only be won with effort, and the companionship of the beings of the Aleph-Beth is worth having. If you are serious about studying the Mysteries, then hard work will inspire you. If the thought of it deters you, then give up the world of sacred science—it is not for you. Together we stand at the beginning of an adventure. The journey is one I have already taken and I will be beside you all the way.

Pronunciation of the Hebrew Letters and Sephiroth

When copying or reading the names and written examples, remember that Hebrew is both read and written from right to left.

There are two main expressions of Hebrew, Ashkenazi and Sephardic. Both are further colored by being adapted to the local/regional accent. I have kept to the one that I was taught and which I recommend, but if you have a preference, then use the way most acceptable to you.

Letter = pronunciation
Aleph = Alef
Beth = Bet/Beis
Gimel = as spelled
Daleth = Dalet
Heh = Heh/Hey
Vav = Vav/Vau
Zayin = Zain
Cheth = Hes/Het (there is no *th* sound, as in *think*, in Hebrew)
Teth = Tet/Tes
Yod = Yod/Yud
Kaph = Hof/Chof (the sound of *ch* in *loch*)
Lamed = as spelled
Mem = as spelled
Nun = Noon
Samech = Samek
Ayin = Eyein
Peh = as spelled
Tzaddi = Zaddee
Qoph = Kof/Kuf
Resh = as spelled
Shin = Shhin with a sibilant *s*
Tau = Taw/Tav

Sephiroth (plural)
Sephira (singular)

Sephira = pronunciation
Kether = Keter
Chokmah = Hokma
Binah = Beenah
Chesed = Hesed
Geburah = Gevoora
Tiphereth = Tiferet
Netzach = Netza/Netzach with a
   guttural *ch*
Hod = as spelled
Yesod = Yesood
Malkuth = Malkoot

~ THE LETTERS ~

ALEPH

Thou art the first, the servant of God,
the ever-becoming One.
Out of the darkness you came
into the pale light of a primal dawn,
bringing the gift of yourself.
Thou art the breath of each new day
that marks the onward march of time,
a new beginning offered without flaw
that we may serve the Most High.
Thou art strong like the ox,
for the earth sustaineth thee.
Thou are the foremost, the leader.
Let me know thy strength, holy Aleph.
Let it become like a tree, rooted within me.
Make me strong,
that I may endure the tests of life with fortitude.
At the Aleph of my birth you were there.
Be thou present at the Tau of my ending.

Image: Ox
Symbol: א
Path on the Tree of Life: 11
Numerical Value: 1

Prayer

The prayer asks for the kind of strength personified by the image of the ox. The virility of the animal and its size and protective instincts toward its progeny make it an ideal father or protector symbol. This fits in with the word *abba,* meaning "father." It begins and ends with the letter A and reads the same both forward and backward. The biblical name *Barabbas* means "Son of the Father." This information can lead you into some deep thoughts and offer new interpretations of the old controversy that a volunteer took the place of Jesus on the cross and that, under the name of Barabbas, he was released and went into hiding; it may also come up during your meditations on this first letter.

The prayer speaks of the first dawn (Creation) and the power of the Aleph as the indrawn breath of the One just before the actual vocalizing of the first creative sound. In one sense, every dawn is a first, for every dawn sees a new life born somewhere, and also a death leading as it does toward a new, unknown experience. No two days since Creation began have ever been the same, nor will they ever be the same; each is unique and is held in the mind of God forever. *Aleph to Tau,* say the Jews, meaning *first to last,* like the gentile saying *Alpha and Omega* or *A to Z.*

The prayer when spoken aloud creates in the speaker the vibrations of this primal letter, summoning the strength and the will to carry on against the odds. It speaks of a new beginning offered without flaw, for often in our darkest times we long for a chance to begin again and erase previous mistakes. When speaking the prayer, stand in the position of the Aleph with your back straight, arms slightly extended from the sides, one hand facing up and the other down.

The earth from which we come and to which we return is one of the four great elements, and is under the regency of Uriel, an archangel deeply committed to the welfare of humanity as a whole. Visualize Uriel standing behind the Aleph in the same attitude and facing you. This is the position in which a dervish dances; as he whirls around, he becomes aware of his inner divine self as the center of a personal universe. One hand, facing up, directs the power of the Godhead to the heart center; the other, facing down, guides it onward to the earth. The prayer seeks the strength of the Aleph, describing the letter as the servant of God, and asks for that strength to be deeply rooted so the tests of the dark night of the soul may be endured. The final lines are poignant for, as the first created independent being, Aleph is present at each birth, as the final letter Tau is with us at death.

The Letter

Aleph is composed of a diagonal Vav from either side of which projects a Yod. One points upward, the other down, signifying that what is above can also be found below. In this way, Aleph is seen as a link between the Creator and its creation and as a symbolic Jacob's ladder. The value of a Yod is ten, making the two of them add up to twenty, plus six for the value of Vav equals twenty-six. This is the same value as the Tetragrammaton, and that again links the Aleph with the Creator. This shape can also be seen as the classic attitude of a religious figure shown by artists in religious paintings—across all denominations we see the same structure, a straight or diagonal line with two extensions in many cruciforms—while the same positioning of hands is found in religious pictures and icons of the medieval and Byzantine periods. The basic shape and form of the Aleph is seen in the symbols of both gods and saints all through the Mysteries.

Once you know what to look for, you can trace the power and meaning of the letter Aleph all through classical art. Most artists of the past were familiar with the symbols of the Mysteries and, of course, Hebrew was a language much used in those times, along with Greek and Latin. When the form of this symbol is understood, you can look for what the artist is trying to express and interpret it in your own way, according to what is obtained in meditation.

The symbol always hints that something in the picture has a double meaning, one pertaining to the everyday world and one to the spiritual world. It certainly makes one look at art in a different way. Take any of these symbols or pictures and use them as a thrust block for your meditation on the letter. By using association chains, your mind will be led from one realization to another. You will find yourself watching as people talk; you'll recognize the Aleph in their stance: hands out, one up and one down, the body between and the head slightly inclined. This body language is saying that though they are telling you one thing, there is a hidden meaning underneath.

The power of the letters leaps out at you from all directions. If they are indeed beings sprung from the primal vibration of the creative Word, then they must contain within themselves the knowledge and understanding of all that is to come. They have much to communicate to us, if we ask. That alone is worth the effort endured to grasp it. They are the sum total of knowledge, because they came into existence already holding all the knowledge that would be in the future. In fact, one might argue that they created themselves. What came first, the letters or the Word?

The Aleph in Hermetic terms could be said to show the three pillars of the Tree of Life. The Vav becomes the Middle Pillar of harmony that combines the influences of the other two. The upward-looking Yod patterns the Silver Pillar of male potency and force, while the downward-facing Yod is the manifesting power of the Black Pillar. The two Yods by themselves exemplify the "as above, so below" teaching in their reflection of each other.

The shape of the Aleph shows itself to be a square, prophesying the four main elements to come. What does this tell us about the fourfold power of the Aleph? The first power is that of balance; the second, strength; the third is endurance; and finally integrity. The ox, the magical image of Aleph, stands square with four feet planted firmly in the earth. Its size and strength warn the unwary to take care. The descending Yod (the Black Pillar of the Temple) speaks of fertility, both physically and in all acts of creativity; creation of any kind needs strength and endurance.

The ascending Yod (the White Pillar of the Temple) aspires to spiritual heights; the Vav holding them together is the Word. When meditating on this letter, one is tempted to keep looking at and concentrating on the whole of it.

When consecrating an altar, each corner is anointed with oil. The symbol of the Aleph is inscribed with oil at its center, so the First Divine Unity as the Echud becomes the foundation of your temple.

Looking at the Tarot trump of the Fool, you will see the same stance. Here the figure steps into a new landscape. One hand holds the wand of power which, because he is a Fool at this stage, is used to carry the bag of memories. The other hand greets the life form that has preceded him.

The Godform of Osiris shows a similar stance, with the arms crossed at right angles. Here we have the middle "spine" or Vav but the extended arms holding the crook and the flail are bent at the elbow with the symbols either crossed or held upright. Nevertheless, the meaning is the same: a central stabilizing power balanced by its two buttresses of force and form, justice and mercy, power descending and power rising. The Calvary cross featuring the crucified Christ shows the balanced power of the physical sacrifice descending into the manifested plane, but both arms (Yods) are raised up as the spirit departs for its natural home.

Do not be surprised to find images that at first glance have no connection. Look deeper and you will find it there. I was plagued by meditational images of orchestral conductors, pianists, and ballet dancers for a whole week before I understood the connection between the Vav (body strength) of the conductor, the pianist, and the ballet dancer. The form and force are needed to keep control of an orchestra, in the hands (the Yods) of the pianist, and in the extended arms and legs of the dancer to provide balance. It comes down to hands equaling strength and will, and the connecting nail equaling body and spine.

Meditations

Try to find time twice a day, once in the morning and once in the evening before going to bed. The longest one should be in the morning when you are refreshed after sleep, and also because the late-night meditation will have sifted through your subconscious during sleep and come up with new ideas.

Aim for fifteen minutes in the morning and ten at night. It's even better if each session can be extended by another five minutes. There are some who find it impossible to sit still for twenty minutes, in which case do not even try. Take an early morning walk instead. The Buddhists practice a walking meditation and so can you. Choose an area where you can walk safely without having to avoid traffic or cross busy intersections. Beaches, parks, or open spaces of any kind are ideal. If you jog or run in the early morning, do it then; you can even meditate while swimming. If all else fails, try contemplation—sit and think about it.

FIRST MEDITATION

Try both kinds of meditation techniques.

Active: 1) Look for and observe the shape of the Aleph in the world around you. 2) When you find such a shape, create a story around it and interact with it in your imagination. 3) Enter the Tarot trump of the Fool and be with him as he begins his journey through the Tree.

Passive: 1) Visualize the Aleph as human size. Watch as it changes color and try to understand what it may mean when filled by a particular color. 2) Be the Aleph. Integrate with it and the being within it.

SECOND MEDITATION

Take this sentence as your first theme: "I will set my hand to the plough of experience and sow the seeds of knowledge."

THIRD MEDITATION

The ox pulling the plough equals strength and endurance. The plough equals the effort. Explore the physical and spiritual meanings of these images.

Pathworking

Path 11 leads from Kether, the point of manifestation, to the first sephira, Chokmah, and is called the Path of the Fool. This is not a derogatory term; its meaning is of someone new and untried coming into the Mysteries. The psalm following the pathworking speaks of the king entering his kingdom, and that is what the Fool is doing. He will lay claim to the world of manifestation. He is a human Aleph, a symbolic Everyman treading the path of physical life. It is an adventure fraught with danger, but the Fool has innocence as a protection. He carries a bag of memories and a white rose as a symbol of hope.

Sit quietly and breathe slowly and deeply for a few minutes. With each breath, allow yourself to sink more deeply into your inner space. Consciously withdraw further and further from the physical world until you can feel the silence within wrapping around you in a warm, soft, safe nest.

You know you are no longer in your own world but outside of time and space. All about you there is a feeling of anticipation and a little apprehension. You can see nothing, yet you know something is about to happen. Far away you see a small red glow; it grows bigger and bigger and blossoms into a blaze of color and light that races across space toward you. You are transfixed.

You are watching the first moments of Creation. Racing behind the light comes the sound. It is like no sound you have ever heard, full of majesty and power; it thunders in your inner ear. It is a voice so mighty, so strong, so powerful, and yet so gentle that you want to weep. (For an emotional and musical comparison, listen to Edward Elgar's "Nimrod" from *Enigma Variations*.)

The light and the sound strike you, sweeping you up, breaking you into a million pieces, then putting you back together again. You are a part of both the light and the sound and something more. The vibrations slow down and break up into smaller pieces, each one of the same substance but subtly different in color, shape, and sound. You see them taking shape, forming and reforming, refining themselves and becoming attuned to their prime purpose: communication.

As things become clearer, the rest of the light and sound vibrations carry on and break up into other forms and shapes. Some are so large you cannot take in the size or make sense of them, others are minute, and all are from the One Source, including you.

You turn back to the shapes you first contacted. They have now divided into twenty-two forms of many colors and shades of colors. Each makes a specific sound as it whirls and dances and vibrates to the ongoing music of the first Word.

One form emerges from the group and draws closer to you. When it was further away it looked your own size; close up it is unbelievably huge. You feel threatened by this and shrink away. It senses your agitation and begins to shrink until it is still large, but comfortably so. The form waits patiently until you feel better, then it makes a sound.

You try to find a way to describe that sound to yourself; the nearest you can say is that it is like a muted silver trumpet, low, vibrant, yet sweet and clear. It lifts the spirit and fires the heart within. The sound comes again. It is speaking to you. It comes closer and waits until you are comfortable with its presence. You can see that it is of a rich glowing red, the red of wine, and along the edge of its shape it glistens with gold. It is the Aleph.

You reach out and touch it. It feels like the skin of a young child. It vibrates with pleasure at your touch and the sound comes again but this time you can understand it. It is touch that is the key. By touching it, you attune yourself to its rate of vibration. Now there is sight, sound, and touch; then you become aware of scent and taste, the smell of earth under a hot sun, a ploughed field on a sunny spring day, and the salty taste of sweat in your mouth. All your senses combine into one super sense and you hear the Aleph's words in your mind:

"You are Life. Welcome, be happy, be strong, endure, and become what you have always been, the inheritor of the Creator's love."

You answer, "Welcome to the world of manifestation, Aleph. With your help, I will become strong, I will endure, and I will be happy. One day I will return to your world. Until then, I ask that you be my companion in my exile from the Creator. With your help I will speak with others of your kind and we will learn together."

Aleph speaks again. "It is for that work that I was created, Life. I will stay with you though you will not always heed my part of the primal Word, or even hear it. But you will learn, and I will learn with you, for I know the destiny that is planned for you."

The other letters come closer and you wonder at their many colors and the wonderful sounds that are their voices. When they speak, it is like distant thunder, yet the power in them is muted so as not to harm you. The Aleph tells you that in time you will get to know and speak with each one of them.

"Ah, Life," says the Aleph. "Let me tell you of myself. I am One, as the Creator is One. I am the first letter of the Ten Commandments and I begin the name of Adonai the Lord God, also Adam the first man, Abraham the blessed, and Aaron the High Priest. I am the crown that you and all humanity will one day wear. That is as it shall please Hashem. Now you must return to your own place of being, but we will accompany you."

The letters gather around and lift you, surrounding you with love and bearing you away through the four levels of existence. You pass through the spiritual level where all is light, then through the mental level that is full of sound and color. In the astral level, you see all the forms, ideas, patterns, and images that have ever been thought of, encased within the matrix of the imagination. Finally, you stand before an archway of stars, the entrance to the physical world.

Aleph moves closer. "Pass through the archway, Life, and may Hashem be with you on your long journey. We will always be near to you; look for us in the world around you."

You turn to look at them once more and smile, for you know that you will be seeing them again, and then you walk through the archway. There is a moment of disorientation, a feeling of falling, a slight bump, and you open your eyes in your own world. However, the memories are still with you. Rest a while and then eat and drink and make sure you are fully aware in your own world once more.

Psalm 24

The Earth is the Lord's and the fullness thereof,

the world and they that dwell therein.

For he hath founded it upon the seas, and established it upon the floods.

Who shall ascend into the hill of the Lord

or who shall stand in his holy place?

He that hath clean hands and a pure heart,

who hath not lifted up his soul unto vanity, nor sworn deceitfully.

He shall receive the blessing from the Lord,

and righteousness from the God of his salvation.

This is the generation of them that seek him, that seek thy face, O Jacob.

Lift up your heads, O ye gates; lift up, ye everlasting doors,

and the King of Glory shall come in. Who is this King of Glory?

The Lord strong and mighty, the Lord mighty in battle.

Lift up your heads, O ye gates, even lift them up,

ye everlasting doors, and the King of Glory shall come in.

Who is this King of Glory?

The Lord of Hosts, he is the King of Glory. Selah [Amen].

Ritual

This ritual shows you how to draw on the power, strength, and endurance of the Aleph. However, when dealing with the first two aspects, understand that the power named is not power over others but over your own negative characteristics. The glory of the Aleph-Beth cannot be denigrated, as the power of the Aleph cannot be corrupted. Neither is the strength to be used against those whom you may see as enemies. Power should be sought in order to control one's faults, or in rare situations to defend one weaker than yourself. Many people who attempt to follow the path of High Magic do so because they want to control the lives of others and because they know deep within they cannot control themselves. To desire power for its own sake is to fall from grace.

The strength of the Aleph is at your disposal to help you accomplish the crowning achievement of your life: to "know thyself." To be able to endure the dark night of the soul with the strength of the spirit is to lift the lower self into the higher self. Approach the ritual with a pure heart and it will open spiritual doors to the eager soul. This book was written to comfort, offer solace, and guide those undergoing a dark night of the soul, so the rituals are designed for one person only. The needs are few and found in most homes. Privacy is important during the work.

A small table and a white cloth will do for an altar; you will also need a candle, a chalice or wineglass filled with wine, water, or fruit juice, a flower, and the letter Aleph. You should learn the prayer of the Aleph by heart. If you cannot do this, record it and place the cassette near your chair where it can be switched on during the ritual. You will also need a bowl of water to which a spoonful of salt has been added. Incense in a burner or a good quality incense stick will help you concentrate. If you do not have a robe, clean fresh clothing is acceptable, preferably in a muted color. Assemble a straight-backed chair with a cushion for your feet and you are ready to begin.

You need to make your working space sacred. Sprinkle the salt and water around the room and, as you circle, speak the following at each quarter: "With salt and water I make this place sacred."

Do the same with the candle, saying: "With flame I illuminate this place of working."

Finally, with incense, circle a third time, saying: "With sweet herbs I hallow this place of intent."

Dip your fingers into the salt and water and touch your forehead, saying: "As it is above." *Bend and touch the floor, saying:* "So it is below." *Touch your right breast, saying:* "I am a child of Light." *Touch your left breast, saying:* "A son/daughter of the Most High." *Clasp hands together on breast, saying:* "And I exist in both the world of the spirit and the world of manifestation."

Place the picture of the Aleph where it can be seen clearly. Take your place in the chair and compose yourself. Breathe deeply and slowly for a few minutes until totally relaxed, then fix your eyes on the Aleph. Look at it intently for at least two to three minutes. Now close your eyes and the after-image should become visible behind your eyelids. Begin to recite the prayer slowly and with meaning. (You should have spent time reading and interpreting the prayer according to your understanding of it before attempting the ritual.) Do not rush it; speak with passion, hope, and desire, as you would to a friend. Open your eyes. Go to the altar, take the candle, and go to the south. Mentally project the shape of the Aleph onto the wall before you. Hold up the candle and draw the Aleph in the air—you do not have to be exact, the outline will do. Say:

"Aleph of the south, the first fire of Creation, I, (your name), come before you asking for your help, as it has been ordained that human beings should do. Ask and you shall receive, we are told. I ask for strength; not the strength I desire but the strength I need in the form that I need it. I do not know myself sufficiently as yet to understand what kind of strength I need. Decide for me until I can decide for myself. Teach me how to use your strength without hurting others. In the name of the One I ask this of you, Aleph of the south."

Bow your head for a minute or two. Return the candle to the altar, take up the chalice, and go to the west. Mentally see the Aleph on the wall before you. With the chalice, draw the shape of the Aleph in the air. Speak:

"Aleph of the west, the first water of Creation, I, (your name), come before you as a supplicant. It has been ordained that human beings must ask for help from our elder brethren and that we will then receive in accordance with our needs. I ask for power; not the power I desire but power in the form I need. I do not yet understand what kind of power I need. Help me to know how to use it wisely. Teach me how to use power safely and without hurting others. In the name of the One I ask this of you, Aleph of the west."

Bow your head for a minute or two. Return the chalice to the altar, take up the flower, and go to the north. Mentally see the Aleph on the wall before you. With the flower, draw the shape of the Aleph in the air. Speak:

"Aleph of the north, the first matter of Creation, I, (your name), come before you as a child of Earth. We have been taught that human beings must ask for help from our elder brethren and that we will then receive what it is needful for us to have. I ask for endurance so I may ride the storms of life and be as a rock for those who need me. Help me to use your gift wisely. Teach me to use it safely and with knowledge. This I ask in the name of the One, Aleph of the north."

Bow your head for a minute or two. Return the flower to the altar, take up the incense, and go to the east. Mentally see the Aleph on the wall before you. With the incense, draw the shape of the Aleph in the air. Speak:

"Aleph of the east, the first word of Creation, I, (your name), come before you as one who would learn. I know that I must ask in order to receive help and blessing from the firstborn. I know that I will be given what I need rather than what I desire. Help me to understand what it is best for me to do. Teach me to fulfill my destiny as a child of the one Creator. I offer my service to the Most High that I may become, in the fullness of time, a true child of Light. Let the power, the strength, and the endurance of the First Breath descend upon me now. In the name of the One I ask this of you, Aleph of the east."

Bow your head and wait for a while, then return the incense to the altar and go back to your chair. Look intently at the Aleph on the altar and impress its form on your retina. Close your eyes and see it in the inner darkness. Try to reach out and contact the being this shape hides. Do not strain, just let it reveal itself to you. If nothing happens, then try again tomorrow. Do not be discouraged. If it does make contact, it may be an image, or a symbol, or by words in your head. Remember and record it as soon as you can.

Open your eyes and go to the altar. Dip your fingers in the salt and water and touch your forehead, saying: "As it is above." *Bend and touch the floor, saying:* "So it is below." *Touch your right breast, saying:* "I am a child of Light." *Touch your left breast, saying:* "A son/daughter of the Most High." *Clasp hands together on breast, saying:* "And I exist in both the world of the spirit and the world of manifestation."

Go to each quarter in turn to bless and thank the Aleph there. Return to the altar and take a sip from the chalice. Put out the candle and the incense and leave the room.

BETH

Thou art my house, my covering,
my place of rest.
Thou art above me and below me
and around me.
Behold, I am enclosed by thee
in the dark of the night
and before the coming of the dawn.
I am surrounded by thy strength
at the ending of the day.
I come unto thee to take my ease
for thou art my foundation
and my encompassment of safety.
The Lord God hath provided many rooms
within thee,
and all are for my delight.
I shall lay down at the coming of night
and take my rest without fear.
For thou art the house of my Soul and
I abideth in thee with joy.

Image: House
Symbol: ב
Path on the Tree of Life: 12
Numerical Value: 2

Prayer

This letter takes as its theme the feeling of safety one has when inside one's home. The very words *home* or *house* give a warm feeling when spoken. Home may be a mansion or a cottage; it can even be the arms of a loved one after a long journey. "Coming home" is a phrase that evokes emotion in almost everyone; we only have to turn to the parable of the prodigal son to know the joy a return can bring and that there is always a welcome, whether it be from people or simply from the land itself.

However, there is more than this within the prayer; there is the need for comfort and the need to return to a place of comfort, consolation, and support. "Behold, I am enclosed by thee in the dark of the night and before the coming of the dawn." This applies not just to the ordinary usage of the words *night* and *dawn*, but more directly to the dark night of the soul. "The Lord God hath provided many rooms within thee, and all are for my delight." In this way I have stated my belief that there are many paths that lead one to the deity; none are derided and all are acceptable in the sight of the One.

The last line can be applied both to the being of Light that empowers the letter and to the One. The latter is the ultimate House of the Soul; the former provides, shall we say, a halfway house offering the promise and the certainty of a welcome ahead. In this way one might regard the Beth as the good samaritan who lifts the weary and beaten soul out of the ditch of self-pity and guides it to a "state of peace and grace" where it can recuperate before going on.

Despite the fact that I travel thousands of miles a year, there is always a feeling of joy when I take the plane from London to Jersey. I see my island coming up out of the sea and give thanks to be safely home. I love traveling and the people I meet, but Jersey is *home*, a place where I feel encompassed by the love of my family and where my family has lived for a hundred years. Home, they say, is where the heart is. When spoken, the prayer surrounds one with the feeling of being blessed by the presence of the deity, and of being protected as by a house. There is a phrase in the Bible that says "and underneath are the everlasting arms." These support and enclose one in safety. This letter also corresponds via its mundane chakra of the planet Mercury to both Hermes, the messenger of the gods, and the archangel Gabriel, who came to Mary in her house in Nazareth to tell her of the coming child.

Stand erect and visualize the Beth before you, life-sized. See Gabriel, or if you prefer Hermes, standing behind the letter with arms outstretched toward you. Repeat the prayer and draw on the power of the letter plus that of the being that ensouls it and that of the archangel; open your heart to receive it. If you are of a different tradition you may wish to use a different form, just be sure that it accords with the inner meaning of the letter.

The Letter

Beth is made of a Daleth and a Vav. It has the value of two but when Daleth and Vav are taken separately it adds up like this: Daleth equals four, plus Vav equals six, for a total of ten. The number ten is seen as a new beginning, nine being the completion before starting again with one.

This letter is the epitome of duality in all its forms and together with the Aleph reminds us of the supernals of the Tree of Life. First there is one; this becomes two, and from the two comes a new beginning, that which is formed by the two and which carries on their influence plus its own added characteristics.

The most obvious duality is that of male and female, husband and wife, for together they make the home into which come their children. In the Western Mysteries, we have the Path of the Hearth Fire, a path considered to be as great in its importance as that of a magus/adept. It is perhaps one of the hardest paths to deal with, for it brings responsibilities as well as heartbreaks and sorrows, joys and laughter. Nevertheless, it also brings some of life's greatest blessings.

This brings us to one of this letter's most significant meanings and powers, for it is the letter that begins the Hebrew word for "blessed" (*Berachah*) and it begins the Torah. The story goes that in the beginning the twenty-two letters adorned the crown of God. When He prepared to create the world, the letters came down and stood before Him, each one asking to be the letter used to begin the Creation. Finally Beth came forward. "Let it all begin with me," it said. "For I begin the word Berachah, then every living thing will use me to bless God." God agreed and so it was. There is a corollary to this story.

After everything was settled, God asked Aleph why it had not come forward to make a claim, for after all it is the first letter. Aleph hung its head and said, "All the other letters stand for more than one; I am just one. I can be no more. I did not think it fitting to make a claim."

God replied to the Aleph in this manner. "Aleph, have no fear, for you were and are the first, you stand before all the rest like a king. You are One and I also am One. It shall be written that I Am and so you will be One with me."

Beth begins many words of importance: *Beth-El* (house of God), *Batei-Midrash* (place of study), *Beth Knesset* (place of gathering). It also begins the name of Binah the third sephira, the great feminine principle, and the lady of the house.

In most cases, a house begins with two people and carries on with the generations that stem from those two. In many countries, a family is spoken of as "a house." We see this shown in many of the ancient writings that speak of the house of Jacob, or the house of Tudor, etc. Some companies in the modern world use the same phrase to indicate they are linked via an overall company, as in the house of Frazier, the house of Dior, etc.

If we look at the shape of Beth, we can see that it indeed has the look of a house with a strong back wall and a sturdy foundation. In the Middle East, most houses in early times were built as two stories, with the day-to-day living space down below and an open-fronted top floor consisting of three walls and a roof where the family often slept at night to keep cool. The front had curtains or reed screens to give privacy. One can see similar houses even today in any Middle Eastern town.

Like the shape of the Aleph, Beth can also be found in art through the ages. In medieval religious paintings, one can see the angled shape of the Beth in the construction of the stable in nativity scenes or in the perfunctory, almost dream-like forms seen in Da Vinci's "The Virgin of the Rocks." Almost 90 percent of medieval paintings have hidden geometry in them, visible only to those with some knowledge of what to look for.

We see in the Tarot card of the Magician something similar to the Beth form. It looks fragile, more of an arbor than a house, but it gives the impression of a structure or enclosure. Here we see the way in which the letters lend each other meaning and power, for the Magus here stands in a very Alephlike way. One hand points up to indicate he draws power from his higher self, the other points down to the elemental weapons on the altar, showing that this is where he will exercise that power. However, he must also exercise caution in his use of that power.

Beth is more than the symbol for a house; it is also a tent. For forty years while they wandered in the desert, tents were the only homes available to the Jews. Each tent was open on one side as a gesture of hospitality to those who passed. However, each tent was turned so that no open side faced another for the sake of privacy.

Beth also symbolizes the house of the spirit, so we can include in this description all sacred locations, from the simple circle of a pagan group to the incredible beauty of Chartres Cathedral, from the austere meetinghouse of the Quakers to the quiet dignity of a synagogue. But there are other houses of the spirit that we cannot ignore: the house of the physical body and the house of the mind.

Human beings vary in their care of the body, from the ultra physical fitness fanatic to the proverbial couch potato who moves only between the table and the television. Some think of the body as the real self and simply live from day to day. They are, in the terms of the philosopher Gurdjieff, the unawakened, and will remain so until, in some future incarnation, they finally wake up. Some wake up intermittently when events in their lives induce a short period of awareness. Some recognize that state as the life they were always meant to live and work toward staying that way. The mind, however, is a different thing altogether, and when it wakes up we can suddenly find ourselves in a very different reality.

Eminent English author Colin Wilson has written in many of his books of the "peak experience." This describes a near-perfect balance between the mind, the spirit, and the body. It can occur when one is at low ebb and all looks dull and hopeless, or it can happen for no obvious reason. We see something, hear something, or some small event occurs that enables us to look at things from a very different angle, almost a different dimension.

In his book *Frankenstein's Castle* (Ashgrove Press, 1980), Wilson writes of American professor of psychology Abraham Maslow, who said, "[I] got tired of studying sick people because they never talked about anything but their illness; so I decided to study healthy people instead."

Professor Maslow soon made an interesting discovery: healthy people frequently had "peak experiences," or flashes of immense happiness. For example, a young mother was watching her husband and children eating breakfast when a beam of sunlight came through the window. It suddenly struck her how lucky she was, and she went into a peak experience. Others Maslow studied began recollecting peak experiences that they had had, but which they had often overlooked at the time. Moreover, as soon as they began thinking about and discussing peak experiences, they began having them regularly. In other words: the peak experience, the moment when the near and the far seem to come together, is a product of vitality and optimism. However, it can be amplified or repeated through reflection, by turning full attention upon it instead of allowing it merely to happen.

The case of the young mother reinforces the point. She was happy as she watched her husband and children eating, but it was an unreflective happiness. The beam of sunlight made her think "I am happy," and instantly intensified it. It is as though we have a mirror inside us that has the power to turn "things that happen" into experience. It seems that thought itself has a power for which it has never been given credit.

I believe, from my work with the letters, that such experiences can be induced if one works with them for extended periods. The Beth of the mind is the temple of thought and, more than that, the temple of *controlled and enlightened* thought. This book is the result of many such moments.

Meditation

Take as your theme the three temples.

There are three temples in which we may worship as a child of Light. The first is the temple of the body. This is like a courtyard where we welcome friends and family and meet and speak with them. We must keep it clean and fresh and make it pleasant to the eye and ear and nose. It should be swept clean and cleansed with water and its walls maintained.

The second temple is that of the mind. This is like an inner room where we may speak together of what is in our hearts and experience the joy of shared knowledge.

The third temple is the house of the spirit, a private sanctuary where we may speak with God and share our innermost thoughts, hopes, dreams, and desires. Seek out the astral level and by the power of thought and the proto-matter (see *Magical Use of Thought Forms* by J. H. Brennan and D. Ashcroft-Nowicki [Llewellyn, 2001]) of the astral, build a courtyard, an inner room, and a sanctuary with as much accuracy as you can. You may use this complex for meditation if you wish.

Pathworking

Sit quietly and gradually withdraw from the world around you. Allow nothing to distract you, just listen to the sound of your own heartbeat and the circulation of the blood in your ears. Deepen the darkness behind your eyes until all sensation is gone and you are alone within the inner silence.

You become aware of movement, the bustle of a crowd of people, noises, dogs barking, cattle lowing, sheep and goats . . . the smell of the animals begins to make itself known to you. Then, as if you had opened your eyes, the darkness lifts and you find yourself in a narrow and very crowded street.

Everyone is going about their business and they take very little notice of you. You walk slowly down the street—more of an alleyway—and look about you. Take note of all that you see and try to remember it for later. You come to the end of the alley and turn into a street almost exactly the same as the one you have left, busier if anything. It is lined with stalls full of vegetables and baskets of hens, ducks, and geese. A stall of bright potteryware catches your eye, and another selling cloth. You wander along, taking in the sights, sounds, and smells.

Now you come to an open space on which some sort of building is taking shape. It is not very big, but bigger than most of the houses you have seen so far. The walls are of bricks made with mud and straw; this is done by women who labor in the hot sun while some of the men carry the dried bricks over to the builders. You offer to help and it is gratefully received. The work is hot and you make frequent trips to the water jar standing in the corner.

Once while you are there you share the wooden cup with one of the young carpenters, who is stripped to the waist in the heat. He has a gentle face and speaks kindly to you.

You work until your back feels as though it might break in two and finally the overseer calls a halt. The sun is now high in the sky and you seek some shade; the workers, seeing you have none of your own, share their meal of bread and cheese and dates with you, with more water. The heat of the day is at its highest and everyone sleeps until it gets cooler. You lie in the shade and try to imagine what the building will be like when it is finished, and drift gently into sleep.

Out of the soft darkness comes a glimmering shape; at first you do not recognize it, but then, in your dream, you sit upright, a smile on your face. It is the Beth. When the Aleph came to you, it felt rather austere, but from this letter there is a friendly, warm feeling, a very feminine feeling. Like the Aleph, it is as big as you and of a warm golden-brown edged with green. It has a welcoming feel, though behind that is an enormous power held in check.

The Beth brings with it a scent, the smell of newly baked bread, and suddenly you remember. Beth-lechem/Bethlehem, meaning the house of bread. There is laughter all around you as the Beth applauds your realization. When it comes, the voice is a low contralto, warm and rich.

"You are Life. Aleph has spoken of you. Welcome, Life, be welcome in my house. All has been prepared for you." The light increases and you see before you a room lit with oil lamps. There are rugs on the floor and woven hangings on the walls. A small table has been laid with a white cloth and on it a loaf of new bread on a wooden platter and a small pile of salt. Nearby is a fish wrapped in leaves, and a cup of wine stands ready to your hand.

"Come and share with us, Life," says the voice of the Beth. "But first let us bless the bread and wine." There is a murmur of sound about you and you know that all the letters are there, unseen but each waiting for the time when they will contact you.

You look at the table and see a small flame hovering over the bread. The choir of the Ashim have come to be with you at this time.

"Baruch Atah Adonoi Elohainu. Melech Ha Olam. Ha Motze Lechem Min Ha Eretz."

The flame moves to the wine.

"Baruch Atah Adonoi Elohainu. Melech Ha Olam. Borai Peree Ha Gafen."

You move to the table and break off a piece of the bread and dip it into the salt and eat it. Next, you take a drink of wine, and then move on to the fish. Try to bring to mind the taste of everything you try. Take your time, there is no hurry. All the while you are conscious of the presences around you in the darkness. When you have eaten, the Beth appears beside you.

"Now, Life, I will come with you back to the building and you will see my powers at work."

There is a feeling of being enfolded in warmth and love and of moving between worlds and dimensions. As you go, you think to ask a question.

"Beth, house of the spirit of God, please tell me—what was it like to be there at the beginning?"

"Ah, Life, it was like being enfolded in living fire, breathing living air, and bathed in living water."

"But what of earth, Beth? Was that not living also?"

"Earth had a far greater destiny, Life, as do you. It was for Life that all this was created. Earth is not just for one form of Life, but also for *all* Life. Earth means not just your planet, but also all places where Life has come into being. Earth was sent out into the cosmos and given a long and heavy task to do. You are a small part of that task. Your Earth strives to accomplish the task set for Her, but you hinder Her."

The darkness lifts and you stand before the finished building. It is evident that it is to be a place of worship. The work has been done with skilled hands and loving care. Everyone has given of their best. The carving on the doors, every hinge, covering, and piece of furniture, including the ornately carved container that will hold the Holy Books, have been prepared. Light fills the building as the Beth enters. Wherever Beth goes the light follows, and the empty building becomes a house, a home. The spirit of place has taken up her abode.

For one fleeting second you see the true form of the Beth, then the memory is gone and you cannot recall what it was like. You want to weep with frustration, for it would have been so wonderful to tell others of the glory that was briefly revealed to you. At your shoulder, the voice is gentle.

"Do not weep. One day you will see me more clearly and on that day I will greet you as a friend, companion, and equal, Life."

Return to your own place now and know that once, in a time long ago, you helped to build a special place in a small town called Nazareth, where a young carpenter lived with his father and mother.

A Psalm for Beth

BASED ON AN ORIGINAL BIBLICAL WRITING

How beautiful are thy tabernacles, O Lord of Light.

My soul longs to enter the courts prepared for me.

My heart crieth out for the House of Love.

Even the humble sparrow hath found a house,

and the swallow a nest for herself

where she may lay her young,

even on the altar of the Lord.

Blessed are they that dwell in thy house, they shall praise thee.

Blessed is the man whose strength is in his house,

and blessed is the woman who is his strength.

They shall go into the courts prepared for them in heaven.

Behold thou art the shield of the humble

and the roof of the homeless.

Let us rise and go into the House of the Lord of Light

And take our ease before him.

The tent of the ancestors shall be lifted and to the weary stranger

it shall be said, "This is my Beth, be welcome."

Bread and wine shall such a one be given.

His feet shall be washed and his hands also,

for the stranger is the Lord of Light

who travels unawares.

Lord, let my heart be as thy Beth and dwell within me.

～

Ritual

You will need the following: a table covered with a white cloth, and a central blue bowl with a small candle in it. Scatter flower seeds over the cloth and surround the bowl with a circle of wildflowers. At the quarters place (south) a candle, (west) a chalice of wine or fruit juice, (north) bread and salt, and (east) a vial of oil. You will also need a mosquito net or several yards of fine curtain net. This should be fixed to the central light fixture or, if you have none, pin or tack the net to the ceiling. The idea is to build the temple in the desert.

Place a picture of Beth where you can see it from your chair set in the east, and a bowl of water and a towel just outside the net. It is important to bathe and put on fresh clothing. Take a staff or a simple walking stick in your hand and begin to circle the altar, keeping as far from it as possible. Make three circles starting and ending in the south, repeating the prayer as you go. Kneel down and lean upon the staff as if weary. Speak:

"I am a stranger in an unknown land; I am weary and would rest. Michael, you who guard the gate of heaven, look upon me and guard me this night, for I have no place to lay my head, no food for my hunger or water for my thirst. Hear me, I beseech you, and lead me to safety." *Stand and make the sign of the menorah, i.e., three half-circles one above the other and a straight line in the center. Then bow and walk to the west. Beginning from here make three circles, ending again in the west. Kneel on both knees and support yourself with the staff.*

"I am a stranger in this land and I am weary and would rest but there is no safe haven for my head and for my body. Gabriel, you who are the messenger of the Most High, grant me safe passage to a place of refuge this night, for I fear to fall among the ungodly." *Stand and make the sign of the menorah. Then bow and walk to the north. Beginning from here make three circles, ending again in the north. Kneel and bow your head to the ground.*

"I am a stranger who travels alone, my body is weak and I am faint from hunger and thirst. Sandalphon, you who were once as I am, look upon me with pity and send a guide to bring me to a place of safety this night. I call you by the name you once bore, Elijah, help me, for I fear I will perish." *Stand, make the sign of the menorah, bow, and walk to the east. From here, make three circles, ending in the east. Bow low before the east.*

"Who will hear me when I call? Will it be you, Raphael, healer of God? Four times have I called upon the angels of the Lord for help. When will my voice be heard? Send me a guide to bring me to a Beth." *Stand, make the sign of the menorah, bow, and get to your feet. Walk as if weary to the south, then look up.*

"I see a star above me; it is a sign that I must follow. *(Walk around to the east, then turn to look at the temple.)* My voice has been heard. Here in the desert I see the Beth of the Lord before me. *(Approach the temple, pause to wash your feet, then open the curtain and enter the House of the Lord.)* Behold, I am made welcome in this house and the table is set before me. Around me are Michael, Gabriel, Sandalphon, and Raphael; they make me welcome and bid me eat. *(To the south, bless the lighted candle.)* Blessed be this light in the name of Adonoi. *(To the west.)* Blessed be this wine in the name of Adonoi. *(Drink the wine and go to the north.)* Blessed be this bread and salt in the name of Adonoi. *(Dip the bread into the salt and eat, and move to the east. Pour a little oil onto hands, feet, and head, and massage it in.)* Blessed be this holy oil that purifies me." *Repeat this variation of Psalm 23.*

"The Lord is my shepherd; I shall want for nothing. He brings me to green fields and tells me to lie down and rest. He leads me to cool water. He restores my faith and leads me along the path of righteousness, for I am his child. Though I walk through a valley filled with shadows, I have nothing to fear, for the Lord of Light is with me. His strength and his power protect me. He prepared a house for me in the middle of a desert, with food and drink for my body and my soul. There was water to wash my feet of the dust and sand and oil to rub into my skin chapped raw by the wind. I know myself to be loved and cherished. Here in his house I will stay and I'll always be ready to welcome the lost and the hungry, as I was welcomed."

Take the picture of the Beth from the altar and place it on the floor. Lay the staff alongside it, then lie down as if going to sleep, using the Beth as a pillow beneath your head. It is good if you can actually sleep, even for a few minutes, as it seals the whole ritual. Then get to your feet, bow to the altar, and snuff out the candle in the south. Leave the temple and make a slow round of the quarters, blessing each angelic guardian. Then leave quietly. If possible, leave the altar light lit until it goes out naturally. Let the Beth of Light stand all night and clear it away in the morning with reverence.

GIMEL

Through thee my life is like a journey
filled with wonder,
with change, and with challenge.
But when I am weary and the road seems
long and endless,
oft times thine image appears before me
in the distance.
Then am I lifted up and my limbs
are eased of their pain.
Like a tired child I am borne onward
and comforted by the motion of thy love.
I dream, and in my dream I see the road ahead,
and I am made strong.
Thy strength prepares me for what is to come,
be it strewn with stones or paved with lustrous marble.
I awake from my dream to find myself beside the road.
I see thee departing in the distance and weep.
For now, I know I cannot be carried forever.
Chastened, I arise and begin to walk
toward the Light.

Image: Camel
Symbol: ℷ
Path on the Tree of Life: 13
Numerical Value: 3

Prayer

The prayer speaks of a spiritual weariness and a feeling of being close to the end of one's strength. Like a child having walked around a large supermarket for too long, the soul cries out to be picked up and carried for a while.

Looking back on my meditations for this time, I had recorded my memories of being carried home by my father after a family Christmas party. This was a very poignant memory for me as my father and I were close. I could recall with absolute clarity the feeling of safety, of being able to relax and trust in his strength. It was this same feeling I asked for and received from the letter Gimel. In a strange link with this memory came the realization that it was my father who had encouraged me to travel when I became an adult. His spiritual interests and beliefs were the inspiration for my life's work. He helped me to see the wonder and challenge in the world around me.

The prayer speaks of dreams and the need for strength to go on when all one wants to do is lie down and sleep. Then the camel appears in the distance and we wait as it draws near, hoping that we can ride for a while and let the ship of the desert do the walking. The hitchhiker traveling a long and lonely road, in bad weather or on a wet, cold night, thinks longingly of a warm car or truck and an affable driver going his way, or indeed any way. It is a very similar situation. We need a lift at times!

Path 13 on the Tree travels between Kether and Tiphereth; we might call them the father and the son, the driver and the car, the destination and the hope.

In terms of the Tarot trumps, it is the path of the High Priestess, the keeper of the Book of the Mysteries. It is her spiritual gifts that enable her to tell when we need help and when we can make our own way forward, weary though we may be.

It is the High Priestess, the knowingness of the inner feminine, that sends out the call for help and brings us to the oasis in the desert and gives us sustenance and rest. But only for a while.

The last lines of the prayer explain we cannot be carried forever; there comes a time when we must take to our feet and walk the path ourselves. We can do this because we know that if it is too much for us to bear for a little while, we will be carried, as my father carried me when I was small.

The Letter

Gimel is made from Zayin and Yod, shown upside down. As a word it derives from the meaning "to do a good deed" (*gemelet hasidim*). Devout Jews try to do acts of kindness in secret and never seek thanks or gratitude for what has been done. The High Priestess hidden behind the veil of the Mysteries enacts this decree well.

The value of Gimel is three, a feminine number (Binah as the third sephira). But consider the fact that the letter is composed of Zayin equaling seven and Yod equaling ten, making seventeen; if taken further, it will reduce to eight. If placed on its side, eight becomes a symbol for eternity, and our journey toward the Ultimate Light will take a long time.

Gimel begins several words of interest: *gamut* equals exile, a state Jewish people know very well; *gan-edan* is paradise; *gamla* is bridge or connection; *gadol* means great. It also begins *gibor* (mighty) and *Geburah,* the God-name of the sphere *Elohim Gibor.* In the Qabalah, Gimel is often seen as the pipe that carries water from the roof of the house and drains it into the earth through its protruding foot. In the same way, the power, love, and understanding of the supernal spheres is channeled from higher levels down to Malkuth, where it will replenish and water the earth.

Look at the medieval paintings depicting "The Flight into Egypt." Nearly always Mary is shown seated on an ass or a donkey. However, it is more likely to have been a camel if they were crossing long stretches of desert; a donkey or even a larger ass could not have made it safely across large tracts of sandy waste.

The two symbols of the Virgin Mother (High Priestess of the ancient Mysteries) and the camel certainly speak clearly of the recounting of the desert journey (taking the brethren up the levels) with which all ritual proceedings begin.

We might look at another desert journey that is perhaps even closer to the path of Gimel, and that is the journey of the three kings who came to offer gifts, advice, and worship in Bethlehem. In fact, the letter Gimel is often found with three small extensions rising from the head of the Zayin, making it look as if it is crowned. They appear in the beginning of the story of Yeshua and his own desert journey toward the final sacrifice and enlightenment. There were moments when the Gimel lifted him and carried him for a short space of time when the physical body grew too weary to sustain itself. The baptism, the transfiguration, the wedding at Cana, the entry into Jerusalem—all were moments when the burden seemed to be lifted and eased for a brief moment. The final easement is seen in the descent from the cross, when the journey has been completed and the final rest attained.

Gimel is the giver of self-reliance and inner strength. We can see Gimel as the water carrier, for the camel is indeed such an animal. Its ability to hold water within its hump and travel for long periods without drinking make it an ideal system of transport in desert regions. We might even look at it as a suitable symbol for the new Age of Aquarius, the man with the water jar, though there is no reason whatever why the symbol should be human—a camel does the job even more efficiently!

We can see the letter as the High Priestess who guides those who come seeking the Mysteries across the desert of their soul toward the spiritual oasis of enlightenment. In the trump itself, we see that she sits between two pillars with a veil between them. When traveling long distances in the desert, a tentlike cover is often strapped to the camel's back and the traveler sits inside with a curtain pulled across for privacy and to keep out the sand. The pillars and the veil can be looked on as a representation of this.

The privacy also indicates the withdrawn aspect of the Priestess. She holds the Book of the Law and maybe that law is the law of survival in both the spiritual and the physical sense. I know it was so for me during my own dark night. Maybe this book is a map of the universe or a detailed exposition of the Great Plan.

Those who have traveled the paths of the Tree of Life have often found the numbering of them to be puzzling. Why do we descend from Kether to Tiphereth on Path 13 before we have had a chance to travel across Path 14 from Chokmah to Binah? Why do we go down only to have to make our way up again? I can only suppose, and this is purely personal and *not* a teaching, that the numbering of the paths has been altered since it first came to light in the fourteenth century, in the form we now use it. There is still much to unravel and we cannot always take what we have been taught as the absolute truth. Time, distance, the vagaries of the human mind, and the difficulty of transmission can cause subtle differences over the centuries. We have no way of knowing if the present order of the Tarot trumps is correct, or if the real one has been forgotten. To really put a fox among chickens, what if the trumps were meant to be moved around according to the need of the moment? Gimel does not only drain water from the roof, it expedites ideas from Kether to Malkuth. It is the water that surrounds the High Priestess, flowing from her robe onto the rest of the trumps and fertilizing them.

Maybe we had better try opening the Book of the Law and see what is inside, rather than guessing or taking ancient ideas as the only ones. Gimel does us a kindness in revealing that there are many answers to every question and all of them can be right. One last riddle: If Gimel is composed of the Zayin (sword) and the Yod (hand), why is the hand holding the sword and what for?

Meditations

First Meditation

Meditate on an act of kindness you would like to do for someone other than yourself, without them or anyone else knowing about it. Think about it very carefully first. Ask yourself if the person would really like, appreciate, or even want your gift.

Second Meditation

Meditate upon an act of kindness you wish someone would do for you. Try to understand what it would mean, how it would affect you and your family. An act of kindness is *not* necessarily giving you a lot of money!

Third Meditation

Meditate on the journey of the three wise men, a journey that would have taken months to complete, and of making it on faith alone. Think of this in the physical sense, then repeat it as a spiritual pathworking on a higher level.

Fourth Meditation

Meditate on the flight into Egypt, looking at it from the point of view of a spiritual journey made by the Priestess, carrying with her the letter of the Law, i.e., the child, the returning sun/son.

Pathworking

Gimel, the path of the High Priestess on the Tree of Life, is a path of great subtlety. Reread the summary concerning the letter itself before taking the path. Settle into your chair and begin relaxing. Establish a 4-2-4-2 breathing pattern, breathing in to a count of 4, holding the breath for a count of 2, then breathing out to a count of 4 and again holding for a count of 2. Then let yourself slip into a light trance akin to a daydream.

Close your eyes slowly as if you are sleepy and see on the mental screen a line of dancing women. Hands held high, they step with a light and joyful energy. Follow them and they will lead you into the space where Gimel waits for you. You know the shape and form of the letter but not the form its power takes.

The dancing women disappear into the indigo shadows of space and leave you looking about. It feels quite cold and you shiver; there is sand under your bare feet so you must be either on a beach or in a desert. Knowing that Gimel has the magical image of a camel, it is a fair bet that you are in a desert.

The moon comes from behind a cloud and reveals the stark beauty of the sand dunes at night. Some distance away you can see the outline of palm trees clustered together, an oasis maybe. In the other direction you can see a slow-moving caravan coming toward you. Some ten or twelve camels moving with their strange swaying gait become clearer as they draw closer. One of them carries a hooded canopy on its back and it halts before you. A blue-turbaned man wearing a matching scarf across his face comes from the shadows and indicates that you are to climb into the strange contraption. At his instruction the beast kneels and you climb into a surprisingly roomy tentlike arrangement.

There is a moment of vertigo as the camel gets up again, but then the caravan resumes its trek and you soon adjust to the movement. You relax into the backrest of the seat and try to collect your thoughts on the subject of Gimel.

Triune in nature, it stands for the three pillars, for the three rays of love, wisdom, and power. The three also links it to Binah, the third sephira and the great feminine principle. You continue to turn over in your mind all the things you have learned about the letter Gimel as you journey on.

After a while you become aware that the camel has stopped. The tent lurches forward, then backward as the animal kneels down. The curtain is pulled aside and the guide helps you get down. Silently he points to a tent standing beside the large pool in the center of the oasis. You walk toward it and enter. Inside it is warm and dimly lit. There is a scent of roses but no flowers can be seen. You sit down on a pile of soft cushions, glad to be away from the lurching motion of the camel. On a small table is a cup of wine, a bowl of dates and grapes, and a plate of *rahat-lakoum* that you recognize as Turkish Delight.

Behind you is a curtain of fine silk, almost but not quite transparent. You feel there is something or someone behind it. This is confirmed when a soft laugh is heard and a rich contralto voice bids you welcome. Instinct tells you that this is the being that ensouls the letter Gimel.

"Welcome, Life. My fellow letters, Aleph and Beth, have said much concerning you; most of it, it must be said, is complimentary. But you have far to go before you have met and spoken with all of us. You are taking this journey through the letters for a purpose: the first purpose is for you to gain an understanding of us and the second is so that we may make contact with you."

You take a hasty sip of wine and compose yourself to ask a question that has been on your mind during your meetings with the first two letters. "Thank you, Gimel, I am happy to be with you and I would like to ask a question that has been puzzling me."

"I will answer if I can, Life."

"Why can I only 'see' the letters as letters and not as angels or something similar?"

"That is easy to answer. You see what human eyes can see, no more, no less. The shape and form of the letter is the physical form, and your eyes interpret the vibrations in the only way your human brain can 'see' it. What you think you see as the letter is not what I see when I look at my fellow letters. I see the glory and the radiance of the forms. You see only those lines, colors, and shapes that your brain can make of it at this time. Think in this way: before you is a glorious Aleph, but you are only seeing 10 percent of what that form really is. The other 90 percent is there, but your brain cannot process the vibrations. But one day, when your physical eyes have evolved enough, you will see more."

You think this over and agree that this is a reasonable explanation. Gimel goes on. "The Creator decreed that I would embody acts of kindness and compassion. You may see my powers at work in the story of the good samaritan. In fact, Life, if you look more deeply at the parables and the psalms, you will be able to pick out the letters in the meanings and secret teachings of those stories. To love was and is the first law of the universe, for the Creator made us all with love, desired our existence with love, gave us a reason for existing by loving us. The more we can love the more fully we can exist, the more fully we exist the more we can understand the reason for our creation. This is true of you, no less than us."

Gimel pauses and then goes on. "In me are combined the feminine desire to arouse, to conceive, and to nurture; to some who seek me out I am the three-wayed Goddess, to others I am a part of a trinity of powers that embody the feminine principles of compassion and tenderness. I am virgin priestess, bride, and wise-woman. I carry and support the unborn babe, the infant child, and the dead son. As the camel carries burdens you cannot, so I carry sorrows that human beings can only guess at. Yet I am also laughter and, like Miriam, I will dance and sing before the Most High. I am many things, Life; your task is to find and understand them."

You try to understand all this and fail; it is too much to hold in your head. Gimel sighs and speaks gently from behind the curtain. "Do not try to remember all of it, it will come to you as and when it is needed. All you have to remember just now is that I am here to hold, comfort, and sustain you when you have need of me. Now return to your own place, it is time."

You rise and turn to bow before the curtain; for a few seconds you seem to see the Gimel, golden as ripe corn and edged with the black of great sorrow. Then it is gone and you are left wondering exactly what you did see.

You leave the tent and find the guide waiting for you. The rest of the caravan has moved on but your beast crouches, awaiting your coming. With the help of your guide you climb onto the back of the camel and draw the curtain across; you have much to think about. Slowly the camel returns the way you came. As you move through the silent desert the moon dips below the horizon and the east begins to lighten. Soon it will be dawn, a new day in which to do a kindness for someone. You slide gently into sleep lulled by the movement of the beast beneath you and wake in your own time and place.

Psalm 23

The Lord is my shepherd, I shall not want.

He maketh me to lie down in green pastures.

He leadeth me beside the still waters.

He restoreth my soul.

He leadeth me in the paths of righteousness

for his name's sake.

Yes, though I walk through the valley of the shadow of death,

I will fear no evil,

for thou art with me.

Thy rod and thy staff they comfort me.

Thou preparest a table before me

in the presence of mine enemies.

Thou anointest my head with oil.

My cup runneth over.

Surely goodness and mercy shall follow me

all the days of my life

and I will dwell in the house of the Lord forever.

～

Ritual

You need a table with a white cloth for an altar. On its place in the east, place a small burner with charcoal and some incense (I suggest pure frankincense). Also put a small bottle of perfume/eau de toilette. It should not be the cheapest, but something you will have to make a small sacrifice to buy. In the south put a lit candle and by it three new candles in different colors tied together with a ribbon. Put a picture of the letter Gimel on the altar. In the west, place a chalice with a small amount of wine or fruit juice and an unopened bottle of wine (this can be nonalcoholic if preferred). In the north put a piece of fresh bread sprinkled with a few grains of salt; also a small bowl with some flowering bulbs in it, tied with a ribbon. The intent of this ritual will be four acts of kindness to people whom you do not know.

Put a seat in the east facing the altar. Bathe and put on fresh clothes or a robe and slippers. Light the charcoal and sprinkle a few grains of incense on it when it is glowing red. Take the incense burner and circle the altar three times, saying: "With the first circle I cleanse this place of worship of all earthly thoughts and emotions. With the second circle I cleanse this place of worship of all unclean desires and feelings. With the third circle I cleanse this place of worship of all influences of my daily life." *Put the burner on the altar, go to the south and pick up the candle, and make three circles.*

"With the first circle I cleanse this sacred space of all anger and hatreds. With the second circle I cleanse this sacred space of all darkness born of deliberate evil. With the third circle I cleanse this sacred space and fill it with light, that I may work in the presence of the Most High." *Put the candle on the altar, pick up the chalice, and make three circles.*

"With the first circle I bless this holy place with the Grail of Love. With the second circle I bless this holy place with the Grail of Sustenance. With the third circle I bless this holy place with the Grail of Light, so I unite myself with this ancient symbol." *Put the chalice on the altar, pick up the bread, and make three circles.*

"With the first circle I consecrate this temple with bread as did Melchisedek when he met with Abraham. With the second circle I consecrate this temple with salt. With the third circle I consecrate this temple with my will. So mote it be." *Put the bread on the altar and take a seat in the east.*

Recite this invocation: "Into this place cleansed, hallowed, consecrated, and made holy in the ancient manner, I invoke the triple powers of the holy letter Gimel: love, wisdom, and power.

"I call upon the presence of the third letter that it may come forth from the crown of God and make itself known to me here in this place. *Pause.* I make offerings of incense and light, of wine, and of bread and salt." *Rise and face the east; hold out your arms.*

"Behold, I have come before thee, Lords of Light. I ask for the power of love to fill me that I might gain wisdom." *Go to the altar and pick up the perfume; offer it up.* "I ask a blessing on this perfume that it may bring pleasure, joy, and lightness of heart to the one who is destined to receive it." *Replace and go to the south; face it with arms out.*

"Behold, I have come before thee, Sons of the Morning. I ask for the power of wisdom to fill me with love for my fellow men. Teach me to guard my tongue that I may speak no words of hurt this day." *Go to the altar, pick up the candles, and offer them.* "I ask a blessing on these candles that, when lit, they may bring light into the home of those who will receive them." *Replace and go to the west; stand facing west with arms out.*

"Behold, I come before thee, Lords of Mind. I ask for the creative power of love to fill me with laughter and joy this day. Grant that I may bring that same joy to others, so they may remember this as a day of promise. Open my heart and let its power flow out to those who have need of it." *Go to the altar, pick up the wine, and offer it.*

"May it lift their spirits and give ease of mind to those who will drink it." *Replace the wine. Go to the north and face it with arms out.*

"Behold, I come before thee, Lords of Form. I ask only that I may be of use to you in the Great Plan. Help me to cleanse my life, my heart, and my spirit that I may prove to be worthy of all that I have been given in my life." *Go to the altar and pick up the bowl.* "I ask a blessing on these bulbs that they may share that beauty with those to whom they will be given. May their colors brighten weary days, may their perfume lift a sad heart, may their strength sustain a faltering spirit." *Replace, return to the east, and sit for a few minutes.*

"Holy Elohim, listen to my words and grant my request that I may be of service. Help me to think of others before myself. Strengthen me that I may help those weaker than myself. Sit upon my tongue that I may speak truth; be my guide in the work that I do in the marketplace, in the home, and in the sacred space where I worship. Fill my days with peace of mind and my nights with serenity of heart." *Rise and go to the altar, pick up the incense, and make three reverse circles.*

"As I retrace my steps, let these circles of power disperse and return to their own place. May all be as it was and peace be on this place." *Return to the altar, sprinkle a few drops of wine on the charcoal to put it out, and with the candle make three reverse circles.*

"As I retrace my steps, so may these circles of power disperse and return to their own place. May this night be one of peace for the whole world." *Return to the altar and snuff out the candle. Pick up the chalice and make three reverse circles.*

"As I retrace my steps, let these circles of power disperse and return to their own place. May the power of love fill this house; may some soul be given gentle release this night, may some child be born tonight with special gifts of the spirit." *Return to the altar and drink the wine. Pick up the bread and make three reverse circles.*

"As I retrace my steps, let these circles of power disperse and return to their own place. May the power of wisdom fill the hearts of those in high places, may they listen to the voice of their spirit and do what is right and good, not what is right for them."

In the morning take the perfume with you. Find someone who serves you well and, during the day, give it to her. Tell her you appreciate her service and that you feel it should be rewarded. Do not give your name and make sure it is someone you do not know personally.

The next day, take the candles and look for someone you think would appreciate them—maybe an older person or a busy and harassed mother, a teacher, or a street person. On the third day find someone to whom you can give the wine. The same conditions apply. Finally, on the fourth day take the bowl of flowering bulbs and give them to an old lady to brighten her day, her room, and her heart.

Do not think your gifts will always be accepted with a smile. People can be suspicious, angry, or bad tempered. You may see your gifts thrown away, smashed, or refused with harsh words. People are not used to kindness. Do not let it anger or hurt you; your gifts will reach the heart of the Creator no matter what happens to them.

Keep calm and accept whatever happens.

DALETH

Thou art the door to joy and tears.
All that lifts my heart and wounds my soul
enters my world through thee.
Thou art the gateway to life and death,
knowledge and power,
deceit and love.
Thy heart is a lock, but where shall I find the key?
Open to me, Beloved,
let me enter into thee and know thy embrace.
Shall I knock upon thy lintel?
If I beg thee, wilt thou open to me?
Thou art the door to the Light,
and the key to the lock is love.
I wait before thee until,
weary with sleep denied, I close my eyes.
When I awake the way is open before me and,
singing praises to God, I enter thy world.

Image: Door
Symbol: ד
Path on the Tree of Life: 14
Numerical Value: 4

Prayer

The prayer for this letter begins with praise for the door as a symbol of all the things we encounter when we enter. Joy and tears can be found within the house once the door has been opened to us. What goes on behind closed doors is a secret; comedy, love, tragedy, lies, and deceits all have their place behind a door. It can be either open or closed, it invites or it excludes.

Omar Khayyam sang: "But evermore came out from that same door wherein I went." Doors are important to us as human beings, not just because they give or deny entrance to our homes and our privacy, but as a symbol that promises freedom, access to the unknown and, above all, challenges.

When doors are locked against us it causes anger and hurt. Why have we been locked out? What is being kept from us? Who shuts themselves away from our outstretched hands? Doors have locks and locks need keys, and keys come in many shapes and forms. As a symbol, the key is as ancient and complex as the door. We may have to forge a key, create one, ask for it, buy it, or, as a last resort, break down the door by force. The only way to open the door of the spirit is to knock and be let in willingly.

When this prayer was written I felt as if I was standing before the door of my spiritual life, a door that I had run out of and left open in my haste to flee from the turmoil inside. Now I was back but the door was closed. I needed to open it but could not find a way to do so.

Should I knock and demand reentry, or would I have to beg the door of my own soul to open? In my meditations I came up against a wall, and yet there was an image that kept recurring, one that had a message for me. It seemed part of me was still within, on the other side of the door. If this was so, then surely it would open to me. But it remained shut.

Then I remembered a television series where a would-be student sat before the door of a Shaolin temple and waited patiently in wind, rain, and heat until it opened for him. I waited in the same way, keeping my mind clear of all thoughts, just waiting. Each day I sat before the image of a closed door; then one day I sat and wept, and the door opened silently. I entered with a deep and profound sense of being welcomed back into my rightful place.

Standing in the inner temple of the spirit, I bowed as usual to the altar light and realized that in bowing my stance was that of the symbol for Daleth. I myself was the door. The door was closed to me because I was closed to myself. When I gave in and accepted the situation, it opened wide. It has never closed again, nor will it.

The Letter

Daleth is built from two Vavs placed head to toe. While its number as Daleth is four, that of Vav is six; six plus six is twelve, so it has a hidden number of twelve, corresponding to the twelve months of the year. But the one plus two equals three, the number of the preceding letter.

This letter with its number of four alludes to the four seasons, the four directions, the four worlds, and also the four letters of the Tetragrammaton. It brings to mind the Square of Chesed, a sphere that holds balance and organization within itself. Chesed is also Gate 49 of Binah (Binah itself making up the fiftieth and final Gate): four plus nine is thirteen, and one plus three brings us back to four.

Daleth opens the word *daa'th* (knowledge) and *devekut* (cleaving to God). Daleth has a connection to the word *dal*, which can be interpreted as a beggar or one who asks for alms. This reminds us that it is right and proper to share what we have with those who have nothing. The open door of hospitality is something that is sacred in the Jewish faith.

In his book *The Wisdom in the Hebrew Alphabet*, Rabbi Munk speaks of the relationship between Daleth and Gimel, according to the Talmud, in this way: "Why does the foot of Gimel extend towards the Daleth? [It is] to teach us that the Gomel (benefactor) should always try to seek out the Dal (the needy one) and offer help without delay."

He also speaks of the Lishkas Chashaim, a special room in the temple where anyone rich or poor could enter, but only one at a time. Those who could spare it left a contribution, those who could not might take what they needed. No one knew who gave or who took.

All too often in this modern world we write out a check or donate through the medium of a credit card when asked for money, but to actually do something ourselves for someone in a personal way is much better and has more meaning.

On the Tree of Life, Path 14 is that of the Empress. The Tarot trump mostly shows the picture of a pregnant woman with or without the trappings of royalty; she is surrounded by flowers, fruits, corn, and the lush green of nature. She is named the Illuminating Intelligence because it is the Chasmal (brilliance or radiance) that is the foundation of the hidden Mysteries.

We can see the symbolism fitting well here, for when a door is opened it lets in the light by which we can see more clearly. Running as it does between Chokmah, the primal masculine principle, and Binah, its feminine counterpart (fecundity), the act of opening a door to new life is to be expected. But it is not just physical procreation that is meant, it is also the manifestation of ideas, inventions, and advances in science and technology as well as those rare beings whose destiny is to bring the great religions into the world.

Here we have the beginnings of Mother Nature in her primal aspect. In terms of the ancient goddesses we are talking of entities such as Ge, Rhea, the Titanesses, the Giantesses of the Scandinavian mythos, and Tiamat in Mesopotamia. There is nothing sweet and gentle about this Empress. She is woman, *W O M A N,* as Peggy Lee famously sang it.

When we look at the shape of the letter we can see another side of the coin, so to speak. When we come into an august presence we normally bow as we enter. When entering a church the custom used to be that men bowed to the altar and women bent the knee. Nowadays this courtesy to the Godhead is often omitted.

When one bows, one bends from the waist and automatically takes the form of the Daleth. In ancient times the door was usually less than the height of the householder; one had to bend to enter. When one enters the door leading to the Church of the Nativity in Bethlehem, one has to bend almost double in order to get through the door. The same posture can be seen when people enter any kind of spiritual scene, presence, or atmosphere, something often portrayed in religious paintings of the sixteen and seventeenth centuries. The bent back and bowed head is indicative of many emotions: sorrow, respect, humility, awe, and fear.

The door of the Mysteries is well known to those who follow alternative paths to the Light, but probably the most famous door of all is "The Light of the World" by Holman Hunt. It depicts the Light of the World (Christ) knocking at a closed door to which there is no handle. One may see the figure as any one of the aeons of the ages, Osiris, Prometheus, Orpheus, and the Oak King, as well as Jesus of Nazareth. If you look closely you will see the door has no handle; it can only be opened from the inside, as I found when I tried to pass through my own door of the soul. When inner divinity is recognized and accepted, one becomes one's own savior.

Meditations

First Meditation

Establish relaxation and breathing rhythms; Abram Abulafia, a highly respected teacher of Jewish wisdom, devised methods of breathing to enable his students to rise on the planes more easily. You are following in his footsteps.

Read the parable of the prodigal son, taking each of the three sections separately. 1) The demand for his inheritance and his departure; 2) his experiences in the outer world and his downfall; 3) the return. Look for symbols, realizations, and an understanding of the text on the physical, the mental, and the spiritual levels. When you have done this, meditate on each section, taking on the character of the son and then of the father.

Record anything of significance.

Second Meditation

Build an image of a wall with a door in the center. Imagine yourself seated before this door. Do nothing else, just wait. If thoughts come, look at them, examine them for relevance to your situation, then dismiss them. Do this for three days. On the fourth day the door will open and you can pass through. Record what you see.

Third Meditation

Meditate on the symbolism of the Light of the World.

Pathworking

The pathworking begins with a time of solitude and silence. Your chair should have a firm back and be of a height that enables your feet to rest flat on the floor. If needed, a cushion under your feet will help. Use a steady, rhythmic breathing to ease yourself into a light trance. Path 14 of the Tree leads from Chokmah to Binah and is symbolized by Daleth the door and by the Tarot trump of the Empress. She is the door to life, the mother image. Close your eyes and build the image of a door with care and precision, for once built it can be used in other ways and for other purposes.

Look at the door. It is old and shows signs of much use. So it should, for this is the door of the Mysteries and where it leads depends on your intent, the degree of your training, and the clarity of your inner vision.

Don't hurry, take your time. Look at the wood and the way time has weathered it. Touch it and feel the roughness and the irregularities of its surface through the medium of your astral senses. Look at the color of the wood. It is unpainted and has turned to a dull brown or grey over the years. Look at the iron hinges, large and slightly rusty. See the nails holding the sections together, roughly made and not as elegant as their modern counterparts. Now see the lock and handle, much larger than those used in our time. Look also at the massive stone wall that supports the door, the archway above it, and the doorstep below it; both have the letter Daleth incised into the stone. All these things need to be fixed in your mind. When you are satisfied with your idea of the door, grasp the circular handle, turn it, and push it open, hearing the squeak and grind of the hinges as you do so.

Before you is an ancient building with a vaulted ceiling. Close the door behind you and walk forward. You are in an obviously sacred place. An altar of stone on which a pair of ox horns have been placed dominates the small room. Oil lamps flicker and throw your shadow against the walls as you move forward. Behind the altar is a plain, lime-washed wall on which someone has painstakingly written ancient Hebrew texts. The writing is very fine and done with loving care and dedication. There is a feeling of devotion, as if many people have worshiped here over a long period of time.

There is a small wooden stool before the altar. Sit here and enjoy the peace. The silence envelops you and as you sink into it the lamps grow dim and finally all light disappears. The wall of writing begins to glow and becomes a doorway open-ing out onto a landscape of cultivated fields heavy with sun-ripened grain. In the middle of the field sits a woman nursing a very young child. The woman wears a coronet of flowers and corn and beckons you to come to her.

You walk through the cornfield to the mother and, when you stop beside her, she holds out the babe to you. The child's weight seems more than it should be but you hold it securely. The woman speaks:

"I am the door to the house of life. All life comes into manifestation through me, for I am the giver of form. Everything that lives is one of my children, and all owe allegiance to the One Creator. I am a door that opens to the stranger, the weary, the forsaken. I open to joy and sorrow, to life and death. You are the seeker who opens the door to others. Take the child with you, for the child is the key."

She rises and walks away from you across the waving corn. The child lies qui-etly in your arms and you begin to walk back to the little chapel, hoping that someone will come and tell you what to do with the child. As you walk, he gets heavier and heavier until you have to set him down on the ground. When you do, the child stretches and turns and grows and becomes a small boy of four or five years old. He takes your hand and looks up at you with dark brown eyes.

"I will open the doors for you," he says. "You are Life as I was once Life. The letters speak of you as one who is ready to open the door of knowledge. Come."

He leads you back to the chapel and lays his small hand on the latch of the door. It swings open and before you is not the ancient, dimly lit room you saw before, but a magnificent cathedral with an altar of marble, gold candlesticks, and an elaborately carved and jeweled cross. There is also a golden menorah and the elaborately carved and embossed container that holds the Torah and the Talmud. Stained glass of incredible richness dazzles the eye. The child leads you through all the glitter and the gold, past the high altar with its snowy-white cloth and gold brocade, to a door behind the altar. It too bears the sign of Daleth, and opens to his touch.

Here is a quiet room with wooden chairs facing a simple table. Several people are seated here, quietly meditating. A woman rises to her feet and begins to speak of the joy in her heart and the peace that fills her life.

"This is a Quaker meetinghouse," the child tells you. "The spirit is here as it is in the others." He leads you past the woman and opens yet another door. It leads into a Buddhist temple where a group of monks are chanting a prayer. The sound of drums, bells, and the whirring of prayer wheels fills the air. The child tugs on your hand and points to a door behind the figure of the Buddha.

Door after door is opened to you; sacred places, where the Creator is worshiped under many names, are revealed: Hindu temples, Masonic lodges, stone circles, Methodist and Baptist chapels, synagogues both ancient and modern, Gothic and Norman churches, deep caves filled with wondrous paintings, and the ruined temples of ancient gods—every one of them sacred in its own right.

"There is no division in the mind of the One," explains the child, who is now more like twelve than three or four. "It is only on Earth that such a thing occurs."

Night is coming and you find a cave in which to shelter. You hold the boy close to you to keep him warm and think about all the things you have been shown. Your mind slides gently into sleep and in the darkness you see the form of the Daleth floating above you. It is a deep blue with gold at the edges and you feel its gaze fixed on you. It makes you feel a little uncomfortable; the letter senses this.

"Life," it says quietly. "Why do you tremble? Am I so terrible to look upon?"

You say no but you feel as if there is something more for you to do, but what?

"Life, dear one," says the Daleth, "you have one more door to open, the door to your own heart, and I am that door. Open me and enter into your own heart center."

You ask how you can do this and the boy speaks from behind you.

"Use me. I am the key to all doors. Just recognize me for who I am and take me into your heart."

You stand, uncertain of what is meant by all this, afraid to do the wrong thing, think the wrong thing. The boy smiles and takes your hand.

"I am the maker of keys. What you see is but a shadow. I am all that was, is, and will be. Your heart is one of the jewels in my crown."

The light surrounding him expands and envelops you. There is a sudden and terrible pain in your heart center, then it goes and your heart is open to the power of the One.

"I am love that has come among you to share myself with you and with yours. I am with you for all time."

"Life," says the voice of Daleth, "I am the door to your heart as long as this incarnation manifests. You may forget that I am here, but I will not forget you.

Open me wide to those you love, and try to open me even to those you do not love! Return now to your own place and be at peace in your heart."

Surrounded by love, you sink into silence and wake in your own time and space.

Psalm

EXCERPTS FROM THE 31ST PSALM OF DAVID

Thou art my rock and my fortress,

therefore for thy name's sake lead me and guide me.

I will be glad and rejoice in thy mercy; for thou hast considered my trouble.

Thou hast known my soul in adversity.

Have mercy upon me, for there is much that troubles me.

I am forgotten as a dead man out of mind.

I am like a broken vessel,

for I have heard the slander of many,

fear was on every side.

They that opposed me took council together against me,

but I trusted in thee, O Lord.

My times are in thy hand,

deliver me from the hand of mine enemies.

Let the lying lips be put to silence.

Great is thy goodness

which thou hast wrought for them that trust in thee

before the sons of men.

&

Ritual

This is a simple ritual relying mainly upon visualization. Nevertheless it will "open doors" for you in a specific way. You will need a table and a white cloth, a blue bowl in the center with a tealight in it, and a candle in a holder at each quarter of the altar: gold for east, red for south, blue for west, and green for north. In addition, you need a small bell (when you buy a temple bell, take your time and try many before choosing; the tone should be sweet and silvery, not tinny or strident) and a small bowl of salt and water, mixed. Place a cushion in each quarter of the room on which to kneel. Incense should be of a kind to induce a light trance. Enter and light the central light. Lift the bowl in both hands and raise it high.

"Praise be to the Creator of all things. Thou art the One of Many Names, all of which are sweet in my ears. In this light you are present in this temple and in my heart. With this presence I hallow the above *(lower the light to your knees)* and I hallow the below. *Turn to the east and hold out the bowl.* I hallow the east and the door to the domain of Raphael, the healer of God *(go to the south and hold out the bowl).* I hallow the south and the door to the domain of Michael, the warrior of God. *Go to the west and hold out the bowl.* I hallow the west and the door to the domain of Gabriel, the messenger of God. *Go to the north and hold out the bowl.* I hallow the north and the door to the domain of Uriel, the upholder of God." *Return to the east and place the bowl in the center of the altar. Take the gold candle in your left hand and turn to the east; hold out your right hand with the palm up.*

"I invoke Raphael, the golden glory of the dawn, healer of the Most High. I stand before the door to thy halls of healing. Open to me, Son of the Morning of Creation, that I may enter and be with thee and bathe my wounded soul in thy healing light. *Walk forward to the east, set down the candle before you, and kneel on the cushion.* I knock upon the door of Raphael the healer and call to thee." *Knock six times on the floor and call out "Raphael, Raphael, Raphael." Visualize a door of brilliant gold opening and light streaming out and bathing you.*

"The door has opened for me. I shall enter the house of light and mercy and be made whole." *Visualize entering through the door and allow the experience to build within you. Try to remember what you see, hear, and feel. Take as much time as you need. If you cannot kneel for any reason, then instead of a cushion place a chair in the east and sit in it for this time.*

"I have walked with Light and been healed by Light, and for this I give thanks." *Rise, turn, bow to the east; take the candle and return it to the altar. Walk to the south side of the altar and take up the red candle. Turn to the south and hold out your right hand, palm up.*

"I invoke Michael, the bright glory of the noonday sun, warrior of the Most High. I stand before the door to thy halls of courage and loyalty. Open to me, Son of the Morning of Creation, that I may enter and be with thee and fill my eager soul with the light of thy flaming sword." *Walk forward to the south, set down the candle before you, and kneel on the cushion.*

"I knock upon the door of Michael the warrior and call to thee." *Knock five times on the floor and call out "Michael, Michael, Michael." Visualize a door of brilliant red opening and light streaming out and bathing you.*

"The door has opened for me. I shall enter the house of strength and justice and be judged by the scales. Unafraid, I offer myself to the discernment of the warrior of God." *Visualize entering through the door and allow the experience to build within you. Try to remember what you see, hear, and feel. Take as much time as you need.*

"I have placed my heart in the scales of justice and have accepted the judgment of Michael. I have stood in the Light and I am made whole and clean." *Rise, turn, and bow to the south; take up the candle and return it to the altar. Walk to the western side of the altar and take up the blue candle. Turn to the west and hold out your right hand, palm up.*

"I invoke Gabriel, the silver radiance of the moon, messenger of the Most High. I stand before the door to thy halls of intuition and knowledge. Open to me, Son of the Morning of Creation, that I may enter and be with thee to listen to thy silver voice and bear witness to the secret knowledge of the ages." *Walk forward to the west, set down the candle before you, and kneel on the cushion.*

"I knock upon the door of Gabriel the messenger and call to thee." *Knock four times on the floor and call out "Gabriel, Gabriel, Gabriel." Visualize a door of intense blue opening and light streaming out and bathing you.*

"The door has opened for me. I shall enter the house of knowledge and communication and become a student of the silver voice. Here I will learn what is offered to me and use it for the good of all." *Visualize entering through the door and allow the experience to build within you. Try to remember what you see, hear, and feel. Take as much time as you need.*

"I have sat at the feet of the messenger and have listened to his words of wisdom. I have walked in the halls of knowledge and been given the gift of understanding. I will strive to be worthy of what has been given to me." *Rise, turn, and bow to the west; take up the candle and return it to the altar. Walk to the northern side of the altar and take up the green candle. Turn to the north and hold out your right hand, palm up.*

"I invoke Uriel, the great archangel of Earth and upholder of the Most High. I stand before the door to thy halls of spiritual enlightenment and compassion. Open to me, Son of the Morning of Creation, that I may enter and be with thee. Teach my soul concerning the wonders of the universe and open my heart to compassion that I may truly love my neighbor as myself." *Walk forward to the north, set down the candle before you, and kneel on the cushion.*

"I knock upon the door of Uriel, the mighty archangel of Earth, and call to thee." *Knock three times on the floor and call out "Uriel, Uriel, Uriel." Visualize a door of intense green opening and light streaming out and bathing you.*

"The door has opened for me. I shall enter the house of enlightenment and compassion, and learn of the love of the Creator for that which it created. Here I will learn to open my heart to all life and come to know true compassion." *Visualize entering through the door and allow the experience to build within you. Try to remember what you see, hear, and feel. Take as much time as you need.*

"I have sat at the feet of Uriel and opened my heart to enlightenment and love. I am blessed by the presence of the Sons of the Morning in all their glory and strength. Truly I will strive to be worthy of what has been given to me." *Rise, turn, and bow to the north; take up the candle and return it to the altar. Lift the center light high.*

"Praise be to the Creator of all things. Thou art the One of Many Names, all of which are sweet in my ears. In this Light you are present in this temple and in my heart. By the power of this Light I give thanks to that which is above *(lower the light to your knees)* and below. *Turn to the east and hold out the bowl.* I bless and thank thee, Raphael, and the powers of the east. Peace be between us. You have permission to depart. *Go to the south and hold out the bowl.* I bless and thank thee,

Michael, and the powers of the south. Peace be between us. You have permission to depart. *Go to the west and hold out the bowl.* I bless and thank thee, Gabriel, and the powers of the west. Peace be between us. You have permission to depart. *Go to the north and hold out the bowl.* I bless and thank thee, Uriel, and the powers of the north. Peace be between us. You have permission to depart."

Return to the altar and replace the center light. Bow and snuff out all candles but the center one; leave this burning for a while longer, then return and put it out.

HEH

When all the world is dark and fear surrounds me,
when my night-blind soul cries out for help,
I turn to thee,
For thou art my opening to the Light and hope.
Like a child crouching in the dark, bereft of love,
I call to thee for succor and for comfort.
How long must I remain in darkness?
How long must I suffer the darkness in others
that threatens to engulf me?
From far beyond the ultimate source of Light
comes the voice of my desire.
I lift my head but remain silent, accepting
what I cannot change,
enduring that which seeks to overthrow me.
Hope, that most beloved of messengers,
comes winging down the paths of morning.
The darkness lifts, and I see beyond the shadows
to the sun.
I look to thee and I behold my beloved.
I open up the window of my battered ark.
And, like a yearning dove,
my heart flies through the opening to freedom
and the Light.

Image: Window
Symbol: ה
Path on the Tree of Life: 15
Numerical Value: 5

Prayer

Prayer is a strange thing; you want to begin but the words are not there, then suddenly the heart opens and the words pour out. Ernest Butler used to teach us that the most powerful prayer in the world was a four-letter word: *help*! There have been times when I have simply not been able to express what I need or want. Then I opt for the simplest prayer of all. I say nothing but simply open my heart and let deity choose the words that best explain my thoughts, feelings, hopes, and fears.

This particular prayer was a turning point during my time of spiritual darkness. In my meditation I had become aware of being in the ark, with the rain beating down and the feeling of the boat rocking under my feet. I am a bad sailor and although I am a fairly good swimmer I have a fear of the sea. So I was less than thrilled to find myself in such a situation.

Knowing I had something to learn from this, I tried to stay with it. Gradually I began to understand that my situation at that time was very similar. I was at the center of a storm, I was in danger, I was feeling decidedly sick and very fearful because there seemed to be no one at the wheel, so to speak. I was wrong—there was someone at the wheel; a very strong hand was guiding the course of my ark at that moment.

Within the darkness and the silence I sent out a call for help. The letter Heh was the answer. I had to find the window and let in the Light. Once that thought crystallized, the enclosed feeling and the sensation of movement ceased. The window had opened and the realization had been grasped and understood.

"Ask and ye shall receive," we are told. As always in situations like this, one is answered by symbols because that is the way of the primal mind. Over the years I have learned that the way to ask is also by the use of symbols. The words of the prayer very much speak for themselves and describe the vision in my meditation very accurately.

The Letter

Heh has a value of five, also the number of the planet Mars. The right-hand part is formed from a Daleth, while the left support is a Yod turned upside down. So we can add the four of the Daleth to the ten of the Yod and get fourteen. If you add one plus four you get back to five again. Interestingly, if you take the four as the four sides of a square, then lift the center point, it becomes a pyramid.

It is with this letter that we come to a controversy. Some authorities say Path 15 is that of the Tarot trump of the Star, while others say with equal conviction that it is the path of the Emperor. Both have their points, but in my book *The Shining Paths* (Thoth Publications, 1999), I used the Star for Path 15, so I will stay with it.

The shape of the Heh, of course, carries on the symbology we have been using in both the Beth and the Daleth. The house is the temple, the home, and/or the stable of the Nativity. The door is the open invitation to the soul to incarnate, either that of an ordinary human being or, more rarely, the soul of one destined to be the aeon of the age. We have also looked at the bent posture of those entering a holy place or a presence as shown by the shape of the Daleth.

The shape of the Heh corresponds to its image of a window, one that is slightly open at the top. It also has a secondary image in the Tarot card, namely that of the five-pointed star. Both of these forms have an important bearing on the way the Heh affects those working with its powers. One affects us in the sense of opening us emotionally, mentally, and spiritually to a personal revelation. We see this more clearly as Nefesh (the physical sense), Ruach (the emotional sense), Neshamah (the mental sense), and Chayah (a Daa'th-like awareness). The second effect encloses us within the symbol itself and makes us aware of the latent power within, so close to the surface and ready to offer itself in those moments of self-doubt and danger, both physical and spiritual. The soft aspirant sound of the Heh indicates that it is a letter with feminine characteristics. It indicates the female ability to create but also the masculine ability to fertilize. The story of Abram and Sarai reveals this as they were childless until God added the creative Heh to their names, Abram to Abraham and Sarai to Sarah. Soon after, though past her natural childbearing age, she gave birth to a son. When placed at the end of a word, Heh doubles its creative power and intensifies its meaning. This makes it powerful when used on magical scripts.

Heh is considered to be specially powerful when appearing twice, as it does in the Holy Name יהוה. The shape is open at the top of the letter. This shows that 1) God has given free will to humanity, and 2) that the door is always open to those who desire to return, as in the story of the prodigal son.

The breathy sound of Heh links it to the sound of the Aleph, thus beginning the name Eheieh and the statement "I am." This is heard in the cry of the newborn child as it takes its first breath and gives out the Heh: "I am, I am born, I am here (*heenayni*). I have form." When a child is born, its head passes through the pelvic circle of bone. Midwives call this moment "the crowning." If you look at the construction of the pelvis, you will see the bone on either side branch out like antlers. In a normal delivery every child is thus crowned with horns, the symbol of the astrological sign Aries, linked to Path 15. Every soul is royal at this time and enters into life with all its potential gifts ready to unfold. The environment and the home into which it is born will determine how that potential will be achieved. Heh as a window admits both light (illumination) and air (communication). This makes it a transmitter of knowledge and creative power.

Anything that is framed stands out; the frame makes a statement, it forces you to look at what is framed and to observe more closely the detail caught in the frame with greater understanding. If the window is closed or obscured, the possibility of a true understanding is lessened. When Noah opened the window of the ark and sent out the raven, he was hoping to "see" if the flood was over. The raven was black, the message was obscured . . . Noah sent out a second bird and this time it was the white dove; the message that it brought back was clear to him.

You can use this technique in everyday life to great advantage. If beset by difficulty or a particular problem, frame it. It will help you focus on what is central to the problem. When you look at the whole thing you get too involved in small details; this prevents a clear understanding. See where the core is, frame it, and look at it closely. You will find that once you restrict your vision to the main cause it becomes much easier to deal with.

I found this so useful that I bought a large photo frame and began to use it as a focusing technique. Sometimes I used a Tarot card to symbolize my problem; other times I used a montage of symbols or drawings, even a Dali-esque sprawl of color and shapes that seemed to express what I was feeling. By framing it I was able to concentrate on the cause and so find the solution.

For even better results simply use a real window and draw a symbol of your dilemma on the glass with a felt-tip pen in the color you think best symbolizes the problem. Don't use words, they do not reach the subconscious mind; always use symbols even if they are just shapes or undefined forms. Then sit and look at it with the light coming through the window, illuminating the problem displayed.

There is a hidden meaning in the word *window*. This symbol stands for an incoming light . . . illumination, realization on a spiritual level. This is the power of Heh. Its creative, fertilizing ability is the result of knowingness, of illumination. The knowledge of the inner divinity becomes clear and real. This is why the Heh is such an important part of the Tetragrammaton. We all know our own name. God knows its own power, glory, divinity, and ultimate Godhood.

Again, go to Renaissance paintings and see how often a window is placed behind or to the side of the subject. Contemplation of what the window frames will open up the thoughts of the artist and his understanding of the person or subject he is painting. The more I became involved with the letter, the more I began to appreciate the knowledge and the understanding of the great painters of the past. I began to look at their work with new eyes and in doing so opened up a new world of color, form, and symbolism that I had not known existed.

Meditations

FIRST MEDITATION

Sit in silence before a slightly open window and observe in minute detail what you can see. Try to understand what is happening within that small square. Think of it in terms of what you know and understand concerning the letter Heh.

SECOND MEDITATION

With a thick felt-tip pen, draw a large Heh upon the windowpane. Do this in the morning when the light is at its brightest. Then sit before it and contemplate the symbolism of the morning light shining on and through the symbol. Try to reach an understanding of the letter through this.

Third Meditation

Draw a symbol on the window glass, or put up a picture or painting so that the light streams through it. Contemplate this and allow the images to rise up. Try this with different symbols and pictures from different traditions and times.

Pathworking

When you are ready, close your eyes and let yourself fall into the inner silence where truth dwells. Heh, the fifth letter of the Aleph-Beth, is aligned to Path 15 from Chokmah to Tiphereth. As the letter of the path of the Star, it is a very powerful being.

By now you know what to expect and you look about you eagerly for the appearance of the letter Heh. It moves slowly and majestically into your view, violet in color and rimmed with silver. It hovers before you and when it speaks the voice is full, rich, and holds a note of command.

"Life, I have been commanded by the Most High to show you a little of the vast creation around you. A creation in which I, Heh, have played a great part."

There is a silence that becomes filled with divine laughter. The violet of the Heh becomes bright red, and it goes on hastily. "Of course it was the doing of the Most High, I merely assisted in a small way."

It pauses and you get the impression that the letter is being gently reprimanded. "A very small way. If you wish you may ride on my back. I am quite strong, you know."

You place your foot on the Yod as if upon a step and the Heh bends lower until you can climb on the top of its Daleth. You feel quite safe here, for although the Heh is inclined to be a little pompous, it is quite fond of human beings. The letter moves off at great speed and the Earth falls away beneath you. You can see the moon before you, growing larger and larger until it fills your sight. The Heh takes you down almost to the surface and now you can see the bits and pieces left behind by the astronauts.

"The moon is quite inert. Life will have to be very inventive to be able to live here," the Heh tells you. "Of course, Life will live here one day soon, but not in the way you live on Earth. Let me show you the beauty of the planet you call Mars." It zooms away.

When Mars comes into view you are breathless with its beauty. The high cliffs and massive valleys, mountains far higher than those on Earth . . . and the color. You could never have imagined how many shades of red there could be. The Heh shows you where the probes have landed and you can see the one that was lost at the bottom of one of the smaller cliffs. Its wheels still turn slowly, but its camera equipment has been shattered.

"Life learns through mistakes, that is the reason the Most High is so forgiving. God knows that mistakes make good teachers. It is when the lesson of a mistake is not learned and the same one is made over and over again that He becomes sad."

The Heh goes on. "Life will come here soon and by that time they will have learned more of the secrets of my form and sound and power and so will be able to use it to survive here. In the far future the Life of which you are an example will change and transmute, as Life was designed to do. It will become native to this planet and forget the time when it was not so.

"Of all the creations of the Most High, Life has been the most wondrous. When a new species evolves He uses my power and sound as a foundation." Heh makes a sound curiously like a human sigh, then goes on. "I am often guilty of being proud of this, but you see it brings me so close to Him I cannot help it . . . come, let us go on."

Heh carries you farther across the solar system, past the orbit of the swiftly moving moons of Demos and Phobos, until the huge bulk of Jupiter comes into sight. This close, it fills the whole of your vision. Fascinated, you watch the turmoil of the great red spot and travel across the paths of the many moons, each so different in its way. All the time you are asking questions and Heh explains that though it knows many things, it does not know everything but will answer what it can.

A friendship is beginning to grow between you and the being that is Heh. Its tendency to self-satisfaction is offset by its frankness. Its total, unutterable love for its Creator endears it to you. As you leave the red planet and set out for Saturn, you ask: "Heh, what is it like to be one of the first created by God?"

There is silence, then: "Life, the joy is such that there are no words for me to use to even come near to telling you. Yet this much I can tell you, though you may not believe me. We were created, my brother and sister letters and myself, to help

God in his great task of creating the perfect universe in which Life has the total experience of existence, from the depths of manifestation to the heights of spirituality. I and my companions will never know this utter perfection, for we came before Life was formed. Each one of us is blessed in some way. Aleph begins and is the leader of us all, Beth is the first letter of the blessing, Daleth is kindness and compassion and so on, but Life will surpass us all.

"I am a creative letter and my power is to give increase in many ways. But the letters were also given to you, Life, so that you could laugh, and sing, and give praise. We grow through your use of us. My sound is that of your letter *H*. I begin the word hallelujah, but also hate. I am the first letter of Hashem, the name a Jew uses to speak of God, but I also begin the words havoc, heresy, hell, and hubris. When Life uses the letters to speak well of others, when we are used to fashion words of love, faith, and trust, we grow in power and experience. When we are used to form words of hate and blasphemy, we are diminished. You do not realize, Life, how much power you have over beings like myself. We cannot refuse to be used by you, but we can be misused. Do you understand? I hope so, for on you depends the Great Plan. We are in sight of the rings of Saturn, are they not beautiful?"

The Heh carries you through the silvery rings, diving and soaring like a bird. You cling to it, terrified and yet exhilarated at the wonders that you see. It is one thing to see these things in a picture or in a photograph taken by a space probe, but to experience them close up, as they really are, is something you will never forget. The words of the Heh are something else you will never forget. You promise yourself that from now on you will choose your words more carefully, respecting the letters that form them.

Your thoughts are heard by the Heh, who curls the Yod that is its foot around you in a gentle caress. "We are all a living part of Hashem and his creation, Life. Let us give joyful thanks for that."

From the beauty of Saturn to the icy coldness of Neptune and Uranus, the Heh takes you onward and you marvel at the precision and exactness of everything around you. There is something awesome about the balance of each planet as it follows the steps of the great dance about the central point of the solar logos. You try to tell the Heh that you are sorry you never realized everything was so ordered, so perfect, and so beautiful.

"Ah, Life, all that Hashem makes is beautiful, even when it appears not to be so when you first look. Even more wonderful is the purpose behind the creation. Do not feel sorry that you have not seen this before; the time was not right for you, as it was not right for me to spend time with you, until now. Seeing your wonder has helped me to see it with your human eyes and for that I must bless you."

As the Heh speaks, you feel the power of its blessing settle upon you, filling you with love, strength, and the creative power that is its own gift to you.

"Look down, Life, there is Pluto, the last of the planets in your solar system. There are other small asteroids, of course, but this is the last planet. Look beyond and you will see the beginning of deep space. One day human beings will set out to cross it. On that day I think a little pride will be well justified."

You look and wonder. The Heh turns for home now and together you make your way back across the miles toward the green and blue Earth that waits for you. A feeling of thankfulness wells up in you and you sing out with joy. The Heh joins with you in a rich bass voice and together you and the letter of God speed across space toward Earth, the shining jewel of the solar system, roaring out a song of praise to the One Creator.

Far below you is the planet of Life, and as the Heh sets down gently you see that you are beside a pool of crystal clear water. A young women crowned with seven stars kneels there, holding two jars of water that she is carefully pouring into the pool. One foot is in the water and the other is on land. You slide down from the back of the Heh and approach her to ask her what she is doing. She tells you:

"I am creating Life. This jar contains the impulse to create form in many different ways. This jar contains the essence of the Most High. When the two came together in the primal waters of the Earth, Life began its long evolutionary journey. The seven stars of my crown represent the seven planetary lords who oversee the whole process. I am the beginning, the plan, the pattern of that which was to come. In you I see my work evolving as it was meant to do."

She rises and walks into the distance. The Heh waits silently. You go toward it, understanding now that what you see with your eyes is not what Heh truly is. You caress it gently, letting love flow from your heart toward it. It explodes into light, dazzling you, but in that one second you come close to seeing its perfection. From the light comes the voice of the Heh.

"Life, I thank you for your gift of love. It will be shared between my companion letters and I. In return, we offer this advice. Look to the letters of your name and their meaning. You will find much in them to help you in your search for self-knowledge."

In the silence that follows, you sense its departure. You take a deep breath and as you let it out, you wake to your own world.

Psalm 119

Verses 33–40, assigned to Heh

Teach me, O Lord, the way of thy statutes,

and I shall keep it unto the end.

Give me understanding and I shall keep thy law;

yes, I shall observe it with my whole heart.

Make me to go in the path of thy commandments,

for therein do I delight.

Incline my heart unto thy testimonies,

and not to covetousness.

Turn away mine eyes from beholding vanity,

and quicken thou me in thy way.

Establish thy word unto thy servant,

who is devoted to thee.

Turn away my reproach, which I fear,

for thy judgments are good.

Behold, I have longed after thy precepts;

quicken thou me in thy precepts.

∾

Ritual

You will need a table with a white cloth; a central altar light; four small tealights in holders at each quarter; four mirrors approximately 12 x 12 inches, no smaller, one at each quarter (you can use a roll of reflective paper with a mirrored surface from a hardware store but the reflective image must be clear). Place a chair in each quarter and make sure that when sitting down you can see yourself clearly in the mirror opposite your chair. If possible make hip-length tabards in the quarter colors and place them as follows: gold in the east, red in the south, blue in the west, and green in the north. Place a small chalice of wine or fruit juice and a wafer on the altar. When all is ready, seal the space with a pentagram at each quarter, invoking the protection of the Light, then approach the altar and light the center light.

"Light of Lights, live within me that I may light the way for those who come after me. I seek to open the window of my soul that I may understand the divinity within and without. *Move to the west and light the candle in that quarter, then put on the blue tabard.* The first level of self-realization I seek to know is that of my spiritual self. I take my seat in the quarter of intuition and look to the east for enlightenment. In the mirror of the east, let me know myself." *Take the western seat and look into the eastern mirror.*

"I summon Raphael, the golden healer of God, to the station of the east. Open the magical mirror of the dawn to my inner eye that I may perceive the divinity that lies hidden within. Let the inner eye be opened and the power of intuition awaken. Let the created Heh within observe the creative Heh without. Let that which is above sanctify that which is below." *Sit silent and still and observe yourself within the mirror before you. You may need to spend some ten to fifteen minutes before realizations begin to open up in your mind. When you feel enough time has elapsed, write down what you have received.* "I give thanks to thee, Raphael, for your help and for your presence. I ask the blessing of the Most High upon you." *Rise, take off the blue tabard, and move to the north. Put on the green tabard, then light the candle there.*

"The second level of self-realization I seek to know is that of my mental self. Therefore I take my seat in the quarter of manifestation and look to the south for clarity of mind. In the mirror of the south, let me know myself." *Take the northern seat and look into the southern mirror. See yourself dressed in green.* "I summon

Michael, the warrior of God, to the station of the south. Open the magical mirror of the noonday sun to my inner eye that I may perceive the majesty within. Let the inner eye be opened and the power of creative fire awaken. Let the Heh without quicken the Heh within. Let that which is above grant wisdom to that which is below.

"Observe the creative Heh without. Let that which is above sanctify that which is below." *Sit silent and still and observe yourself within the mirror as before. When you feel enough time has elapsed, write down what you have received.* "I give thanks to thee, Michael, for your help and for your presence. I ask the blessing of the Most High upon you." *Rise, take off the green tabard and move to the east. Put on the gold tabard. Light the candle there.*

"The third level of self-realization I seek to know is that of my astral/intuitive self. Therefore I take my seat in the quarter of spirituality and look to the west for the clear sight of the seer. In the mirror of the west, let me know myself." *Take the eastern seat and look into the western mirror. See yourself dressed in gold.* "I summon Gabriel, the messenger of God, to the station of the west. Open the magical mirror of the setting sun to my inner eye that I may perceive the majesty within. Let the inner eye be opened and the power of the spirit awaken. Let the Heh without observe the Heh within. Let that which is above grant clear sight to that which is below. Let that which is above hallow that which is below." *Sit silent and still and observe yourself within the mirror as before. When you feel enough time has elapsed, write down what you have received.* "I give thanks to thee, Gabriel, for your help and for your presence. I ask the blessing of the Most High upon you." *Rise, take off the gold tabard, and move to the south. Put on the red tabard. Light the candle there.*

"The fourth level of self-realization I seek to know is that of my physical self. Therefore I take my seat in the quarter of courage and look to the north for the power of the manifested magician. In the mirror of the north, let me seek myself." *Take the southern seat and look into the northern mirror. See yourself dressed in red.* "I summon Uriel, the seneschal of God, to the station of the north. Open the magical mirror of the midnight sun to my inner eye that I may perceive the true self within. Let the inner eye be opened and the grace of love awaken. Let the Heh without contemplate the Heh within. Let that which is above grant self-knowledge to that which is below. Let that which is above consecrate that which is below." *Sit silent and still and observe yourself within the mirror as before. When you feel enough time has elapsed, write down what you have received.* "I give thanks to thee, Uriel, for your help and for your presence. I ask the blessing of the Most High upon you." *Rise, take off the red tabard, and move around to the east, clockwise. Bless the wine and the wafers. Lift the wine high.*

"I lift up my heart to the Light of Lights. Share with me, thou greatest of Mysteries, this offering of wine. Let it be a sign of love between us." *Drink and replace chalice; take up a wafer and lift it up.* "Likewise, let us share bread together and let it be a sign that we shall henceforth exist One within the Other." *Eat the wafer.* "All is accomplished, the servant of the Light of Lights departs now in peace and with a full heart."

Snuff out all the candles. Reverse the quarter pentagrams and retire.

VAV

Thou art the teacher and the giver of the piercing wound
by which we learn and understand.
How sharp is thy point and how deeply
 it embeds itself in my heart.
I cry out, petitioning mercy and surcease
from the agony of learning.
I am alone in my pain. But where art thou?
My Creator, hast thou also forsaken me?
I try to escape but I am nailed by thee
upon the foursquare Cross of the Elements,
nigh fainting from the pain of your intent.
Heartsore, I hear thy voice and look to see
I am not bound by aught save love itself.
It is thy lesson of love that wounds me,
that keeps me near and suffering.
The pain I feel is the pain I cause to thee,
and so causing must endure.
Nothing holds me here but the lesson I must learn.
If this be so, then will I endure.
For out of pain will come experience.
I will fill a chalice with my tears
and offer it to those who come after me.

Image: Nail
Symbol: ו
Path on the Tree of Life: 16
Numerical Value: 6

Prayer

This is a prayer of pain and panic. The lessons we learn in life can be very painful and often during such times we feel bereft of comfort, hope, and help. This is often so when the dark night of the soul comes upon us. We become so blinded by our pain that we cannot see what it is trying to tell us. This happens on the physical level of the body as well. We feel a pain and grouse about it, take some medication, and when this alleviates the pain we go on with what we were doing. We ignore the fact that the pain is the body's way of asking for help in that area. We are either too fearful of what it might mean or too concerned with other things to bother with our health. As above, so below; as with the body, so with the spirit.

We often ignore spiritual pain in the same way and instead of seeking the cause we override it with complaints and pander to it with placebos. If, however, we take time to be silent and seek within for the real cause, we often find that the pain is caused by our own actions. We do not have enough spiritual trust, neither do we take time to cure our spiritual ills.

"I am alone in my pain. But where art thou?

My Creator, hast thou also forsaken me?"

Even Yeshua had a moment of doubt and panic . . . but at last, said with perfect love and perfect trust (the words with which every member of the Craft enters sacred space), "Into thy hands I commend my spirit."

Once we face up to the cause of spiritual pain, we find that it is an illusion we have fashioned ourselves (shades of the Tarot trump of the Devil). But because nothing that happens in this universe is ever lost or wasted, the pain can be transmuted into understood experience. This is something that can be handed on to others undergoing their own dark night. Ernest Butler, the founder and creator of the Servants of the Light School, taught us never to regret anything that happened to us, but to use the experience to offer support and help to those going through similar circumstances. He said: "You can then offer not pity, or even sympathy, but true understanding and support; this makes your own experience a blessing in disguise." His words inspired the last lines of the prayer: "I will fill a chalice with my tears and offer it to those who come after me."

The Letter

On the physical level, a nail (Vav) holds things together. It facilitates building houses, furniture, the doors and windows already discussed, and many other things. It is an essential path of what in the Western Mysteries is known as the Path of the Hearth Fire, or everyday life. In fact the male phallus is a uniting Vav in the act of coition, connecting male to female as it does. It is a conduit of life at the beginning of conception, as the female vagina becomes the conduit into the world at the end of pregnancy.

On the astral level it is the link between the imagination and the matrix of the astral world. It is the dream, the desire, the wish, and the hope that seeks out its astral counterpart and joins with it to become a wish fulfilled.

At the mental level it can be a union of two minds, two hearts, two souls coming together to make a union of bodies, emotions, and spirits. The power of the Vav is the power to unite things *and* make them work together. Notice the emphasis on the word "and" in the last sentence. "And" is very much a Vav word because it unites other words; for example, this and that, black and white, good and bad, and so on. At this level it also brings together the inspiration (mental), the pattern or prototype (astral), and the final manifestation (physical).

At the spiritual level, when contemplating the name of God, notice that the Vav joins the first Heh to the final Heh, linking and doubling in power the blazing, creative energies of God. In the phrase "As above, so below," the word "so" links the above and the below. Yeshua via the Vav as the implement of His death connected the spiritual world to that of matter.

The painting of the Creation by Michelangelo on the ceiling of the Sistine Chapel shows the moment of Adam's creation. The hand of God reaches out to the hand of Adam, and the energy that flows between the fingertips is a perfect example of the Vav as an energy link.

A study of the Tarot trump of the High Priest, or Hierophant, is also worthwhile. We see here another form of the uniting Vav energy, for the two figures kneeling before him are united and drawn together by the teachings he is imparting. As the High Priest, he becomes the conduit of power emanating from Kether on its way to Malkuth. Thus he is of himself a Vav or junction point between the levels. Any form of mediating ability provides the same energy: mediums, mediators, prophets, and oracles, etc., down the ages have exercised this same joining and conducting power.

Meditations

FIRST MEDITATION

Visualize the symbol of clasped hands and meditate on the image. Look at the shape of Aleph; see that the Vav is a uniting agent for the two Yods, and meditate on what this suggests to you.

SECOND MEDITATION

Meditate on how the central and invisible force between two magnets creates an unseen but powerful bond.

THIRD MEDITATION

Meditate on love as a Vav between a man and a woman, on conception as the Vav between man, woman, and child, and on the spiritual link as the Vav between a priest and his or her congregation.

Pathworking

As you enter the silence, fill your mind with the thought of unity and how the whole world in which you live depends upon unity at some level or other. Now broaden that thought and see how the universe is also united, each tiny piece locking into another and in turn becoming part of something else. The whole of Creation, once it has manifested, depends upon the power and energy of the Vav, for without a unity of purpose it would all fall apart.

Open your inner eyes on a small village, in a time about fifteen hundred years ago. You are walking between the roughly made houses on a track beaten by many feet. You can hear the sound of a hammer on metal and you follow it until you come to a forge. The smith is not a very tall man but he is powerfully built. He is intent on his work and you stand watching him. He is fashioning some nails, drawing out the iron into thin strands and cutting them into different lengths. He makes each one carefully, using hammers of different weights and with different heads. Finally each one is cooled in the water bucket and set aside. Then he looks up and smiles.

Under the dirt, dust, and sweat you see that he is quite young and with a pleasant if ordinary face. He greets you with courtesy and, surprisingly, has been expecting you. He offers you water and asks you to wait while he puts on something more suitable for the journey you will both be taking. He goes into the house, taking the nails he has just made with him.

You sit and wait quietly. By now you are used to such surprises and have no fear or apprehension concerning whatever will happen. The smith reappears in a homespun robe of dark red with a twist of the same material about his head. He carries two bundles and two leather satchels and gives one of each to you. The satchel contains a loaf of bread and a waterskin. From a corner he takes two staffs and hands one to you. Then you set off down the track and out of the village.

As you walk the smith talks. "You are here to understand the power of the letter Vav. It is more than just a nail; it connects everything to everything else. That is why it was placed in the name of God, and why it is a part of so many of the other letters. Think of a chain and you will see a symbol of Vav power. Think of handcuffs on a prisoner, the wedding ring on the finger of a bride, and you see Vav. We are all connected by and through the power of the Creator. The One is the primal unifying power of this universe. Would it surprise you to hear that there are other universes? Oh yes, you know there are other galaxies, but they are a part of this universe. There are others, many others, and they all work on the same principles." He stops and points to a large tree just ahead.

"Look at that tree. You see only the trunk and the leaves, but underneath there are thousands of connecting roots that link the tree to the earth. That is Vav energy and power. Look at the grass there and the cow eating it. The grass is nothing like milk, yet the cow acts as a link between grass and milk. Fruit, vegetables, plant life—all are links between the mobile life forms of this planet and the earth on which they both live. All those links are one aspect of the power of Vav."

You walk in silence as you think this over, then you begin to make links yourself. "The clothes I wear, the sandals on my feet, link me to the wool and the leather from which they are made, to the sheep through the wool and the ox through the leather. The earth is a link because it receives and holds and links all that grows in and on it. We are all dependent upon each other. Is that what you are saying?"

"Yes. Nothing stands alone. When the One created the letters, he gave to each of them an energy, a power, and a purpose. He set all the letters into his crown as a symbol of the power of his Word. Those letters, which make up his many names, have a direct link to him—the letters of the Tetragrammaton especially. By placing the uniting Vav between the two powerful Hehs, he created what you will call in your time an alternating current. In your world you use solar energy with the aid of something you call a panel. Think of the Creator as the central Sun of Suns, the primal point of light, sound, color, and energy throughout the entire universe, then think of everything else that lives, breathes, and has existence in whatsoever form as a panel, a receiver of his energy and power. This is achieved by the connecting power of the Vav within, that minute particle of himself that was given as an eternal gift to Life in the very beginning."

While you have been walking and traveling, the afternoon has slipped into early evening. You make camp by a small stream where a group of trees offer shelter from the night wind. By a small fire you break bread and eat plump, juicy olives and dates from the satchels. You sit quietly and think over the revelations that have been given to you. It has expanded your view of the world you live in and the solar system, and even what lies beyond. As the night draws on, you wrap yourself in the snug sheepskin that was your bundle and fall into a deep sleep. The smith keeps watch.

In this sleep that is a sleep within a sleep, you open your dream eyes on a different world. Beside the fire a presence stirs and unfolds itself. No smith, but a radiating Light that is also a sound and a color. A flash of silver edged with scarlet and green towers above you as the Vav takes on the shape of its letter.

"I greet you, Life, in the name of the One. I have given you words, now I shall give you sight for a few minutes so that you may see the universe as it really is. For this you must enter into my world; it is a level that you will not be able to sustain for more than a short span of time. Try to remember as much as you can, and understand as much as you can. I will be close by so you will come to no harm."

There is pressure on your eyeballs, your throat, your heart center, and your solar plexus. You feel wrenched as if your body has convulsed; there is a moment of pain so brief it is gone before you can react to it. Then you are floating free in a place so different you cannot find words to describe it, even to yourself. You look at your hand and see every molecule like a tiny solar system, yet linked to every other molecule. The edges of your form are blurred into several layers; vaguely you understand that this is because you are existing in all dimensions simultaneously. The impressions crowding your brain are being received from a multitude of personalities, all you and all existing in a different level of being. Yet you are all one.

You look around and see the universe from the letter's point of view. Instead of emptiness it is filled with suns, double and even triple, and solar systems of all kinds. Gas clouds as big as galaxies and in between matter, stardust, God particles floating, changing, transmuting, forming, and reforming, and all linked to those around them. Each one gives out its own note, filling space with glorious sounds like millions of voices singing. It is a shining, silvery, universal net of living matter and all of it a living whole. Finally you grasp the true meaning of a phrase you have heard and read about so often and never before fully understood. This, *this* is the House of the Net.

You try to see as much, understand as much as you can, then it begins to dim and fade. You cry out, weeping, begging for a moment longer, but knowing that even if it were possible you could not exist in this place. The sounds and colors fade into darkness, a wrench convulses your astral body, and you are aware of the Vav beside you. Desolate from the loss of such beauty, you weep, and the Vav speaks gently.

"Why do you weep, Life? Have you not understood the greatest answer of all? What you have seen is your inheritance, the inheritance of all Life. You will come into it one day, it is not lost to you, just kept safe until you complete your training as a child of God. Keep me in your mind and heart, Life, for I am the link between you and the Most High, between you and what you have seen. Like the smith I can forge links between you and all other Life. Take these three nails—see, I will place them in your third eye, your throat center, and your heart center. Here they will stay so you can remember, speak of, and feel what you have experienced, and teach it to others. Farewell, Life." You are enclosed in warmth and love and slowly begin to feel the weight of the physical about you. Open your eyes and rest.

Psalm 91

He that dwelleth in the secret places of the Most High
shall abide under the shadow of the Almighty.
He is my refuge and my fortress, in Him will I trust.
Surely He will deliver thee from the snare of the fowler
and from the noisome pestilence.
He shall cover thee with His feathers, and under His wings shalt thou rest.
His truth shall be thy sword and thy buckler.
Thou shalt not be afraid of the terror by night,
nor for the arrow that flieth by day.
Nor for the pestilence that walketh in darkness,
or the destruction that was at noonday.
A thousand shall fall at thy right side, and ten thousand at thy left hand,
but it shall not come nigh thee. There shall no evil befall thee,
neither shall any plague come nigh thy dwelling.
For He shall give His angels charge over thee to keep thee in all thy ways.
They shall bear thee up in their hands, lest thou dash thy foot against a stone.
Thou shalt tread upon the lion and the adder.
The young lion and the dragon shalt thou trample under foot.
Because He hath set His love upon me, therefore will I deliver Him.
I will set Him on high because He hath known my name.
He shall call upon me and I will answer, deliver, and honor Him.
With long life shall I satisfy Him and show Him my salvation.

≈

Ritual

You will need an altar, a white cloth, and a center light in a blue bowl with four smaller lights surrounding it: gold in the east, red in the south, blue in the west, and green in the north. In the east, place a small burner of incense of your own choosing and a length of gold ribbon, enough to tie around your waist. In the south, place a menorah with red candles or a multiple candleholder and enough red ribbon to go across your shoulder from right to left. The west holds a glass of pure water and enough blue ribbon to go across your shoulder from left to right. The north has a basket of freshly baked rolls or matzos and a green ribbon to go around the neck and hang to the waist. The intent of the ritual is to unite oneself with the four elements through the power of the Vav.

Enter your sacred space and bow to the altar. Make sure you have everything you need. Turn to the east and make the sign of three plus three, that is, two interlaced triangles making a six-pointed star, for six is the number of Vav. Speak:

"By the power of the divine within, I open the gate of the east and welcome Raphael, regent of air; Paralda, elemental king of air; and the element of air itself. Be welcome into this sacred space." *Move to the south and repeat the star.*

"By the power of the divine within, I open the gate of the south and welcome Michael, regent of fire; Djinn, elemental king of fire; and the element of fire itself. Be welcome into this sacred space." *Move to the west and repeat the star.*

"By the power of the divine within, I open the gate of the west and welcome Gabriel, regent of water; Nixsa, elemental king of water; and the element of water itself. Be welcome into this sacred space." *Move to the north and repeat the star.*

"By the power of the divine within, I open the gate of the north and welcome Uriel, regent of earth; Ghob, elemental king of earth; and the element of earth itself. Be welcome into this sacred space." *Move to the east again and go to the altar. Light the center light and the smaller gold light.*

"I light the altar light with reverence and with love. May it shine throughout this ceremony and remain in my heart as a constant beacon for those less fortunate than myself." *Take two steps back from the altar, and with incense make the sign of the six-pointed star before the altar.*

"By this sign and by my will, I summon the presence of Paralda, elemental king of air. *Pause and visualize the king between you and the altar.* My intent is to make a peaceful and holy alliance with the powers of air through the uniting intelligence of the holy letter Vav, that I may truly understand the power of the first Word. I bless the element of air and its presence within me. May the power of the Vav be with us in this ritual. *Step through the astral image of the six-pointed star up to the altar, bow, and replace incense.* I take up this gold ribbon and bind it about me as a sign of the covenant between me and the element of air. Selah." *Move to the south, light the smaller red candle, take up the menorah, and take two steps back. With the candles, make the sign of the six-pointed star.*

"By this sign and by my will, I summon the presence of Djinn, elemental king of fire. *Pause and visualize the king between you and the altar.* My intent is to make a peaceful and holy alliance with the powers of fire through the uniting intelligence of the holy letter Vav, that I may truly understand the power of primal fire, the creative desire of God. I bless the element of fire and its presence within me. May the power of the Vav be with us in this ritual. *Step through the astral image of the six-pointed star up to the altar, bow, and replace the candles.* I take up this red ribbon and place it across my shoulder from right to left as a sign of the covenant between me and the element of fire. Selah." *Move to the west, light the blue candle, take up the chalice, and take two steps back. With the chalice, make the sign of the six-pointed star.*

"By this sign and by my will, I summon the presence of Nixsa, elemental king of water. *Pause and visualize the king between you and the altar.* My intent is to make a peaceful and holy alliance with the powers of water through the uniting intelligence of the holy letter Vav, that I may truly understand the power of intuition. I bless the element of water and its presence within me. May the power of the Vav be with us in this ritual. *Step through the astral image of the six-pointed star up to the altar, bow, and replace the chalice.* I take up this blue ribbon and place it across my shoulder from left to right as a sign of the covenant between me and the element of water. Selah." *Move to the north, light the green candle, take up the bread, and take two steps back. With the basket make the sign of the six-pointed star.*

"By this sign and by my will, I summon the presence of Ghob, elemental king of earth. *Pause and visualize the king between you and the altar.* My intent is to make a peaceful and holy alliance with the powers of earth through the uniting intelligence of the holy letter Vav, that I may truly understand the power of form and growth. I bless the element of earth and its presence within me. May the power of the Vav be with us in this ritual. *Step through the astral image of the six-pointed star up to the altar, bow, and replace the basket.* I take up this green ribbon and hang it about my neck as a sign of the covenant between me and the element of earth. Selah." *Move to the east and go to the altar.*

"For inasmuch as I, (your name), have this night voluntarily and with love and trust entered into a covenant with the four elements, their regents and kings, to sustain their elements within my physical body for this incarnation, I ask the Most High, the Creator of Heaven and Earth, to bless those regents, kings, and elements for their work within me and around me. May the power and support of the holy letter Vav be a lasting part of this intention and may its inner presence be a living part of my life from now on." *With an incense stick, turn to the east and make the sign of the six-pointed star. Step through it and bow to the east.*

"Let the gate of air in the direction of east be closed and may all concerned be at peace. May all beneath this roof sleep deeply and well." *With the incense stick, turn to the south and make the sign of the six-pointed star. Step through it and bow to the south.*

"Let the gate of fire in the direction of south be closed and may all concerned be at peace. May all beneath this roof sleep deeply and well." *With an incense stick, turn to the west and make the sign of the six-pointed star. Step through it and bow to the west.*

"Let the gate of water in the direction of the west be closed and may all concerned be at peace. May all beneath this roof sleep deeply and well." *With an incense stick, turn to the north and make the sign of the six-pointed star. Step through it and bow to the north.*

"Let the gate of earth in the direction of the north be closed and may all concerned be at peace. May all beneath this roof sleep deeply and well." *Return to the east and replace the incense. Snuff out all candles but the center one. Leave this to burn for half an hour. Take off the ribbons and place them in a bag and leave them on the altar overnight. Wear them when doing any of the rituals in this book from now on.*

ZAYIN

Sword-Bearer, I come to thee
with my hands open.
Be not wrathful with me,
but stand beside me as a protector.
In the presence of my enemies,
be thou my shield and my armor.
Thou art my jackal,
smelling out the spoor of those who would wound me.
They come upon me like flies seeking my blood.
But thou art my champion and I lean upon thy strength.
We two will stand together
and the darkness shall not overcome us.
Give me thy hand, let me feel its power.
Give me thy love, that I may be like unto the pomegranate
and bear seeds of greatness.
Separate me not from thee,
but let me dwell with thee in love.
Two of a likeness, from above and
from below, we will stand together.
From the mountaintop comes the voice of the Lord:
"With the Zayin shall I cleave thine enemies
and scatter their bones in the desert."

Image: Sword or Spear
Symbol: ז
Path on the Tree of Life: 17
Numerical Value: 7

Prayer

There are times when anger is the only thing that serves the immediate purpose. There are, after all, only four cheeks on the human body that one can turn! When the pressure becomes too great to bear, one might be forgiven for venting one's spleen as an alternative to raising the blood pressure to dangerous levels. After all, even Yeshua got steamed up in the court of the money changers!

This prayer came at such a moment and putting it on paper was immensely satisfying. It was a moment when apathy and despondency gave way to rage, rage at myself for allowing things to get me to such a low state. This was followed by a steely determination to rise above the situation. To those who find themselves in a similar predicament, let me say that the situation is only as bad as you want to make it.

To become angry is to raise the level of one's value of the self. It is the level above apathy and that means you are on the way up. This is not a prayer asking for your hand to be held, it is a demand for backup in a just cause. "Be thou my shield and my armor"—this is fighting talk! It is at such a time that one finds there *is* someone beside you. It may be your own higher self, or a presence from the angelic world. It can even be someone you knew and loved and who has gone before you. I have known many instances when a much-loved relative or friend has returned to give help in such times. Accept it, it is your just dues.

"We two will stand together and the darkness shall not overcome us." When you can feel that there is someone/something behind you, you are on your way. The prayer makes it quite clear that you are dealing here with what the Bible calls "righteous wrath"; this is not, I repeat *not*, for anyone who simply feels they would like to have a go at their boss or the man next door with the dog that barks all night. Once the link is made between you and your companion, you will begin to feel a lightness of spirit. This is the point where you begin to see the light at the end of your dark night of the soul.

The Letter

The letter really does look like its image of a sword. In some books on the Aleph-Beth it is described as a spear, but the shape, with the hilt and the blade, is well defined. In fact it can be seen as anything with a sharp point capable of inflicting a wound, or piercing, or dividing, and because it divides that which is one, they become two and then three and so on.

Zayin is placed on Path 17. Astrologically this is the place of Gemini the Twins, and there is certainly enough duality here to underline that choice. Castor and Pollux, Cain and Abel, Romulus and Remus, all famous twins. But the Lovers are also well represented. You can find them in many of the events of the Old Testament. Ruth and Boaz, Jacob and Rachel, Abraham and Sarah, Soloman and Sheba, and David and Bat-sheba. (The prefix *Bat* was the original name for Hathor, the Egyptian goddess of love and desire. She is now seen only as the ornamental weight or *menat* holding the heavy ceremonial necklaces in place.) You might do well to reread the story of Noah's ark and the gathering up of the animals and birds two by two, male and female, with all the potential for increase that this implies.

The Tarot trump of the Lovers, the Gemini, shows in fact three figures—the man and the woman plus the spiritual aspect of their union. This is often depicted as an angelic figure, but it really should be the Shekinah, for it is she who blesses the marriage bed.

With the Tarot trump of this path being that of the Lovers, it may appear strange that the letter symbol is a sword, a symbol of division. However when we look at the biblical story of Creation, we can see a very real division in the allegory of the rib (sword, spear, and of course yet another phallic symbol) taken from the side of Adam and used to create Eve. Whether you view the Bible version as true or as a legend that has grown out of tales and suppositions from earliest times is not the point. Which came first—the chicken or the egg, the male or the female—does not matter. The story holds a symbolic teaching; it tells us that there was a time in evolution when a separation, a distinction, between the sexes became essential for survival. Give Mother Nature her due, she does nothing without a reason.

The division of labor—one to carry, bear, and nurture, and one to provide food (and in some species the male *is* the food!) and to protect—would have seemed to give the young a better chance of survival. The sword therefore can be seen as a necessary part of evolution in this sense.

We see it in the fiery sword with which the angel drove Adam and Eve from the garden of Eden. From the single hermaphroditic cell with no worries about seeking and finding a mate, fending off other males, etc., to the more complex lifestyle that separate male and female units had to face would certainly have been traumatic. Yet the separation also brought about the chance to develop emotions that come with such a change. The emotion of bonding between couples and between parents and offspring brought into being the higher emotions of love, gentleness, caring, and the desire to protect and nurture. From this sprang desire, passion, and the emotions that go along with them: jealousy, lust, and the desire to own, possess, and subjugate.

One of the lessons of this letter is that you cannot learn without conflict. The most effective learning comes from bitter experience. As the saying goes, "Wisdom is recognizing the mistake when it happens for the third time!" The sword, the spear, and the nail (Vav) are therefore teaching letters with a particular message for the soul.

Pain is a necessary evil that warns us when to pay attention. Physical pain tells us when something is wrong with our body; without it we would not know to take our hand away from a hot plate, or take advice from a doctor when our appendix becomes troublesome. (This is when the sword becomes the surgeon's scalpel, separating the diseased part from the healthy body.) There are a few people who suffer from a condition that blocks feelings of pain. As children they have to be watched carefully in case they are injured and do not know it.

Mental or emotional pain makes us pause and look at our lives to see where we have gone wrong. Or it may be the pain of separation from a loved one by death or from other causes. It is a pain that is hard to bear but its teaching is that life must go on, that nothing can be taken for granted.

Some forty years ago a disaster in Europe occurred when a circus tent caught fire; most of the many dead were children. In many cases whole families died; the grief of the parents was terrible. One mother lost her only son, a boy of ten years. Her grief was compounded by the fact that they had quarreled just before he left for the circus and she had not kissed him goodbye. This incident has stayed with me all this time and I have taken it to heart. I try never to part from my loved ones on a bad note.

Spiritual pain can result in a loss of faith, hope, and even the will to live. It is the separation from that which made us and still lives within us and constantly strives to stay close to us. Spiritual pain is always caused by ourselves, and stems from our inability to understand the plan laid out for us. Separation from the One, the inability to admit that there is something greater than ourselves "out there," is true spiritual pain. When Lucifer, the Son of the Morning, gave up heaven and the presence of God, the spiritual pain of separation would have been something the human mind could not imagine.

One of the manifestations of the grail is that of the spear, another form of Zayin. When Percival comes to the grail castle, he beholds the wondrous procession when the grail maidens process through the castle. One carries the Cup of Cups and another carries a spear that continually drips blood. This is the spear of Longinus, the Roman soldier who pierced the side of Yeshua as he hung upon the cross. In this we have a complex set of symbols to decipher: the Son of Man nailed by the Vav to the cross of manifestation, pierced by the spear of the Zayin at the moment of liberation from the physical world before going on to the higher.

There is pain here, physical, emotional, and spiritual, and each one is a lesson in itself—the need to physically and painfully die in order to be lifted to a higher existence; the emotional pain of taking on humanity's debt; and the spiritual pain of the moment, when even Yeshua wavered: "My God, why hast thou forsaken me?"

For Catholics there are the seven (Zayin's number) swords piercing the heart of Mary, the crown of thorns, the sacred heart, and other symbols, many of which depict the Zayin in various forms. We see this "pain in order to learn" teaching not only in the Christian tradition but in the Jewish, the Buddhist, the Hindu, the Pagan, etc. Was this separation the lesson we began at Babel? Must humanity be forever at odds with each other over their belief systems? God is God by whatever name it is called or gender it is seen as. That is the *point* of it all—the Vav of it, the Zayin of it, the learning experience of it—to know the One is *there*.

Meditations

FIRST MEDITATION

Contemplate the supernal triangle. The manifesting power of Kether splits into the male and female principles of Chokmah and Binah. See them as Osiris and Isis, their powers merging into the focal point of Daa'th, the child. The power strikes down into Tiphereth (Horus) and becomes one with the spiritual son energy. On to Yesod, a symbol of the moon (womb), opening the way to Malkuth. The birth of Horus, the new aeon, forms the shape of the Zayin (sword) as well as the Calvary cross (below).

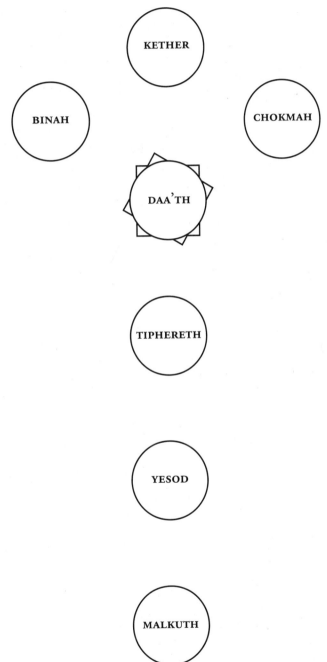

SECOND MEDITATION

Contemplate the twin nature of the human body: two legs, two arms, two testes, two ovaries, two kidneys, two adrenals, two lungs, two parts to the thyroid, two eyes, two ears, two parts to the neocortex. Taken together they make the royal road to the brain. The spine is a road of sensation, learning, experience, understanding, and finally wisdom, leading to the adytum of the brain where it manifests as the burst of power we know as the rising of the kundalini. It has been said by those who have experienced it that this rising can be both pleasurable and painful. Without pain we cannot recognize pleasure.

THIRD MEDITATION

Meditate on the sword as a symbol of justice and as a giver of mercy; for example, as a coup de grace.

Pathworking

As you slip into a trance, you become aware that you are walking on a long and deserted road. On one side there is a flat expanse of moorland, and on the other a landscape of rolling hills that gradually rises toward a range of mountains. At the foot of the tallest hill you can just make out a castle of golden stone with turrets from which flutter a host of brightly colored banners.

Ahead of you there walks a figure that looks familiar. It is dressed as you are, dressed in a woolen robe with a leather belt and leather sandals. Yours is in a soft green, the figure ahead of you is in white. For a while you walk in silence, then as you turn to look at the scenery you find there is a third figure walking behind you. It, too, seems familiar and is dressed in a similar fashion but in a dark brown color.

You stop and wait for the third figure to catch up to you, but although it keeps walking toward you, it gets no nearer. You begin walking again but keep turning back to look. Finally you bump into something. It is the one who has been walking in front of you. With a sense of shock you realize why you thought these figures were familiar. They are you.

Brown Robe comes up and together you go and sit by the side of the road and talk. White Robe tells you that he/she is your higher self and, far from being distant, is always close to you. Brown Robe laughs and says that he/she is your lower self and also is closer than you think. White Robe opens a satchel he/she has been carrying and sets out bread, cheese, fruit, honey cakes, and wine. You all eat and drink together and, finally replete, you lie back on the sweet-smelling grass and just talk.

You ask Brown Robe, the lower self, to tell you why it is important to have a lower self. It tells you not to confuse the word *lower* with *less*. The work done by the lower self is just as important as that done by the higher self. Part of that work shows you how to enjoy the simple things—food, wine, the laughter of children and companionship of friends, the perfume of a summer night and the cool feel of snow on your face in winter. Brown Robe speaks of the simple love of your pets and the casual affection of your fellow workers, then goes on to speak in reverent tones of the love between you and your partner, of the way in which desire rises and grows into a demand for the sharing of love between you, the touch of hand on hand, and mouth on mouth, the feel of the loved one's body against yours and the moment of union; the pleasure that goes on and on and then bursts into a flame that carries both of you into the realm of White Robe, the realm of the spirit.

You listen and realize that making love is as much a prayer as when you place your hands together in church, that you can praise the Creator by creating love between you and your "twin."

White Robe agrees and speaks of the spiritual joy that such love creates on the high levels. "Such a moment becomes for that space of time a radiance that lights up Creation. It is a moment in heaven when the choir sings not just for the One, but for Life. It is a moment when you, Green Robe, are closest to God. The higher self watches, waits, and gives help, but only when and if asked. I am untouched by what you do, I remain pure, so that on the day you recognize that I am always within you, the melding will bring nothing but joy."

Brown Robe takes from his/her pocket a flute and, putting it to his/her lips, begins to play. The tune is sweet and silvery and brings many memories to mind. You lie back on the sun-warmed grass and let the music wash over you. White Robe begins to sing:

Where did I meet you first, my love?
Where did we first meet?
Was it in Babylon, my love?
When I first sat at your feet?

Or was it on the winding Nile
As the royal barge went past
That I first heard your voice, my love?
For the first time and the last?
I found you on the Delphic chair
Where I had come to find
The key that I had long mislaid
To ease my troubled mind.
Again in Crete and then in Gaul
We lived and met and died
And I have loved you every time
And close to you did bide.
Down through the years I've followed you,
Sometimes you've followed me
And I will love you still, my love,
Through all eternity.

Silence falls and the evening lengthens into night, and you wait with the certain knowledge that there is someone else for you to meet. In the deep silence of the starlit night the presence of Zayin makes itself known to you. The scarlet and black of its colors stand out against the white track of the road.

"I have been waiting for you, Zayin."

"As I have been waiting for you, Life."

"I would like to ask some questions."

"When did Life not have questions?"

"Why it is important to have a lower self? Why not just a higher self?"

"Do not confuse the word *lower* with *less*. The work done by the lower self is just as important as that of the higher self. At this point in your growing, you cannot accept the fact that in reality you are not separated, it just seems to be so. But when the time is right and you are willing to understand that there is no division, then there will be no higher or lower, for all will be one.

"What they are and what you are will become what is. The division is in your mind, Life, it is not real. You are one now and always have been. You decided at some time in your many lives to see yourself as separate and that was what brought me into your consciousness. There is still much to learn before you can see this, but it will come. You see, sometimes a whole has to be divided before it can comprehend its many parts. A young soul is unable to understand its unity until it has seen itself as many. A jigsaw puzzle would not understand what its pattern or picture is until it is put together; it is the same with you, Life. Come with me, I want to show you something."

Zayin goes before you, casting no shadow and not even bending the grass. You follow until you stand below the walls of the castle you had seen in the distance. You look up and wonder at the beauty of the golden stone and the architecture of its turrets and towers. Zayin speaks. "This is the dwelling of the integrated soul, Life. This is a symbol of the beauty of the soul that has come together in perfect love and perfect trust."

You look and wonder. White Robe speaks on your right side. "When the time comes, Green Robe, I will rejoice to know that you have recognized my presence within you."

Brown Robe speaks from the left side. "As will I, Green Robe. Together we will rise to the heights of wisdom and understanding and, as Chokmah, Binah, and Kether, we will be one."

Zayin's presence surrounds all of you and for a moment you know what it is like to be fully aware. Then it is gone, but you have the memory. Zayin's laughter is a gentle sound.

"Life, you continually surprise all of us in the Aleph-Beth. The One surely gave you the greatest gift of all of us who were with him in the Morning of Time. He made you to be his image and gave you the power to imagine; the child is so like the Father. Farewell." The darkness surrounds you and within it you are transported back into your own time and space.

Psalm 121

I will lift up mine eyes unto the hills,

from whence cometh my help.

My help cometh from the Lord

who made heaven and earth.

He will not suffer thy foot to be moved:

He that keepeth thee will not slumber.

Behold, He that keepeth Israel shall

neither slumber nor sleep.

The Lord is thy keeper;

He is thy shade upon thy right hand.

The sun shall not smite thee by day,

nor the moon by night.

The Lord shall preserve thee from all evil.

He shall preserve thy soul.

The Lord shall preserve thy going out,

and thy coming in from this time forth

and forever more.

≈

Ritual

You will need a table for an altar; white cloth; a bowl and a candle for the center light; a thurible of incense; in the east a piece of charcoal; an apple and a sharp dagger in the south; a chalice and a medium-sized bunch of grapes in the west; a freshly baked bread roll and a sharp knife in the north; a second, smaller chalice half full of water; a pinch of salt; a small candle in a holder (lit); and an incense stick (lit). The intent is to divide and to reunite. (It is a good idea to have a box of moist towelettes at hand.)

Make sure you have all at hand and then begin. Take the dagger in hand. Go to the door and make the sign of Zayin with the blade. Speak:

"With the dividing power of Zayin, I seal this space from all outside influence. *Go to the east and make the sign of an equal-armed cross with the dagger.* I call through the door of the east to the glory that is Raphael, Son of the Morning, one of the first born. Come thou, Day Star of the Horizon, to the place prepared for thee, and open the gates of the element of air. By the power of the Zayin that guards the gate of heaven, I call thee and welcome thee." *Go to the south and repeat the sign.*

"I call through the door of the south to the glory that is Michael, Son of the Morning, one of the first born. Come thou, Radiance of the Noonday, into this place prepared for thee, and open the gates of the element of fire. By the power of the Zayin that guards the gate of heaven, I call thee and welcome thee." *Go to the west and repeat the sign.*

"I call through the door of the west to the silver-voiced messenger that is Gabriel, herald of the Word of the Most High. Come thou, Keeper of the Word of Creation, into this place prepared for thee, and open the gates of the element of water. By the power of the Zayin that guards the gate of heaven, I call thee and welcome thee." *Go to the north and repeat the sign.*

"I call through the door of the north to the glory that is Uriel, Son of the Morning, one of the first born. Come thou, Living Symbol of the Earth, come into this place prepared for thee, and open the gates of earth. By the power of the Zayin that guards the gate of heaven, I call thee and welcome thee." *Go to the altar, pick up the charcoal, and hold it in your fingers.*

"With the power of Zayin, I divide this object that I may know the strength of the Zayin. *Hold both pieces to the flame of the center light.* By the power of the Light I shall multiply its uses to create more Light. *Place both pieces in the thurible and wait until it is hot enough to take the incense.* Let the scent of herbs and spices mount up to heaven that the air may be hallowed with its fragrance. Raphael, accept this gift of perfume and place it before the throne that the element of air may be glorified and be united with fire." *Go to the south and take the dagger and the apple. Cut the apple into four quarters and hold them up.*

"With the power of Zayin, I divide this apple that I may likewise divide my time on Earth and make it fruitful. *Pass the pieces through the center flame.* By the power of the Light, I shall multiply these seeds to create more of itself. *Take a small bite of one piece.* I take the fruit, ripened by the heat of the sun to its full sweetness.

I offer the taste of this fruit to thee, Michael. Let it be pleasant in the mouth of the Most High that the element of fire, the heat of the sun that gave it ripeness, may be blessed and united by its juices to the element of water." *Go to the west and pick the grapes off the stalk.*

"With the power of Zayin, I divide this fruit from its vine. *Squeeze the juice into the chalice. Sprinkle a drop on the flame, taking care not to put it out.* I take the wine and offer it to the messenger of God that it may be taken and placed in the hand of the One. Let its strength be added to that of the hand that gave life to Adam. Let it be a token of welcome to the stranger in my tents and thereby bless the element of water." *Go to the north and cut the bread into pieces.*

"With the power of Zayin, I divide this bread and share its essence with the holy angels who surround us. *Sprinkle a pinch of salt on the bread and eat it.* I offer it to the keeper of the Earth, Uriel, that it may be taken and placed in the hand of the One. Let its strength be added to that of the hand that gave life to Adam. Let it be a token of welcome to the stranger in my tents. As the manna sustained us in the desert, let this bread now become a gift to he who created all things. Let it be blessed in its making and in its eating, thereby blessing the element of earth." *Go to the east; take the chalice of water and sprinkle a little of the salt into it. Douse the candle from the south in it, and then douse the tip of the incense stick in it.*

"Earth and water, fire and air, combine together, united as in the beginning when nothing was separated one from the other. With the Zayin did the Lord divide the waters from the earth, and the above from the below. He divided the earth into many parts and made them multiply. Likewise did he separate Life into many kinds but in the fullness of time all shall be united in him. Selah."

Douse all candles and leave.

CHETH

Enclose me within the power of thy radiant glory.
Surround my trembling soul with unbounded grace.
I am a field waiting to be sown with seeds of wisdom.
Listen to the words of my mouth, O Lord,
as they fly like a flock of doves to thy hand.
My soul is bound to the Light with silken bonds of love
as a horse is bound to a chariot.
Thy words are like spears to mine enemies
and my heart seeks shelter in thy presence
for it cleanses me of wrongdoing.
I am a city awaiting the coming of its king
in triumph.
Behold, I open the gates of my soul
to the coming of the One,
the Most High, the Ever Loving.
I surrender, I accept, I adore, I praise.
Bid me lay palms beneath His feet
and dance like David before the Ark of the Covenant.
Rejoice, for He enters the citadel of my heart
and I am conquered by Light.

Image: Fence
Symbol: ㄇ
Path on the Tree of Life: 18
Numerical Value: 8

Prayer

Cheth is given the magical image of a fence. The words of the prayer enhance the feeling of being ringed around with safety and protected by a divine strength: "Enclose me within the power of thy radiant glory" and "surround my trembling soul with unbounded grace."

When we are children we feel most safe when we are held by our mother or father. Within the circle of their arms we are hidden from anything that may hurt or confuse us. As adults we are braver and can deal with our fears most of the time. But even when grown up, no matter how old we become, there are times when we feel a need for enclosing arms, the surrounding strength of something greater than ourselves.

These are the moments when even the bravest resort to prayer, and often to childhood prayers taught us by our mothers: "Gentle Jesus, meek and mild." Soldiers wounded and dying on battlefields far from home often cry out for their mothers in those final moments, seeking their early memories of gentle comfort and the promise of safety.

The Tarot trump of the Chariot would seem to be far removed from a mother's arms, but if we look behind the chariot, we see the walls of a strong and well-fortified city. The Charioteer has emerged from his stronghold and stands ready to offer safe transport if we need it.

The letter itself is often seen as being composed of two spears/swords or Zayins, a symbol applied to the tongue in the line, "Thy words are like spears to mine enemies." The prayer looks to the Creator as a giver of grace to those who have sinned and of being like a city whose gates are opened to receive those that once fled its authority.

David threw off his garments and, dressed in the sacred ephod, danced before the ark of his God. So we may rejoice when the gates of the soul open and allow the divine to enter. Only then can we know the truth of the words "unbounded grace."

The Letter

Cheth is the eighth letter and has the value of eight. If seven is the magical number pertaining to the spiritual aspirations of humanity, then eight looks to that which lies beyond what we think of as our limitations and encourages us to surpass them. There have been many recorded instances of such events. We refer to them as miracles, and they occur when least expected and under conditions that defy any attempt to analyze them.

In the days of the ancient Mystery Schools, it was the custom for children to be brought to the temple at seven years of age. They were tested to see if they would be suitable for training in the work of the temple and if accepted were educated, trained, fed, housed, and clothed for the rest of their lives. For a poor family, this would have been a wonderful opportunity for their child. Plus, in a large family it eased the burden of feeding and clothing another child. The following year, when the child was eight years old, would represent the beginning of their new life as a potential priest/priestess with all that it entailed, i.e., the beginning of their spiritual life as opposed to the hard physical labor that would otherwise have been their lot.

There are two descriptions of the makeup of Cheth. The first (*beis josef*) holds that it is comprised of two Zayins side by side and linked together. The second, attributed to Arizal, speaks of a Zayin linked to a Vav. The symbolism of the two swords can look, at first glance, very similar to the letter Heh—that is, until we look at the disjointed link between them.

CHETH MADE FROM ZAYIN AND VAV

CHETH MADE FROM TWO ZAYINS JOINED

The Heh has an opening that allows the mind and spirit to leave the mundane and seek the divine, or conversely to look up and perceive the illuminating Light descending to earth. The Cheth, however, has a broken and distorted shape (see right) that can cause the Light to become refracted. This means its message can be misunderstood, and that may cause a fall from grace.

When we look at the second example of the letter, we see a sword and a nail. This offers a very different symbolism to the inquiring mind. The sword divides and the nail unites what was divided. When thinking this over, it occurred to me that to understand this seemingly contradictory letter one must accept both versions, for out of contemplation can come an explanation.

If, through a misinterpretation of the message of the Cheth as depicted by the double sword, one misuses one's power, commits a sin, and falls from grace, then one must retrace one's steps and right what has been done in error. If this is attempted in the right state of mind, the Cheth of two swords becomes the Cheth of the sword and the nail. Why and how? Simply because the nail unites what was divided by the sword.

This means that Cheth, besides having a double presentation, also has a double lesson to teach us. Whatever is done in error intentionally or unintentionally can be corrected and reconciled with its original and intended action by the uniting power of the Vav. There is a subtle symbolism in the sword and the nail linked together. It reminds us that it was the sword of the stubborn human will—that would not yield to divine will—that caused division in the first place. Though the nail will rectify the mistake, there will always be a weakness that must be watched carefully in the future.

Cheth is pronounced in a similar fashion to *cheit,* meaning "sin." A sin can be seen as cutting oneself away from the Creator via the "sword" or Zayin of selfishness. For the esoterically minded Christian, the "nail" or Vav of the crucifixion becomes a symbol of the forgiveness of, and a way back to, God. This applies if one is not a practicing Christian or if you worship the Creator as Hashem, the Goddess, Osiris, Mithras, Cernunnos, the Horned Lord of Fertility, or any of the multitudinous names of God. This letter begins Ch-okmah, Ch-esed, and ch-aim (life).

The image of Cheth given in the Western Mysteries is that of a fence. If you look at the variations of this letter, then at the image given on the illustration on page 318 of this book, you will see the sword shape in the pointed railings of the fence. You will also note that the letter encloses only three sides, leaving an opening on the fourth side. This suggests to the contemplative mind a structure used to enclose and protect sheep or animals from inclement weather, especially those structures where the wall of the house provides a fourth side. In the same way, the Creator encloses Creation within a set of laws designed to keep life safe. Life does not always want to be safe and seeks to escape, more often than not, and falls prey to whatever is waiting outside the "Cheth."

Sometimes the temptation to sneak out and see what is beyond the fence is irresistible. One need only look to the legend of the unicorn to see how this works. Legend states that a unicorn can only be captured if tempted by a virgin. It is then trapped within a fence and slaughtered. One would think that after a certain length of time the unicorns would see through this trick and refuse to go anywhere near a virgin. But they must have been more than usually stupid, albeit beautiful, because they are now extinct!

Rabbi Munk has this to say: "Ever since man was banished from Eden he has had to balance two contradictory Zayins: [the Zayins of] passive trust and . . . active enterprise." Within this statement lies the answer to the riddle of Cheth.

Path 18 on the Tree of Life links Binah to Geburah, and is the Tarot trump of the Charioteer, or the mother and the warrior bearing out my words on the dying soldier calling out for his mother. But there is another link that needs to be understood: the mother is also a warrior. It is she who guards the child in its babyhood—she who will, if necessary, kill to defend her young.

It has been my experience that when it comes to the sphere of Geburah many people tend to shy away from its symbolism of the sword, conflict, etc., and the archangel assigned to it, Khamael, is sometimes seen as the angel of death. Geburah, lying beneath the sphere of Binah, needs to be studied in the light of the virtue of Binah, understanding. It is because of the power of understanding that justice may be applied impartially.

The Charioteer is more than he seems to be. He is the guardian, the defender, the ruler, and the dispenser of justice for the city behind him. He *is* the law; he and the chariot are immovable. But with the application of justice comes the mercy of grace. With such rich symbolism to delve into and explore, it is no wonder that the Qabalah and the Tree of Life have become so important in the Western Mysteries. The system encompasses all traditions within itself and illuminates their meaning.

Meditations

FIRST MEDITATION

Read carefully what has been written concerning Cheth, then contemplate this symbol. A flight of seven steps floats before you in space. On each step is written one letter, beginning with Aleph and ending with Zayin. Then there is a large gap, further than you can leap, and another flight of steps, the first of which is engraved with the letter Cheth. Your task is to find a way to reach that next step.

SECOND MEDITATION

Take each letter of C- H- T. Cheth + Heh + Tau; change them to their images, fence or enclosure + window + *T* cross or crook. Link all three together in any way you like, using your knowledge of their meanings and symbolism. Contemplate your findings and use the virtue of Binah to seek out their inner realizations.

THIRD MEDITATION

Look up the definition of the word *grace*. Contemplate it in as many ways as you can. Apply it to different uses, descriptions, objects, etc. as you can find. When you have exhausted these, contemplate the word itself and allow it to fill you with its power.

Pathworking

Close your eyes and allow yourself to drift into a light trance, softly pronouncing the word *Cheth* to yourself. Say it using the *ch* sound as you would in Loch Ness, slightly guttural. Keep saying it as you drift deeper. The darkness begins to lift and you find yourself on a wide plain with mountains behind you. It is early evening and in the distance you see the lights of a city surrounded by walls. You pause for a moment and contemplate your goal, leaning on the staff you carry. You can feel the weariness of your limbs after crossing the high mountain pass and look forward to food and rest. In the distance you see a cloud of dust approaching and wait to see if it will be friend or foe.

It is a chariot drawn by two horses: one black and one white; the driver halts his team and steps down to greet you. A tall, well-built man of mature years, he wears a golden circlet on his head and is richly dressed. He greets you with hands outstretched and a friendly manner. He has come to meet you and take you back into the city as his guest. Even so did Abraham run to greet his guests when he was visited by the angels of the Lord.

You take your place beside him in the chariot and return with him to the city. You are conscious of a third presence but as yet cannot define it. The city is large, with well-built houses and open spaces where the people walk, meet, and carry on their business. Shade trees line the streets and there are fountains and gardens where children play.

Your friend takes you to his house where you are given a comfortable room and food. A bath is prepared and you soak weary limbs and relax. From a balcony you look out over the city under a full moon. There seems to be a celebration going on and you go out from the house and into the streets to see what they are doing. As you leave the house the presence you felt earlier manifests beside you. You know at once that it is the letter Cheth. It gives off a feeling that your senses translate as "steel and silk." There is laughter from the streets as people hurry past, carrying lanterns and bottles of wine. The silver and black presence beside you also laughs.

"Steel and silk—you are becoming very astute, Life. That is a very good description of my powers. Are there any other symbols you can apply to me?"

You shake your head and the two of you carry on toward the square in the middle of the city. The festival is in full swing so you and your companion wander from place to place enjoying the music, the laughter, and the noise of people having a good time. You are aware of the silver and black color of the Cheth beside you and of the strength that emanates from it, yet there is also a feeling of swiftness and agility.

You pass a booth where a young girl is dancing. She is dressed in brightly colored silks and holds long strands of ribbons in her hands. As she dances she weaves patterns with these ribbons until they seem like a flock of colored birds flying around her. Her movements strike a chord of memory in you and you turn to the

Cheth. "She has grace, it is there in her movements and her interpretation of the music. That is one of your meanings, is it not? That there is grace in the youthfulness of the physical body?"

"Indeed, but not just in youth. There is physical grace all around you. See that elderly couple over there, look at their entwined hands. They are gnarled and wrinkled with age yet there is grace in those hands, the grace of their love. Youth is held within the aging body that in itself is grace. Look there, on the roof of that house, a cat lies sleeping in the sun. Even in sleep the grace of its relaxation can be seen. Over there, see the young man on the horse, see how it prances and how easily he maintains balance and control. That too is grace, linked to strength. See if you can see anything else that reminds you of my powers. But do not just look, Life, you must observe."

You do as the letter suggests. You look and observe what is going on around you. The architecture of the city is based on a classical Persian style and you find grace in the fluted columns and curves of the stone arches. The domes and soaring minarets speak of the skill of their architects.

The Cheth approves your observations, then directs your attention to a street artist drawing likenesses of people around him. A group of young men saunter by, their youth and muscular strength also displaying grace and strength combined.

Then the Cheth draws you to a corner of the square where a young man and a young woman are demonstrating the art of swordsmanship. They use two swords apiece and the speed with which they encounter each other is akin to lightning. The swords clash and sparks fly and the sound is like silver fire.

They leap and turn and twist in a display of grace, skill, strength, and cunning that leaves the crowd breathless with excitement. The two then demonstrate their control over their weapons. Using tall bundles of reeds tied together as targets, in turn they step forward and in precise diagonal, vertical, and horizontal sweeps cut the bundles down gradually to a mere few inches.

They use fruit flung into the air and cut into halves and quarters before they have touched the ground. Finally they set up a row of lit candles on a trestle table. The young woman steps forward and sweeps her weapon in a graceful arc, cutting the wicks off every candle, snuffing them out. The crowd applauds wildly.

Now it is the turn of her brother. He kneels and closes his eyes in concentration and remains utterly still, while the crowd waits in silence. Then with the speed of a cobra striking its prey he leaps to his feet, his sword flashing from its sheath and along the line of candles. They remain standing.

The crowd draws in its breath in a single sound of disappointment. But the girl goes along the row of candles and tips each over. They have been cut at a point where the candle joined the metal of the holder. The crowd roars its delight and throws money in homage to their skill and grace. The Cheth draws you away.

"You have seen skill and grace at work, and seen the 'steel and silk,' as you so aptly put it, of my powers. Let me now show you another grace."

The presence draws you into a quiet candlelit building where a group of people kneel at prayer. The air is filled with incense and the sound of whispered prayer. Before the altar is a curtain of fine silk, so sheer you can see through it to the altar.

On the altar is an object that shines with such brilliance you cannot determine exactly what it is. From somewhere beyond the altar comes the sweet silver sound of a bell. A man gets up and goes to the curtain, steps inside it, and kneels before the object. There is silence . . . then the light from the object expands and flows over the penitent, enclosing him with its radiance, then recedes. The man comes back to his seat, face aglow with peace and serenity. Gradually each one takes their place within the curtain.

You wait, then turn to the Cheth beside you. You do not ask in words, but through your heart. "May I approach?"

"Do you need to receive grace, Life? Have you sinned and are you sorry? Can you face what lies within the curtain? Only you can make the choice; remember, there is steel within the silk. Grace will be offered, but nothing comes without cost."

You must at this point make a choice to go behind the curtain or not. What you will encounter is only for you to know and experience. When you have made that choice, whatever it was, you and the Cheth leave the building. Outside is the chariot and its driver. Silently you climb in and look back at the Cheth, a great love for these elder brethren who willingly offer you so much sweeps over you.

"Be blessed for what you have taught me," you tell the Cheth.

The letter glows with light, then lifts its voice and sings out your blessing as a hymn of praise. Its radiant form soars into the night like a shooting star. The charioteer takes you back to your meeting place and you part with words of friendship. You begin to climb the steep path using the staff you have kept throughout your time on this path. The thought comes that soon you will be encountering the letter Samech, whose image is a staff. The darkness enfolds you and a star shoots across the sky. Take a deep breath, make a wish, and open your eyes.

Psalm 13

How long wilt thou forget me, O Lord?

Forever?

How long wilt thou hide thy face from me?

How long shall I take counsel in my soul,

having sorrow in my heart daily?

How long shall mine enemy be exalted over me?

Consider and hear me, O Lord, my God.

Lighten my eyes lest I sleep the sleep of death,

lest mine enemy say I have prevailed against him

and those that trouble me rejoice when I am moved.

But I have trusted in thy mercy.

My heart shall rejoice in thy salvation.

I will sing unto the Lord,

because he hath dealt bountifully with me.

~

Ritual

You will need four small tables; four cloths, one each in gold, red, blue, and green; flowers in gold, red, blue, and a small bunch of green herbs, tied together; eight small candleholders; eight small candles, two each in gold, red, blue, and green; a small clay bowl in which to burn incense; some charcoal; a mortar and pestle; herbs or spices of your own choice; a candlemaking kit; some perfumed oils; a couple of incense sticks; matches; a small bottle of red wine and, if possible, a vial of Jordan water. This is often obtainable from a shop selling Jewish supplies, or if you live or have friends in the capital, from an Israeli or Jordanian embassy. If you cannot get it at all, then leave a bowl of water out under a full moon and use that. Finally, you need a two- to three-year-old sapling of an indigenous tree.

There is a lot of preparation to do for this ritual. You will need to make an incense for your own use. This involves looking up herbs, spices, and oils, and their correspondences to the sign of the path/letter (Cancer and the moon), and the blending to get the proportions right. You need to make a candle specially for this ritual and perfume it with a scent that will mix with the incense. The wine should be opened an hour before the ritual and two drops (no more and no less) of the water added to it. The sapling should be bought on the first day of a new moon and kept watered and ready for the rite, which should also be performed on a new or waxing moon. The intent of the ritual is to take your ritual work one step beyond the usual level, so extra effort must be made in the preparation of the room, the items used, and yourself.

On the day chosen, set aside two hours when you will not be disturbed. Bathe thoroughly (something that should be done before any ritual), wash your hair and clean your nails, etc. When dressed, gather all the things you will need and make them ready. Place a small table in each quarter and dress them as follows:

East: gold cloth, two gold candles in holders, gold flower; small bowl with earth or sand in the bottom, charcoal, and the incense you have made; one stick of incense, matches, bowl of salt, and water.

South: red cloth, two red candles in holders, red flower, special handmade candle in holder, matches.

West: blue cloth, two blue candles in holders, blue flower, chalice with wine and water, matches.

North: green cloth, two green candles in holders, matches, a bunch of green herbs tied together, the sapling, a chair light enough to be carried from quarter to quarter.

When all is ready, begin by sealing your sacred space off from the everyday world. With salt and water, make a circle around the room.

"In the ancient way with salt and water, I cleanse and make sacred this place of working." *Take one of the gold candles and circle the room.*

"In the ancient way with light and fire, I cleanse and make sacred this place of working." *Return the gold candle and take up the incense stick.*

"In the ancient way with sweet herbs, I cleanse and make sacred this place of working." *Return to the east and douse the incense stick in salt and water; put the chair in the east. Sit in meditation for five full minutes on the subject of self-healing, then rise and go to the eastern altar. Make the sign of the double triangle.*

"I open the gate of the east within my spirit and invoke the presence there of Raphael, Son of the Morning. Take my request, Raphael, and place it before the Throne of Thrones that it may reach the ears of the One. I ask to be shown the way forward through the gate of the east, to be guided to the step beyond the seventh that I may lift up my higher self and be found worthy of grace. *Light the gold candles.* I give Light that I may receive Light. *Light the incense in the burner.* I offer incense that I may be hallowed by the breath of the One. *Offer the flower.* I offer beauty that I may behold the beauty of the One reflected in my own higher self. Open the way of the east to me in my dreams and in my meditations that I may attempt the crossing from the seventh to the eighth level of enlightenment. If I am not yet ready for this step, then give me the patience and the understanding to wait until I am ready." *Return to your seat and meditate for five minutes. Rise and take the chair to the south. Meditate for five minutes on the subject of courage and loyalty, then go to the south altar and make the sign of the double triangle.*

"I open the gate of the south within my spirit and invoke the presence of Michael, Son of the Morning. Take my request, Michael, and place it before the Throne of Thrones that it may reach the ears of the One. I ask to be shown the way forward through the gate of the south, to be guided to the step beyond the seventh that I may lift up my higher self and be found worthy of grace. *Light the red candles.* I give Light that I may receive Light. *Light the special candle and hold it up.* I offer sacred flame that I may be made sacred by the love of the One. *Offer the flower.* I offer life that I may be filled with the life of the One and my higher self made aware of this. Open the way of the south to me in dreams and in meditations that I may attempt the crossing from the seventh to the eighth level of enlightenment. If I am not yet ready, then give me the patience and the understanding to wait until I am ready." *Return to your seat, meditate for five minutes, then take the chair and go to the west. Meditate for five minutes on intuition and power. Go to the west altar and make the sign of the double triangle.*

"I open the gate of the west within my spirit and invoke the presence of Gabriel, Son of the Morning. Take my request, Gabriel, and place it before the

Throne of Thrones that it may reach the ears of the One. I ask to be shown the way forward through the gate of the west, to be guided to the step beyond the seventh that I may lift up my higher self and be found worthy of grace. *Light the blue candles.* I offer Light that I may be enlightened by the voice of Gabriel. *Offer and drink the wine.* I offer and share wine and water that my spirit may commune with that of the One. *Offer the flower.* I offer the vibration of color that my life may be colored by the glory of the One. Open the way of the west to me in my dreams and in my meditations that I may attempt the crossing from the seventh to the eighth level of enlightenment. If I am not yet ready for this, then give me the patience and the understanding to wait until I am ready." *Return to your seat, meditate for five minutes, rise, and go to the north. Meditate for five minutes on regeneration, then go to the north altar and make the sign of the double triangle.*

"I open the gate of the north within my spirit and invoke the presence within of Uriel, Son of the Morning. Take my request, Uriel, and place it before the Throne of Thrones that it may reach the ears of the One. I ask to be shown the way forward through the gate of the north, to be guided to the step beyond the seventh that I may lift up my higher self and be found worthy of grace. *Light the green candles.* I give Light that I may receive Light. *Offer the herbs.* I offer growth that my higher self may likewise grow in the power of the One. *Offer the sapling tree.* I offer this tree to beautify the Earth and as penance to replace those that are destroyed. Open the way of the north to me in my dreams and in my meditations that I may attempt the crossing from the seventh to the eighth level of enlightenment. If I am not ready for this step, then give me the patience and the understanding to wait until I am ready." *Return to your seat and meditate for five minutes. Then rise, take the chair, and return to the east.*

"I have offered incense and candles made by my own hands, I have drunk wine and water with my deity, I have replenished the Earth by a small amount. Let these things be accounted, Holy One, when I come to the end of my life. I give praise to the universe that caused Life in all its myriad forms to be. Bless me with serenity in my life, bless me with love in my dealings with family and friends, bless me with the courage to face adversity, bless me with intuition that I may understand the world about me. Bless me, Holy One, with the forgiveness of my transgressions and grant me peace of mind. In you I will place my trust now and through all the years of my life."

Meditate on grace, then light the incense stick, go to the east, and make a double triangle. "I bless the east and Raphael, Son of the Morning. Let there be peace between us. Depart to your own realm."

Go to the south and make a double triangle. "I bless the south and Michael, Son of the Morning. Let there be peace between us. Depart to your own realm."

Go to the west and make a double triangle. "I bless the west and Gabriel, Son of the Morning. Let there be peace between us. Depart to your own realm."

Go to the north and make a double triangle. "I bless the north and Uriel, Son of the Morning. Let there be peace between us. Depart to your own realm."

Go back to the east and make three circles. "I bless all here, seen and unseen. It is done. Let there be light and peace and grace within this house and within my heart that I may be found worthy of the work upon which I have set my heart and my desire. Selah."

Douse all the lights with the exception of the center light, which should be left to burn for an hour, and leave the temple. Plant the sapling as soon as possible.

TETH

Thou art the master of disguise,
the weaver of illusions.
Yet do I see thy true image within
the mirror of my mind.
You tempt in order to teach,
deceive that we may learn to choose wisely,
misunderstood by those who cannot see.
Thou art reviled and thy head is set
under the heel of man.
But thou shalt ever rise victorious
and radiant in thy true guise as a being of Light.
You lift my soul when I am beset by darkness;
you light a flame of hope before my eyes.
I am uplifted by thee,
like the serpent raised in the desert.
Raise my spirit, mighty Seraphim,
for I am oppressed by fear.
Show me thy light,
O Son of the Morning, that I may overcome that fear
and tame the Lion of Baseness.

Image: Serpent
Symbol: ט
Path on the Tree of Life: 19
Numerical Value: 9

Prayer

Illusion is something we all have to deal with in our lives. We can be so easily taken in by words and deeds and faces that are only masks for the darkness and treachery that lie beneath. But, as with all things, illusion has another side to it. Sometimes things need to be hidden from us, and even disguised as something else, so we are forced into seeking out the real thing beneath.

Deception in our time is a way of life from the most minor (perfume, makeup, and hair coloring are examples) through making prints of paintings, copying antique furniture, and reproducing art in plastic and fiberglass to forgery on a grand scale. Most of the time the first two examples are harmless; we use makeup to "enhance nature," we buy a print of a Monet painting because it pleases us and we cannot afford the original, and this provides ways for all of us to enjoy beautiful objects. On the other hand, deception can be a deliberate act to cause harm and betray the good nature of the unwary. Is there a difference between illusion and deception?

I think so. Deception is mostly deliberate and often the work of those intending to cause trouble for their own ends. We often apply illusion to ourselves, refusing to see the truth of what is in front of us. Therefore deception finds us an easy target; we cannot believe what we see so we collude in our own deception.

When we begin to tread the way of the Mysteries, we begin to see more clearly. We begin to observe, when we observe we become aware, and awareness, being a form of understanding, leads to wisdom. We gradually become aware that not everything we are told to believe is true. Before we "see in a glass darkly," afterwards we are enlightened.

The ways of deity are mysterious, as we have been told time and again. Neither does God make it easy for us. There are therefore instances when deception is used in order to make us work harder at observing and finding a way through conflicting symbols to the truth. The symbol of the scapegoat is such a deception. When one combines the scapegoat and the willing sacrifice, the hidden truth begins to shine through; then, quite often, panic sets in and we run from what has become clear to us.

If we look at the symbol of the yin and yang, we see that in every act of goodness there is a seed of darkness that can destroy it. In every act of evil there is a point of Light that can overcome it. This is cosmic balance, that without evil one cannot recognize good or learn to desire it. Without darkness we cannot see the stars. If we can bring ourselves to look through darkness to the core of it we will see the morning star.

The Letter

Teth is given the image of a serpent and indeed it looks like one. The letter combines a Zayin linked to a Kaph, the tail of which is curled over and tucked in. The number of Teth is nine, and if you combine the seven of the Zayin and the twenty of the Kaph, making twenty-seven, then add the twenty-seven together again (two plus seven), it brings us neatly back to nine.

Strangely, although the image is that of the serpent, a much maligned species in both the Bible and literature, the letter Teth begins the word *good.* It also begins the word *tzadoka,* which can be interpreted to mean "alms" or "donation." But such good works must be done in secret so that the one receiving it is not made to feel beholden.

This brings me back to the prayer in which the Light of the Morning Star is hidden and does its work in secret and is often blamed for not showing his angelic form. But the work of the Morning Star has to remain unknown and hidden under veils in order that we, Life, may have a free choice.

If we look at the symbolism of the Zayin (sword) and the Kaph (palm of the hand), we can see that the two go together very well for it is the palm of the hand that holds the sword and directs its force. But the image of the whole letter, the serpent, reminds us that the bite of the serpent can be dangerous.

Teth also begins the word *teshuvah,* which means "repentance" or "rebirth," something that anyone can achieve no matter what they have done. But it must be truly meant. Just repeating the words is not good enough.

Looking at the serpentlike form of the Teth reminds us of the twin kundalini aspects of Creation, the reproductive side and the imaginative side. One enables us to reproduce our own kind and enjoy the pleasures of family life. The other has been the source of great works of art, literature, poetry, architecture, and the great discoveries in the sciences.

When someone sets out to discover a new way of doing something, they achieve success by making mistakes. Strange but true. They try this and that, then something different. Each time they fail, they know a little more about the subject, the problems, and the cause of the failure. The next try will be nearer the goal and they keep on trying until they get it right. True experience lies hidden in our mistakes. To reach a goal after great effort is by far the most satisfying way to achieve success. Teth the serpent, the disguised Morning Star, the one who encourages us to make those seeming mistakes, is really working for us, not against us. Every mistake is a bit of experience and the more experienced we become the better we will be. One must build a house slowly and carefully so it does not fall down in the first storm. Teth, whether it wears the face of the Son of the Morning or that of the kundalini of creative effort, is one of the greatest teachers you can have. Do not believe all you hear or are shown; learn to make your own judgments. Events that are ordained by divine decree are always heralded. The trouble is we often mistake the heralds for enemies. Maybe this is the origin of the saying "Don't shoot the messenger!"

This is Path 19 on the Tree and joins Geburah to Chesed. It reminds us yet again of the double nature of Teth: serpent and angel, justice and mercy, prosecutor and defender, and the creativeness of both sex and the artistic mind.

Meditations

First Meditation

Read Exodus, where the Jews begin their wanderings in the desert. Moses raises a serpent nailed to a Tau cross so that all may look upon it and be saved from the

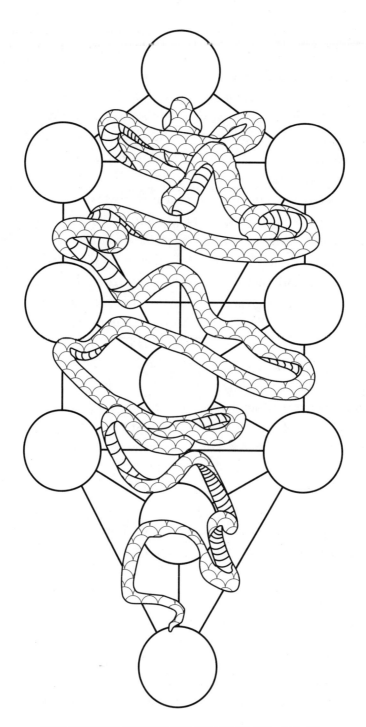

THE SERPENT OF WISDOM ON THE TREE OF LIFE

bite of the asp. Contemplate this story and see what connections you can make with 1) the prayer, 2) the scapegoat, 3) the morning star, and 4) the crucifixion and the nailing of the world's savior to a cross.

SECOND MEDITATION

Read the myth of Asclepius, the Greek god of healing, whose symbol was a serpent twined about a staff of wood. Meditate upon this and upon the serpent as a symbol of healing, both then and now.

THIRD MEDITATION

Meditate upon the forgiveness of sin where it concerns learning to forgive yourself. Ask yourself if you need to forgive yourself for anything and if so, do it.

Three points to think on:

1) Satan was originally the title given to the angelic prosecutor when a soul came before God to be judged. His task was to recite the sins and wrongdoings that soul had committed on Earth, rather like the Weigher of Hearts in the Egyptian Book of the Dead. It was the early church fathers who created the Satan of hellfire and damnation.

2) The Tarot trump of this path is that of Strength. It takes great strength to control the twin powers of the kundalini, both sexual and artistic.

3) Look at a picture of the serpent on the Tree of Life (left) and compare it with this chapter.

Pathworking

Sometimes parents find it necessary to encourage their children to fly the nest; sometimes they have to be thrown out and the door locked behind them. In this pathworking you will be reliving a different version of the Adam and Eve story.

Close your eyes and allow your thoughts to focus on a long stretch of road. You are standing in the middle of it. Before you the road is misty and hard to see. This is the road into the future and as yet has not been defined enough to show an exact path. The road behind you goes straight into the distance where a large grey and white cloud sits on the horizon.

You begin to walk toward it and more quickly than you had anticipated you arrive at the cloud. This divides your own time from the time you will be going into. Walk into it; you will find it rather damp and clammy but not unpleasant. In a few moments you begin to see the cloud thinning and you step out into a garden full of flowers, trees, fruits, and sweet-smelling herbs. The grass beneath your feet is smooth and cool and somewhere you can hear the sound of water. There is a feeling of newness and serenity here and you wander amid the glorious colors of the plants.

You come across animals as well. Some are domesticated and some are wild, but none offer any danger to you. They come readily to your hand and allow themselves to be touched, stroked, and played with. Now and then you see what seems to be pillars of radiant light in many colors moving through the gardens. Sometimes they stop and watch you, sometimes they just pass by. Sometimes there is a feeling of something immensely powerful watching you and it makes you a little afraid.

One of the brilliantly colored pillars now comes toward you; it is green and gold and deep red. It stops beside you and you can feel the pulsating power of the being all around you. It offers its name, Teth, and asks yours. You answer Adam (if a male) or Eve (if a female). It asks why you have not explored the furthest part of the garden. There are trees there with fruit more sweet to the taste than any other.

You reply that you were told not to touch those trees by the Lord who owns the garden. Teth tells you that if you eat the fruit of that tree you will be as wise and as powerful as the Lord of the garden, eventually. Teth offers to take you there and you follow rather apprehensively. When you come in sight of the trees you can feel your mouth water. The fruit is round and red and ripe. It feels smooth to touch, and its scent is sweet. But still you hesitate and finally you sit down under the tree and try to sleep. You are joined by another of your kind, but of the opposite gender, and you tell the other what Teth has told you. You talk it over but decide not to touch the fruit. Eventually you settle down and doze in the hot sun of a sleepy afternoon.

While you sleep two voices converse. One is the voice of Teth, low, musical, and sympathetic. The other is deep, powerful, full of energy, and forceful. They are discussing you and the tree.

"Lord, they are very obedient to your rules. They do not want to touch the tree or eat of its fruit. They are doing what you told them to do."

"Yes, that is true, but I also gave them free will and they are *not* using it. I told them not to eat of the fruit because I hoped they would find the courage to defy Me. Then they would give Me the excuse I need to turn them out of the garden and put them on Earth, where they can begin to grow mentally, physically, and spiritually back toward me, but with all the experience of the physical world within them. Then they can teach me how it feels to be manifested."

"Lord, what do you wish me to do? Tell me and I will do it."

"Teth, you are a Son of the Morning, and beautiful beyond words. But what I need will test your courage and your love for me. I want you to tempt these children into eating the fruit and disobeying my orders. They will hate you for this and so will their children and their children's children, down through the ages. You see, they will not understand that sometimes you have to disobey to learn wisdom, and sometimes you have to sin in order to grow and change through the pain of disobeying.

"Only then will they know the joy of repentance and being forgiven. They will know I love them no matter what they do, even though it may seem otherwise at the time. All this will be brought about by your sacrifice, one of the greatest sacrifices of all time, only surpassed by one other. I will send you from Eden to continue the tempting of humanity. You will not see my face again until all has been accomplished. Do you love me enough to do this?"

There is a long pause and you hear the sound of tears shed by one of the first born. The loving voice of the Lord soothes the anguish.

"I will know, and your brothers and sisters will know the truth. Wise men and women down through the ages will puzzle it out and wonder at the strength of Teth the serpent. But only if you can have the strength to do this for me. If it is not done, then these, my children made in my image, will remain in a state of innocence. They will never know the struggle to gain knowledge of manifestation, to be able to judge between right and wrong; they will always be children and never the divine children I created them to be."

Teth the serpent speaks low and with a sorrow that is almost unbearable. "Lord, I will do as you ask, though my heart breaks with the weight of my sorrow. I will go now for if I hesitate I will not have the courage."

You wake to find a serpent of Light twined around the tree. It speaks softly: "Children of the garden, see this fruit—if you eat of it, you will become as gods. You will know things that even I cannot foresee. It was meant for you to eat sooner or later; it might as well be now."

You take the fruit and smell its perfume, then bite deep into it. As first it seems like any other day, warm and sunny, but then a cloud moves across the sun and the Voice thunders through the garden.

"You have disobeyed Me, you have eaten the fruit of knowledge. For this you will be driven from Eden and will live upon the Earth. You will have to work for every mouthful of food, you will have to learn the ways of manifestation. You will no longer be young and immortal but will grow old and die. But in death you will find a friend, for it will return you to Earth time and again in order to learn. One day you will know all that there is to learn and then, on that day, you will return to Me."

A mighty wind sweeps through the garden and two great angelic beings appear with flaming swords. They drive all three of you from the garden and the gates close behind you. Teth waits until your tears dry and then begins to show you how to build a shelter, what is good to eat, and what is not. Though you blame Teth for your banishment, it remains with you until you can live without its help. Then it withdraws.

At this moment you find yourself back on the road and beside you is Teth. You look at the letter and deep within you there grows an understanding of what all this means. There was and is a reason for the Fall; without it you would never have had the opportunity to grow and learn and search for the divine inner. It has been hard, it still is hard, it will go on being hard for a long time, but one day you and the shining serpent will return to the garden together.

The Teth flames into a rainbow of sound and color as it senses your understanding. You reach out and gently touch the being who gave up paradise to help you realize the Creator's dream for His children. It flows around you like a multi-colored ribbon of light. Above and around you there appear choirs of spiritual beings singing praise and thanksgiving, for a piece of the eternal truth has been recognized by a child of Earth. Through it all comes a Voice, deep and resonant and full of love. "It is well done, Son of the Morning."

You are enclosed in joy, laughter, and wonderment, and in this way you wake to your own world.

Psalm 32

Blessed is he whose transgression is forgiven,

whose sin is covered,

and in whose spirit there is no guile.

Day and night the hand was heavy upon me;

my moisture is turned into the drought of summer.

I acknowledged my sin unto thee, and my iniquity I have not hidden.

I confessed my transgressions to the Lord

and He forgave the iniquity of my sin.

For this shall everyone that is godly pray unto thee

in a time when thou mayest be found.

Surely in the floods of great waters they shall not come nigh unto Him.

Thou art my hiding place; thou shalt preserve me from trouble.

Thou shalt compass me about with songs of deliverance.

I will instruct thee and teach thee the way in which thou shalt go.

I will guide thee with mine eye.

Be ye not as the horse or as the mule, which have no understanding,

whose mouth must be held in with bit and bridle.

Many sorrows shall be unto the wicked; but he that trusteth in the Lord,

mercy shall compass him about.

Be glad in the Lord and rejoice, ye righteous,

shout for joy, all ye that are upright in heart.

Ritual

You will need a center altar with a white cloth and a tealight in a plain glass bowl; a small thurible with charcoal and incense; a red candle in a holder; a chalice with wine or fruit juice; and a wooden plate with a fresh bread roll on it. You also need a small altar in each quarter (a cardboard box will do; stand it on end and put a cloth over it). Each altar needs the following:

East: A gold cloth, a gold-colored bowl with a tealight in it, a stick of incense in a holder, a small mirror, a chair.

South: A red cloth, a red bowl with a tealight, a stick of incense in a holder, a clay pot half full of sand, a small fire on the sand made from a pile of matches (these are to be lit only when you are told in the ritual), a chair.

West: A blue cloth, a blue bowl with a tealight, a stick of incense in a holder, a seashell with sea or salt water, a chair.

North: A green cloth, a green bowl with a tealight, a stick of incense in a holder, a bowl of earth with seedlings or bulbs in it, a chair.

The intent of the ritual is to go directly to the Godhead within and without.

Make three circles round the room, ending in the east. Go to the center altar and light the center light, the incense, and the candle. Stand quietly and go as deeply within as you can. Concentrate on the head, heart, and lunar chakras. The point of God within is to be found at the point of the coccyx, for where else should the God of Creation be found but where the kundalini lies coiled and sleeping? At this point, visualize the letter Teth as the kundalini twined about the base of the spine; see it as a glowing red and gold that becomes green and gold, then blue and gold, and then gold that becomes pure light. Feel its heat grow with each color change. Now it feels like a hot but not uncomfortable coal at the center of your genital area.

Look directly at the center light and imagine it as the outer aura of the Divine Presence. Within, the bright heart of the light contains the unimaginable power and beauty of pure Spirit. See it as a living link between your inner divinity and the Divine Being who passed it to you.

Take the bread and bless it. "I take and bless this bread that it may become a link between the God within and the God without, the fruit of the Earth created for humanity that we might eat and in eating remember that which created us."

Take the wine and bless it. "I take and bless this wine that it may be the symbol of a binding promise between God and humanity to uphold the Divine Plan instigated from the beginning that humanity should be in the fullness of time the inheritor of divinity by virtue of being created from the primal Divine Spirit." *Eat and drink and set the glass and plate aside.*

"I hold within me the divine grace. It will sustain me through my life, in my comings and in my goings, in my work and in my leisure, in my youth and in my time of age. May the One be praised for that which has been received. *Lift the incense.* To thee, O Lord, I offer this incense as a symbol of the breath of my life. Let this be a sign between us that as the smoke rises, so does my aspiration to be pure. *Replace the incense, and lift up the candle.* To thee, Creator of all things, I offer this flame as a symbol of the love that we share for each other, though it may sometimes be less visible than it should be." *Replace the flame, walk to the chair in the east, and sit facing east. Light the incense and the candle and take up the mirror; look into it.*

"I behold in the mirror the reflected image of God, for I was made in that image that I might know myself to be a child of the One. As I see myself I see one that has taken on the task of gaining experience of manifestation in order to offer that experience to the One Creator. I see one who has taken on the suffering human form entails in order to discover the eternal self. I see one who has learned through the making of many mistakes. To my higher divine self and through that self to the Creator, I offer my experience in this life." *Meditate for a few minutes, go to the south. Light the candle, incense, and the small fire, and look into the flames.*

"I see in the fire the creative power of my Creator. I feel within my own body an echo of that divine fire. I inherit my Father's power, though as yet I cannot wield it. I shall be as a sword of flame for the weak and the oppressed. I shall bring the divine fire from the above to the below, and there I will kindle it. It will be as a beacon for those who have lost their way, for those lost in darkness. Behold, I am a flame of the Mysteries. Within me the Light manifests and remains untouched in my higher self." *Meditate for a few minutes, then go to the west. Light the candle and incense and set the shell and water in the middle of the altar.*

"In the waters of the great ocean of space and time, my spirit was formed. From the deep oceans of Earth, I and all life on this planet emerged. Within the richness of the sea, life came to be. The matter of my body belongs to the great tidal forces of the universe. My spirit comes from the One Creator. I cleanse myself with the waters of the Great Mother. *Take some water in your hands and pass it over your head and face.* I lift these waters to the Great Above. *Lift and offer the shell and water.* Water is life, water is the womb of life, water is the sustainer of life." *Meditate for a few minutes, then go to the north. Light the candle and incense, and set the bowl of seeds in front of you.*

"All life has purpose, all life is sacred, be it the green life of earth or the younger brethren, the seemingly inert stones of the mountains and the shore. By whatever form in whatever part of the universe, Life is engendered and nurtured by the love of its Creator. In the times to come, we may meet and speak with Life in many forms."

Lift the shell and pour water on your head, hands, and face. Meditate for a few minutes, then go to the north, light the candle and incense, and set the bowl of seeds in front of you.

"All life has purpose, all life is sacred, and I acknowledge our kinship. I bless these seeds and offer their beauty to the One." *Meditate for a few minutes, then return to the central altar. Lift the light and offer it.*

"I am a child of the One, I have left the garden to learn of the world of manifestation. I remain in contact with my higher self and with my Creator. I am my own priest/priestess, I am sheltered by the hand of the One, and I will try to live according to the plan laid out for me. I am responsible for my deeds, thoughts, and actions. I accept that responsibility."

Repeat the three circles around the temple, bowing to each quarter as you pass. Then leave the temple. Leave the candles burning for half an hour, then douse.

YOD

Touch me with the hand of love, and absolve me of all sin.

Let thy finger point the way ahead,

that I may know the Path ordained for me.

I am uplifted and fulfilled by the crown of Kether.

I am made straight by the rod of Chokmah.

I am cleansed by the waters of Binah.

Thou art the hand of God,

the instrument of the One,

the chastising instrument of the Father.

Touch thou my soul, O my Beloved.

Let me know thee

in the deep recesses of my soul.

Thou art myself uplifted and perfected.

Thy hand outstretched protects me

from the arrows of mine enemies.

My shield, my sword, my way ahead,

my water in the desert,

my shelter from the sun at noon,

my Yod, my Seed of Light.

Image: Hand
Symbol: י
Path on the Tree of Life: 20
Numerical Value: 10

Prayer

We all need a helping hand at times, especially when things go wrong. It is not for nothing that so many welfare and health organizations choose an outstretched hand to feature on their logos.

The prayer calls out for the hand of God to guide and help a soul in danger of losing faith in itself. "Touch me with the hand of love," it begs, "let thy finger point the way ahead." Sometimes all we need is someone to tell us that we can do it, even if the way ahead looks forbidding.

The hand can also chastise when it is necessary. If we look at the crossed crook and flail held in the hands of the Egyptian pharaohs, we can see both the helping (the crook) and the chastising (flail) aspects of an absolute ruler. Justice needs to be tempered with mercy, and guidance has to know when to apply punishment. The hand delivers both. In this day and age when a well-deserved spanking for a naughty child can land a parent in jail, the power of the hand as a guiding and disciplinary tool is sadly lacking. Being sent to one's room is no longer a punishment when that room contains a television, a computer complete with Internet access, a CD player, and a mobile phone!

The hand as a symbol of protection is shown in the prayer, as it "protects the soul from the arrows of its enemies." But it is more than that. The cupped hands can hold water for the thirsty, they can deflect the sun from weary eyes and support faltering footsteps. Such a prayer might have described the feelings of the man who, battered and bleeding, was left to die by the wayside and was lifted up by the hand of a stranger and cared for with love and compassion. Perhaps when next we offer a hand in greeting we should draw a Yod on the palm!

The Letter

The hand of God is featured in many works of art depicting the deity as an artificer, perhaps the best known being William Blake's portrait of God as the Great Architect. What else do we know about the hand as a magical, creative appendage?

We have the hand of Fatima (below), a talismanic symbol known and used throughout the Mediterranean cultures where Western Traditions touch and overlap those of the Middle East. Then there are the beautiful *mudras* or sacred gestures of the Hindu, Buddhist, and Far Eastern religions.

The latter are divided into two main groups: the first is concerned mainly with ritual and, like those in the Western Mysteries, are used to summon, invoke, command, and supplicate. The second group are indicators pointing to a specific Godform or a myth pertaining to a Godform. There are almost 300 listings for the first group: 164 for those of the matrix world (similar to our astral), and 131 for the diamond or spiritual world. However, among these are many that are so similar as to be almost identical.

We may look at the image of this letter either as a hand or as a spermatozoa; both are concerned with helping life to get a foothold on manifestation. It is also the shape of an embryo a few weeks after conception, or even the form of a humble tadpole. While thinking about this you need to read the Egyptian story of Creation. In the original version Atum births himself from the Nun (the primal ocean of space) and manifests himself as a God. Because he is alone in the universe he makes a womb of his hand and ejaculates his sperm into it, thus creating alone and

HAND OF FATIMA

unaided his two children, Shu and Tefnut. In the city of On, later called Heliopolis, one of the many temples was dedicated to Iuessus, the wife (womb-hand) of Atum.

The hands of a mother, father, brother, sister, or lover can express love and support. We depend upon our hands for so many things that we are practically helpless without them despite the advances in artificial limbs. We watch with pride and joy as a young child learns to reach for, grasp, and finally hold on to objects. A baby's grasp is strong enough to support itself when holding on to the fingers of an adult, a relic of the early days when babies had to cling to their mothers' backs for transport—something primates still do today.

Hands can build, weave, spin, paint, create pottery, and cook food. They can heal, play instruments, braid hair, and plant a garden. Is it any wonder that the hand of God the Creator is still such a powerful symbol after thousands of years of evolution?

The path from Tiphereth to Chesed is the Tarot card of the Hermit, who carries the Light (lantern) in his hand. He is the guide for all who seek their higher selves. It is also astrologically the path of Virgo the Virgin, and this symbolism takes us back to the idea of the Yod as a spermatozoa and on to the idea of the virgin birth. If we take this idea and apply it to the seeker, we can see how it fits in.

The seeker lies, all unknowing and unknowable, in the unmanifest of inertia. Uncaring, ignorant of the wonders around, just existing day to day in an endless round of work, home, eat, TV, sleep, work, home, eat, TV, sleep, etc., etc. Then one event, one happening, one little nudge and the soul stirs, wakens, and hears the call.

The Yod, the sperm of Light, enters the mind and heart and suddenly the old life is no longer enough. Everything comes tumbling down and out of the chaos of dissolution the seeker is renewed and sets out upon the age-old quest for the personal grail. As in all the best fairy tales, sooner or later the hero will meet up with the old wisewoman, or the hermit in the wood, or in this case on top of the mountain.

Yod is the smallest letter. Small is beautiful and important, for it is the letter that begins the God name Jah, in Hebrew spelled יה. It also begins the word *Israel*. Numberwise it stands for ten, the new beginning after the completion of nine, and thus begins the next phase of ten, twenty, thirty, forty, and so on.

It is also a feisty little letter, for, so the story goes, it got upset when God changed the name of Sarai to Sarah. It complained that because of its small size it got omitted. To appease the letter, God offered to change the name of Hosea to Joshua, thereby putting the little Yod at the forefront of the new name of the great leader. This apparently was sufficient to calm the little Yod down! Yod begins the words *yetsirah, yom* (day), and *yesod*.

If we go back to the first letter and look at it again, we remember that it is made from two Yods on either side of a Vav. Look at what has been said about the Aleph and contemplate it in the light of the single Yod we have been discussing. You will find that whenever the Yod is part of another letter it adds the strength of the hand to it. It may also add a little fire to the power already there.

Meditations

First Meditation

As befits the image of the Yod, all these meditations are combined with mudras or sacred gestures (see *Mudra* by E. Dale Saunders [Princeton/Bolligen, 1985]). The first set are called JO-IN, the Gestures of Concentration.

A (below, left) is often referred to as the Gandharan Dhyanamudra, B (below, right) is considered to be the oldest. Practice these gestures as part of your daily work.

On the first day give five minutes to each one in the morning and again in the evening. This mudra gives calm and inner tranquility. Link it with a meditation on the form of the Yod. Color the Yod green in the A.M. and blue in the P.M. On the second day give it ten minutes and use red in the A.M. and yellow in the P.M.

JO-IN, THE GESTURES OF CONCENTRATION

MUSHOFUSHI-IN, LEFT, AND ONGYO-IN, RIGHT

SECOND MEDITATION

The mudra is called Mushofushi-in and symbolizes the triple mystery. Allow the same times morning and evening for the first and second days. The meditation subject is the geometric figure of the triangle. On the first day apply the virtues of love, wisdom, and power to the three angles. On the second day use the energies of the supernals Kether, Chokmah, and Binah.

THIRD MEDITATION

The third mudra is Ongyo-in. The left hand is closed into a fist and the right hand, with fingers extended, is held over it. It is called the Mudra of Hiding Forms and is said to cloak the meditator within an aura of isolating calmness. The same times must be allowed as for the others, and the meditation subject is the hand of Fatima. (See *Mudras: The Ritual Hand Poses of Buddhists* by Tyra de Kleen [Keegan Paul, 1924].)

Point to ponder: A fist can hurt and damage, caress, stroke, and comfort. It can hold a sword, a needle, or a scalpel. Never underestimate the power of a hand, especially when held out in friendship, but beware the one who hides the other hand behind his back!

Pathworking

Enter into a state of deep concentration. Allow your thoughts to arrange themselves so that before you is a long narrow passage. At the end there is a bright light. Begin to walk down the passage. Halfway there you hear a voice calling you by the name all the letters have called you: *Life . . . Life . . . Life!* You look around but see no one and continue walking. The voice now sounds impatient: *Life . . . here. Look down.* You look down and see the Yod, small, black, and shiny with an edging of gold. It is small, but its voice and its self-confidence are big.

"Place me on your shoulder, then we can speak more easily," it instructs you.

You do this and find it is a great deal heavier than you expected.

"That is because you see me as a letter and not what is behind the letter. It is true that the Lord made me small but that is so all small things can know their true worth despite their size. Being small does not mean being unimportant! The Lord made me the first letter of His name, JAH, and he also gave me a voice equal to those of my brethren. It is my task to show you that all Life is equal—black, white, and all shades in between, and all species, too. When you begin to travel beyond your own world you will find Life in many forms. That will appear strange to you. The Creator made us all different because He likes variety."

All this time the Yod has been riding on your shoulder and you have reached the end of the passage. Before you is a huge expanse of something you do not immediately recognize. The Yod prods you impatiently with its tail.

"Look, look closer—do you not see what it is?"

The shape finally makes sense: it is a hand, a giant hand. Everything is perfect: the skin, the color, the nails, and the lines on the palm. The Yod prods you again, and you move forward. Each line is as wide as a country lane, clearly marked and following exactly the lines on your own hand. Compare them.

The Yod speaks excitedly. "This is your hand and you must walk each line in order to understand what your life is all about. I will be with you to help you see things clearly." It sounds very important and loving it. "We will begin with the life line. Place your feet here, where it ends, for you must walk it in reverse and go back into your early life. You may begin now."

You set your feet on the giant life line and as you do everything else becomes dim and misty. All you can see clearly is the line before you. Slowly you begin to walk. As you do, images and conversations pop up around you and in your inner ear. At first the images are of last week, last month, six months ago. But as you continue you find yourself reliving happenings and events going back in time.

You see yourself at various ages—20, 10, 7, 5, 3, 2 years old. Incidents you thought you had forgotten are played out before you. Every now and then, when something seems important to understand more fully, the Yod stops it and replays it until you are satisfied. Although you cannot change what has already happened, you can understand the circumstances much more, and now you will know how to avoid the same thing in the future, or you will be able to help others to see similar things more clearly. You can also replay times of great joy and times when people you have lost can be near you again. The Yod will help you if you need anything explained. Ask and it will answer.

At the end of the line you watch yourself being born and bless the child that you will grow up to be. The line disappears and you find yourself at the beginning of the line of the head. On this line you become aware of your innermost thoughts, the ones you have pushed down because you did not want to face them: the way you think about people, about yourself, even those you love or have loved. You can see the patterns of your thinking and your reaction to them, and how thought has influenced you in your life. You see examples of wrong thinking and where it caused trouble, and how to avoid it. The Yod gets a little caustic at some points, but it will help you if it is asked.

When this line fades it leaves you feeling that you know yourself a lot better than before, and your subconscious mind feels clearer—and cleaner. As it fades, the heart line appears. You see those who have loved you and whom you have loved in return; you can tell them how much you love them face to face. Pets you have lost will be there, too. This can be a joyful line to tread. Childhood toys you once adored and perhaps lost or which were eventually thrown away will also appear. The Yod shares your joy and will, if asked, bring objects to you to be wondered over and handled again. At the end of this line, just sit and talk to the Yod for a minute or so; it can be exhausting.

The fate line is next and it is the last for this working. There are many others you can tread if you wish, but leave them for another time. Four lines are enough to cope with at the moment. The fate line will show you how and where and some-times why you took a certain turning. You will see and enact again certain moments in your life when things could have gone in a different direction. If you ask the Yod, and if it thinks it will serve a purpose, it can show you, briefly, how a different decision would have turned out. But it will not always do this, so do not insist. At the end of the path you find yourself back in the passageway. The Yod lights your way back to the entry.

"Well, Life, you have traveled far and seen your life in a deeper perspective. Have you learned anything of value?" You must answer the letter truthfully.

"If you wish, you can tread these lines more than once. Sometimes it is too much to take in at first. I am ready to guide you as often as you wish. This is, or can be, a new beginning of understanding and knowing yourself, Life. I am your helping hand, your guiding hand, your loving hand—use me, I am here for you." It begins to move down the passage and you call after it. "Yod, thank you and bless you. We will meet again."

It pauses and, in a voice more friendly than before, replies, "I am sure we will, Life, and I thank you for your blessing. I will share it with my brethren. Farewell."

It is time to return to your own dimension. Note that you may wish to break this working into two days. This is acceptable and will give you a wider viewpoint and more time to assimilate things you see and experience.

Psalm

Into the hand of my Creator I will put my soul,

for that hand is the source of my spiritual strength.

Into the hand of my Creator I will put my thoughts,

for then they will be judged worthy or not, as He may see fit.

Into the hand of my Creator I will surrender my dreams,

for I know they will be guarded with gentleness.

Into the hand of my Creator I will put my earthly life,

for it came from that hand and will return to it.

Into the hand of my Creator I will place

those that speak against me

that all may be judged with a true justice and with mercy.

I came into life with potential my only possession;

I will leave it rich in experience, a gift for Hashem.

≈

Ritual

This is a very different type of ritual than those that have gone before. It is not done in a temple at all, but for all that, it must be done with a sense of holiness and humility. Because the symbol of Yod is a hand, this is all to do with how your hands are used and what you can accomplish with them. The ritual is completed over five days and must be done on consecutive days.

You will need:

1) An old tarnished piece of brass or copper; a plate, cup, vase, or ornament; cleaning materials and old cloths.

2) A place where you can safely build a fire and keep it burning for at least an hour.

3) Collect some washing, preferably white, that has to be done. Not easy, flimsy stuff, but something that will take a lot of scrubbing.

4) A spade; some flowering bulbs, a sapling, or a small bush; salt; water; oil of frankincense; soap; towel; a small amount of incense in a thurible; charcoal; and a pair of white cotton gloves.

On the evening of the first day, an hour or so before you go to bed, prepare a bowl of warm water and sprinkle into it a teaspoon of salt and let it dissolve. While waiting, light the charcoal and when ready put on some incense that should contain a little hyssop. With the soap and water, wash your hands very thoroughly for several minutes. Hold your washed hands in the smoke of the incense for several minutes, turning them to allow the smoke and scent to hallow every part. Now anoint your hands with the oil, pouring a little into each palm and smoothing it well into your skin. (Try a little on your hand a few days before to make sure you are not allergic; if so, then use a mild oil such as lavender, rose, or neroli.) Now put on the gloves and keep them on until the next morning. Try, if you can, to memorize the following prayers; if you can't, don't worry.

1)
Lord, I give thanks for two strong hands.
Today I want to offer You the work of those hands.
I am going to do the best I can and as I work
I will praise you using whatever name
Comes most naturally to me.
Look upon me as I work and accept my labor
As a thanksgiving for my hands.

2)
This piece of tarnished metal is how I see myself at this moment.
Underneath there is beauty but it is hidden by the grime of neglect.
By my work and my industry I will make it clean and bright once more
And make it shine as brightly as I hope my spirit will one day shine.

3)
Constant movement, constant pressure and patience.
Accept these as my offering. Help me to keep my spirit
Clean and bright so it will shine like this metal.
I have set myself this task. My will must be the polish,
My hands will give the pressure,
But you, Lord, will be the cloth that makes the whole thing shine.

Rise early on the second day and begin to polish the metal. Do not hurry, it has to be perfect. If the object is intricate, it will take time, skill, and patience to clean it properly. Use a cloth for the main part and a small brush for the smaller areas. Rub in the polish well and allow it to dry, then begin to polish.

As you work repeat the prayers or, if you wish, use some of your own words. The prayers are using your breath, the element of air. Think of your physical work as a prayer in itself. If tempted to hurry, imagine you have been given the grail to polish. At the end of the day, repeat the preparation of the hands.

On the third day rise early and build a fire well away from the house, somewhere quiet and secluded. Gather the wood and ring it with stones, then set the fire going. As you strike the match, speak the prayer to Michael, the regent of fire.

Keep it going, feeding it with wood for at least an hour. All the while sit and contemplate the flames and the smoke and think about the virtues and the dangers of this element. Think of early humanity having to live without its comforts and protection. Watch your hands as they lift, carry, gather, and hold things. This gift has made humanity the prime species of this planet.

4)
Michael, lord of fire, I give praise for this gift of flame.
On a winter's day I will remember this moment. I understand

The greatness of the gift of fire that has been given to us.
The hand of the Creator is like my hands, for I was made in that same image.
The fire of the spirit within me rises up, as do these flames.

5)
The winged lion is the ruler of creative fire.
Show me, Holy One, the true meaning of this element,
Let me know its energy, its purpose, its power.
Let me find the strength to use it with purpose and honor.
Let the fire of my spirit warm those who have no warmth of their own.

At the end of the day, repeat the cleansing of the hands. On the fourth day rise early and take the washing. You are going to wash it as women used to wash clothes, in cold running water using a stone to slap them against. This will help you to understand their work and their lives. They are your ancestors and would have been amazed at something like a washing machine. (By the way, did I tell you that this task is for both men *and* women?) You will have to work really hard to get the clothes white and clean and your hands are going to sting and get sore. The cold water will make them swell and turn red, but you will learn the hands are the servants of the will. From being servants they become the holders of power, because they have learned to serve.

6)
I will be clean and fresh to go into the house of light.
With the labor of my hands I will be clean.
I know now the effort and the pain of righteous labor
And I am humbled before those who serve me.

7)
My garments are clean before the altar of light.
Their cleanliness is my offering,
For it is the work of my hands and the sweat of my body
That have provided for me. Look upon the work of my hands
And my heart and accept it, O Lord,
For it is done with faithfulness and love.

Repeat the cleansing of the hands at night. Rise early on the fifth day and take up the spade and go into the garden and dig the earth—three cubits in length and two in width. Prepare the earth to receive the green and growing things you have brought with you. Plant each one with a prayer of your own making and a blessing. Give it permission to grow tall and strong. Plant a mixture, if possible, of herbs and flowers so that the eye and the nose and the tongue may each take pleasure in the fruits of your work. Take pride and joy in your labor and, when the work is done, take pleasure in relaxing. Wash and clean your hands and rub them with balm. They have served you well, as the Yod serves the Godhead. It may be the smallest of the letters but it has great importance, for without it the name of God cannot be spoken.

KAPH

Help me to understand the mystery of my life.
Help me to grasp that which eludes me.
Bring me to a full understanding
of the divine inner,
for thou art the letter of the law
that brings evil to its judgment,
the eternal wheel of karma that
demands retribution.
I shall fear no evil with thee beside me.
Take my hand and lead me toward the Light.
And along the way help me to forgive
what I cannot forget.
Hold me, for I am a child frightened of the dark.
Preparest thou a table before me,
that I may take my God into me.
Thou art the hand of the High Priest of Priests.
Outstretched in blessing it covers me.
I rest beneath it, content and at peace.

Image: Palm of Hand
Symbol: כ
Path on Tree of Life: 21
Numerical Value: 20

Prayer

This letter and its prayer is all about trust. The trust we place in others is sometimes misplaced and causes pain and sorrow. But when trust is fulfilled, the joy one feels is unbounded. To find just a few in whom one can place full trust is a gift beyond measure. Such people are to be treasured and the trust returned in like manner.

It can be very hard to trust when everything seems to be going wrong and each new day brings new worries and new threats to one's peace of mind. It is at such times that one needs to trust in one's deity. This is probably the hardest thing of all. Rather you feel like screaming and shaking your fists and saying, "You don't exist, you are never there, it's all your fault," and so on. We have all done this at some time or another, but if, and it is a big if, you can sit down, look at the situation and assess it, and go back to where it all began, you begin to realize something. That nine-tenths of your predicament is your own fault!

This is not what you want to hear. It is much more satisfying to believe that you are the victim and you are owed something. But it does not work like that because along with free will comes the corollary: *Be responsible for your own actions.*

The prayer asks for understanding in order to grasp what is asked of the seeker. It also implies trust in divine law that whatever happens will be a learning experience. A hard one maybe, almost inevitably, but a lesson learned nevertheless. Nothing we do, say, cause, or experience is wasted, even if it is wrong at the time. We will *learn* and that is the whole point of existence.

Like a child we want a hand to hold on to when the going gets tough and we are stumbling in the dark. It is often the time when, as that lovely poem *Footprints in the Sand* tells us, we are carried in the arms of God, though we do not know it at the time. But children grow up and learn to walk unaided. When they do, we call them "initiates."

The Letter

The shape of the Kaph is formed by two Vavs facing each other and joined head to head. Kaph being the palm of the hand, the two nails of the Vav will have an immediate significance for esoteric Christians. It also implies strength, for while one nail will hold two pieces of wood together, two nails will make it even stronger.

Rabbi Munk says there are three crowns: priesthood, kingship, and Torah. He goes on to say there is a fourth crown, that of a good name, and this is the highest of all. What has this to do with the image of the palm of the hand?

To become a priest there must be one of authority who lays his hands upon the aspirant's head. In a coronation the head of the recipient is blessed and anointed with oil before the crown itself is bestowed. In Jewish law, the Torah is paramount and in a sense the yarmulke that every Jewish man wears is like the hand of Hashem upon him, covering him and blessing him for keeping the law of the Torah. The crown of a good name is given, it cannot be bought, but it can be lost. It can be damaged and be redeemed. It is the palm of the hand of Hashem that then crowns the fortunate one. As was the case of Baal Shem Tov, the Master of the Good Name, Kaph begins the name of Kether, the crown and the point of manifestation.

The letter shows a bent shape that, in form at least, is similar to that of Beth. The image and the meaning are different, of course, but think about this. One curls the palm of the hand into a fist to knock upon the door of a house. When the door is opened, an outstretched hand, palm uppermost, greets you and invites you inside. Palm to palm is a gesture of friendship and goodwill as we enter the house of a friend or neighbor. Wouldn't it be nice if it were always that simple to be friends? With this in mind and because it seems so appropriate I have included here my poem written and published in 1992 and reproduced here by permission of Random House Publishers.

The Return

Let there be peace between us, said the Jew, taking the hand of the Arab.

From the thigh of Abraham we both emerged; let there be an end of hate.

I am weary of the sword, said the Arab, offering bread and salt to the Jew.

Let us water our gardens from the Jordan and feed our children together.

I need to know you as a brother, said the Tamil to the Parsee offering grain.

My fields hold a fine harvest; if you are hungry share my bread.

I name you the son of my father, said the Parsee to the Tamil in return.

Never shall your family lack shelter in the season of the monsoon.

Let me mend your broken plough, said the Hindu to the Muslim farmer.

While I work you shall use my plough and my oxen in your fields.

A blessing on your family, said the Muslim farmer to the Hindu.

In return I and my sons will help you harvest your crops.

Forgive me my past injustices to you, said the White man to the Red.

Let me honor your ways, smoke your pipe, and walk in your moccasins.

Come into my hogan, sit and eat with me, said the Red man to the White.

Let us fill the peace pipe and make plans for the future of the land.

Let me bind your wounds for you, said the Black man to the Yellow.

I have doctors and medicine for you and your children.

For this help I will teach you ancient secrets, said the Yellow man to the Black.

Together we will strive to learn the secrets of the eternal Dao.

Lord God, now I understand why you created humanity, said Lucifer.

Father, forgive me, may I return home? You never left, said God.

—Dolores Ashcroft-Nowicki, ©1992

∾

The laying on of hands is something with which we are all familiar. There are many alternative healing techniques that require it: osteopathy, acupuncture, Shiatsu massage, aromatherapy, Reiki, and many others. A gifted diagnostician can, through their hands, tell exactly what is wrong with the patient.

During an ordination ceremony, the palms, thumbs, and forefingers are anointed with oil so they may hold the Host with clean and consecrated hands. The hands are then joined in prayer and a white cloth is wound about them. Finally the hands of the bishop are laid on the head. The sensitive chakra points in the palms direct the blessing and the power into the head center to awaken it to its purpose.

It is well known that stroking the appreciative and responsive body of your pet can reduce stress and lower blood pressure. Some retirement homes actually have a scheme whereby people living nearby can bring their pets in on certain afternoons to meet, play with, and comfort the elderly.

Skin is an organ. It is incredibly responsive to touch unless we are deeply asleep or unconscious. It reacts to cold by making us shiver if we touch ice or stay too long in cold places. If we sense something or someone approaching on a dark night or in a secluded spot, the hair on the back of the neck stands up. Blind people need only the lightest touch to read Braille, whereas the sighted can only feel raised bumps on a piece of paper. While on the subject of skin, let us not forget that when the first parents were sent from the garden of Eden, God clothed them in garments of skin, for until that time their bodies were made of a much finer and purer matter.

The Tarot card associated with this letter is the Wheel of Fortune and lies on Path 21 from Netzach (power) to Chesed (mercy). On this path we must learn to trust in the power of the Creator, that whichever way the wheel turns there is a reason for it. We rise and fall continually. As the wheel of life turns we must, inevitably, turn with it. In a temple the floor is covered with black and white tiles so the initiate can learn to deal with the dark times as well as the light.

Gareth Knight says, "The Wheel of Fortune is a symbolic pattern of evolving destiny." Then he goes on: "Traditionally the palm of the hand is not only a chart of one's destiny, but is also that part of the Divine Anatomy that was nailed to the cross" (*Practical Guide to Qabalistic Symbolism*, Helios, 1969).

Meditations

FIRST MEDITATION

The seven main chakras of the body are well known, but there are other chakras. One lies in the center of each palm. In the etheric body this center exudes power, and the more highly trained one becomes, the more power is forthcoming. When a priest or priestess of any religion of the Light holds out the hand in blessing, a stream of light and power issues forth and rests on the head of the recipient. Meditate on both these actions. Be the one giving the blessing and the one receiving it.

SECOND MEDITATION

Place the palms together and pray, but not with words. Simply open the heart center and allow the letters of the Aleph-Beth to form themselves into a prayer of their own volition. Do not attempt to read or understand what they are saying; let them say it for you. This is very effective when you are feeling too overwhelmed or simply cannot find the words you need to express your feelings either of joy or sorrow at that moment. Human words can be very inadequate at important moments in one's life. However, the words formed by the beings of the Aleph-Beth, because they are the actual words of Creation, are perfect for any occasion.

THIRD MEDITATION

Visualize the following scene, allowing the meaning of it to seep into the subconscious mind. You are in a dark, quiet room. Above you is a window through which a ray of sunlight falls at your feet. Study this ray of light and see in it tiny dust motes dancing. As you watch they change and become the letters of the Aleph-Beth. They dance and twirl, sometimes two join together, or three, then they separate and dance alone. Watch them. Do not seek to understand messages in the couplings, just watch them dance. This may seem strange but it will prove to be very effective. A similar meditation was used by the ancient prophets of Israel thousands of years ago.

Pathworking

You will need a chair with a straight back or place a piece of board behind your back, anything that will enable you to sit still and very upright. For a few days before this working, I want you to find something that weighs around three and a half pounds in weight: a book, sand or pebbles wrapped in cloth to that amount, even a bag of something like sugar or flour will do. I want you to wear this weight on your head for at least twenty minutes first, then half an hour, and then for as long as you can bear it. *Why?* you may ask.

The Talmud's interpretation of Kaph says that "God will place a crown upon your head." This is not the crown of kingship or of priesthood, but the "crown of a good name." This path is an enactment of a crowning. Thrones tend to be hard, high-backed, and uncomfortable to sit in for any length of time. The Royal Crown of England probably weighs three and a half pounds and maybe more. This is a lot to carry on your head and neck muscles for several hours. The coronation of an English monarch takes many hours, at least five or six in the Abbey for the actual service, then the drive back through London, appearances on the balcony of the palace, etc. The strength needed to carry such a weight is remarkable.

Under the gold and jewels of the actual crown there is a cap of purple velvet. This is called the Cap of Maintenance and covers the anointed head of every sovereign. Because every king or queen of England is also the head of the church, he or she receives a token ordination during the coronation service.

Wearing the weight on your head will instill into you a very real sense of the actual weight, how it feels and how such a sense of weight and responsibility affects you. Try carrying the weight sitting, walking, and standing.

The weight of such a crown is carried not just physically but mentally and spiritually. The crown you will carry from now on (the crown of the good name) will be with you spiritually for the rest of your life unless you renounce it ritually. It lays upon you a responsibility. If you do not wish it, then do not do the pathworking.

What is this responsibility? To keep your name and reputation without stain from now on. An easy thing, you might say. But think about it. Then decide. If one sullies one's own name, the crown will be taken. If others sully your name, they will be called to account.

Arrange low lighting or if possible semidarkness. Take your place in the chair and begin to detach yourself from the everyday world. After a while you begin to feel many presences about you. These may be of the living and the dead but they will be people you have known and loved. Solemn music can be heard faintly and as it swells, the darkness lifts and you find yourself at the entrance to a vast cathedral-like edifice. It displays no symbols of any particular religion but there is an overwhelming sense of majesty and power.

The place is filled with those you have known and loved down through the ages, and as you enter you see at the far end of the aisle a white mist. You, yourself, are robed in white and barefooted with no ornaments of any kind. From the side comes a man of great age leaning on a staff. He is bearded and has white hair that flows over his shoulders. He speaks sternly but with compassion. He asks you to think about the ceremony ahead of you. If you have any doubts about it, it's better to withdraw now if you are not sure, and return in the future.

You are given time to think. What is in a name? How good is your name in your community? Have you done anything to destroy it? Have you ever tried to destroy the good name of another person? If so, withdraw. Can you give yourself a promise that if you go ahead you will do all in your power to maintain your good name? When you are ready, answer yes or no.

If it is no, return to your own time and place, and go on to the next part of the work. If it is yes, the old priest will ask you to follow him. Together you process down the long aisle between the crowds who have come to wish you well. Many wear the same crown that today you have come to accept as your right. They cheer you on and support you in this great moment. As you draw near, a fanfare of trumpets rings out to welcome you. You pass through into the sanctuary and the mist fades.

Before you is an altar dressed with a cloth of gold. On it lie a scepter and a sword, and, on a red cushion, a simple gold crown. Around its base is your name engraved in Hebrew letters. From behind the altar comes a presence greater than any you have yet encountered. It exudes an aura of power and grace and instinctively you kneel before it and bow your head.

There is a pressure of hands on your head and the warmth from them fills your body. The presence pours oil of frankincense on your head and hands, and above you a voice murmurs a blessing. From the other side of the altar comes a presence, one that you know without being told is the letter Kaph. It shines with a clear blue light ringed with gold where the two Vavs join, and it carries a linen cloth with which it dries your head and hands of the excess oil. Its voice is sweet, low, and gentle.

"Be of good cheer, Life, this is how human beings were meant to be, uplifted by their Creator. There will be times when you fall, but do not despair, try again. Each fall is an added experience, each try a triumph of will and spiritual strength."

It stoops over you and folds your hands into a special mudra. Place your palms together, then interlace your fingers. Extend the two forefingers and press their tips together. Now the two little fingers in the same way. Now align the two thumbs side by side and spread the extended fingers as wide as possible. This is the mudra position of love, wisdom, and power.

Open your heart center and silently invite the letters of the Aleph-Beth to enter and combine to form a united song of praise for the blessing of this day. Let the power of the letters and their many voices speak for you. Their song fills your heart with joy.

You hear a voice above you but cannot make out the words. It creates within you a desire to be worthy of your good name. There is a weight on your head as the crown is lowered. It is much heavier than you had imagined. The letters in your heart sing out and gentle hands raise you up. The presence has gone but the priest is there.

He places in your left hand the Scepter of Rule. Now you must rule your own inner kingdom. In the right hand he places the Sword of Will, so you can be an example of the virtues of discretion and discrimination. You turn to those in the hall, all wearing the crown of a good name, and they welcome you to their company. You walk between them, trying to balance the weight on your head. You think of the old saying, "On your head be it." Now it *is* on your head.

You turn to thank the priest and the Kaph. Where there was an old man there is now a winged being with a crown of wheat, poppies, and vine leaves. You know him. Once he was Elijah, now he is the archangel Sandalphon. The Kaph is a brilliant blue with a lily of gold at its heart. The scepter disappears into your forefinger with a tingle, the sword into the right finger. They will remain there. The crown melds into your skull but you know it is still there, reminding you of your responsibilities. You thank and bless your companions and ask them to carry your blessing to those who attended and to the great presence. They understand and will do so. You turn and walk into a soft darkness and come, at last, to your own place.

Ain Soph

Ain Soph, uncomprehended in the thought
Of man or angel. Having all that is
in one eternity of Being brought,
into a moment. Yet with purposes
whence emanate those lower worlds of time
of Force and Form. Where Man with one wing caught
in clogging earth, becomes an angel in a freer clime.
From partial blindness into partial sight
We strive, yearn, and with an inward hope sublime,
Rising or mastered by down dragging might,
And groping weakly with an ill trimmed light
Sink, quenched.
Ain Soph was manifest, as dim
And awful as upon Egyptian throne
Osiris sits. But splendor covered him
And circles of the Sephiroth tenfold,
Vast, and mysterious, intervening rolled.
—A. W. E. O'Shaughnessy (1844–1881)

Ritual

You will need a central altar; a small altar in each quarter (they do not have to be actual tables; storage boxes on their side and covered with a cloth will do). The central altar has a white cloth, the others have gold, red, blue, and green, as per quarter. On each one, place a central candle in the right color, and an incense stick in a holder. Also, you need a small glass with a little wine; a piece of bread on a napkin; and salt and water in two small jars. You will need to make five crowns. Use a simple shape in cardboard and cover with gold foil. Decorate with a few stones in quarter colors. The central crown is left plain.

When ready, enter and prepare for the sealing. With salt and water, draw the Star of David on the door with the intent of sealing it from seen and unseen intruders. Circle the room, sprinkling salt and water as you go.

"With salt of the earth and water from the endless oceans, I set a circle of protection about this place of working. *Go to the altar, take the incense, and walk around the altar.* With sweet-smelling herbs I prepare this place of working. May my mind remain clear and my intent true. *Take the light and circle the altar.* May the power of fire energize this place of working. *Return to the altar.* I state my intent to invoke the regents of the quarters and to receive from them the elemental crowns, by which I may safely work with those elements." *Go to the eastern altar and make a six-pointed star.*

"I invoke Raphael, regent of the element of air. Come forth from the courts of the morning and open to me the gate of the east, that I may know the joy of each new day as it is created. I summon Paralda, elemental king of air. Lord of the winds, grant to me the crown of air that I might safely go forth into the hurricane and the storm and be unafraid. Come to me, ye elementals of the air, be at peace with me and together let us praise that which created us both. I give praise to the perfect Word that created all life and to the first breath that caused the Word to be. *Take the crown and salute the east, Raphael, and Paralda.* Bless this crown that I may wear it in humility and peace." *Put the crown on your head, kneel in homage to the Giver of Power, and ask a blessing in your own words. Replace the crown on the altar and proceed to the south.*

"I invoke Michael, regent of the element of fire. Come forth from the house of the noonday sun and open to me the gate of the south that I may know the warmth of the sun on my face and the blessing of the solar logos. I summon Djinn, elemental king of fire. Lord of the creative fire, grant to me the crown of the element of fire that I might safely go forth into the flame of faith and be unafraid. Come to me, ye elementals of fire, be at peace with me and let us praise that which created us both. I give praise to the Creator. *Take the crown and salute the south, Michael, and Djinn.* Bless this crown that I may wear it in humility and peace." *Put the crown on your head, kneel to the Giver of Power, and ask a blessing in your own words. Place the crown on the altar and go to the west.*

"I invoke Gabriel, regent of the element of water. Come forth from the land of the setting sun and open to me the gate of the west that I may see the beauty of each succeeding sunset. I summon Nixsa, elemental king of water. Lord of the oceans, grant to me the crown of the element of water that I might safely go forth into the storm and the waves and be unafraid. Come to me, ye elementals of water, be at peace with me and let us praise that which created us both. I praise the primal ocean of the unmanifest from which in turn came the unknowable. *Take the crown and salute the west, Gabriel, and Nixsa.* Bless this crown that I may wear it in humility and peace." *Put the crown on your head and kneel in homage of the Giver of Power, and ask a blessing in your own words. Replace the crown on the altar and proceed to the north.*

"I invoke Uriel, regent of the element of earth. Come forth from the valleys and the mountains and open to me the gate of the north that I may know the greatness of the One who provides for all. I summon Ghob, elemental king of earth. Keeper of the seeds of life, grant to me the crown of the element of earth that I might understand its needs and the younger brethren that dwell with me. Come to me, ye elementals of earth, be at peace with me and let us praise that which created us both. I give praise to the planet of Earth, to Gaia the Earth Mother. *Take the crown and salute the north, Uriel, and Ghob.* Bless this crown that I may wear it in humility and peace." *Put the crown on your head, kneel in homage to the Giver of Power, and ask a blessing in your own words. Place the crown on the altar and go to the center altar.*

"I invoke Metatron, guardian of the throne of God, in whom resides the breath of the Spirit. Come in the chariot of fire and let me behold thy shadow for I am not worthy to see more. In your gift is the crown of the Spirit that will purify my soul in its light. I ask that there may be peace between us. Bless me in his name, for it lies within you. *Take the crown and offer it.* I offer this crown to you to keep until

I may be found worthy of it. *Replace the crown and take the light; make three circles around the altar.* May I and all who lie beneath this roof sleep in peace tonight. Blessed be all who are close to me. Blessed be those who have helped me in this rite."

Put out the candles as you circle the room. Unseal the door, bow to the central light, and depart.

LAMED

Why do you goad me so fiercely?

If I go slowly it is so as not to miss the wonders around me.

I am like unto the sheep to the shepherd,

the lamb to the ewe, the ox to the yoke.

Patient I must be and enduring,

for you demand so much of me.

What is the lesson you would have me

learn in this life?

I see the unending road before me and

my soul grows weary.

Lay not thy lash upon me, I beg thee.

I am but human and therefore frail of heart,

and my burden is heavy; give me some ease that I may rest.

Judge me not harshly for my spirit is still learning.

Temper me and let me pass onward to the Light.

Image: Ox Goad
Symbol: ל
Path on the Tree of Life: 22
Numerical Value: 30

Prayer

We all have times when we sit down and say to our God(s), "Enough is enough, I've had it with you. You don't realize that 'down here' is very different to 'up there.' I have worked hard, been as good as I know how, remembered to thank you on the few times when you seemed to be listening . . . and what do I get when I need help? Zilch."

If you have never taken your God to task in this way, you are a remarkable person. When I wrote this prayer I had reached such a point and was ready to throw in the towel. Not getting any satisfaction from Him, I then had a go at the contact behind the school I represent.

"Have you any idea how a human being feels at this low an ebb? Don't you realize I am at the end of my rope?"

"Yes," replied the contact. "We know, we were just wondering if you did! You seemed so willing to go on . . . so we waited for you to find your absolute limit!"

This of course was not what I wanted to hear, but it is typical of people who work in the Mysteries that they often do not know when to stop. Conversely they just as often stop when they need to press on. That is where Lamed comes in. The biggest problem in this work is inertia, an inability to get up and get going. Humans are basically lazy—all of us, with no exception. The Lamed, the tallest of the letters, has a tilt to its head so it looks down on the Earth rather like the eye of God. It also has very good eyesight and an equally good memory.

The prayer complains bitterly and offers a variety of reasons why one should be given a little latitude. The road is long and unending, you want to stop and look around you and see what is going on, you are tired, you are human and fragile, etc.,

etc., etc. Often, and I have found it to be so many times in my case, it is because the time has been spent doing the easy things, instead of getting down to the hardest things first and getting them out of the way. Lamed is well aware of how much we can stand, and when we finally feel guilty and start doing the important things, we tend to drive ourselves into a stupor with overwork. As the contact said, "You were willing to go on . . . so we let you."

Lamed is very much a teacher on how to pace yourself in this kind of work. Sit down and think about what you have done, how you have done it, and if it could have been done better. Invariably the answer is yes.

The Letter

The letter is formed from a Kaph and a Vav and the value of these two letters add up to twenty-six but the value of Lamed as a letter is thirty. Add all of them together and you get eleven, a number that is almost as magical as seven, and one that is never diminished in numerology.

The Lamed's shape is very like that of the *shofar*, the ritual trumpet used in Jewish ceremonies such as Rosh Hashanah, when there are three groups of thirty blasts given on the shofar with another ten added to make up the hundred.

If one looks at the magical images hidden in the letters of Lamed, one finds a goad, plus water, plus a hand or opening. Lamed, when used as a meditation symbol, will often push your mind into realizing things that open hidden doors of understanding (watery intuition). Lamed also looks like a quill pen, the implement of writing, and therefore the passing on or preserving of knowledge. It is the middle letter of the twenty-two and the fulcrum of its balanced wisdom, and is often seen as the heart of the Aleph-Beth. It begins the word Lamad (למד). This holds the meaning of both learning something and then, having understood its meaning, teaching it to others. But there are, as always, other meanings.

But simply to study for its own sake is not enough; one must put what is learned into practice. Quoting from Rabbi Munk, "The Mishnah teaches . . . if one's deeds exceed one's knowledge, one's knowledge will endure. But if one's knowledge exceeds one's deeds, one's knowledge will not endure." This underlines our Western saying, "One is known by one's actions, not by one's words."

Lamed also begins the phrase *lashon hara,* meaning "slander." This is regarded as one of the worst of all sins. "Be not like a fly seeking out sore spots, but cover your neighbor's faults and reveal them not to the world" is the advice given.

Lamed can also denote progression toward a goal or aim in one's life. This may be as simple as wishing to be a good person, not looking for riches or power, or it might be an ambition to become a surgeon and achieve not only the joy of healing others, but to make a good life for oneself as well. There is nothing wrong in seeking to become the best you can be. It means the soul has found its place in manifestation and wishes to become as perfect as it can in that place. If it brings wealth and possessions, then they have been earned; however, if those things have been achieved through misuse of position, power, and knowledge, then one risks losing everything, including the crown of the good name already discussed.

There have been many discussions among gentiles as to the reason for the success of Jews in the world of business, but Jewish children are encouraged to learn and grow in knowledge from the time they are born. The family is of great importance; children feel secure and their religion provides boundaries and rules that both support and encompass them. They are taught that to grow both physically and mentally is natural. They see it in the word *Israel,* for it begins with the smallest letter, Yod, and ends with the tallest, Lamed.

This letter is associated with Path 22 on the Tree of Life, and is ruled by Libra the Scales, which is appropriate for the middle letter of the Aleph-Beth. Its Tarot trump is that of Justice. In the SOL Deck, this card shows the figure of Anubis, the Weigher of Hearts in the Halls of Osiris. The figure is enormous and in the original draft of the artwork a human figure reaching just to the top of the dais was to be seen. However the scale of contrast was such that it actually aroused a feeling of fear. This was not what we wanted, so the figure was taken out. The picture is full of brilliant light with no shadows anywhere. This reminds us that when it comes to the weighing of the heart there is no place to hide or to run. Though there may be apprehension there should be no dread, for the scales are just, and though we may fail to answer all the questions of the forty-two assessors correctly, yet we will pass into the Light.

The last question of all is this: Is there one person who is glad that you were born? There are very few who will fail on that question. There is nearly always someone who is glad you were born and their answer opens the door.

Appropriately enough, Path 20 leads from Tiphereth to Geburah and is the path associated with judgment in the afterlife. The path from Netzach into Tiphereth is that of death and therefore links with Path 22 as it crosses Tiphereth diagonally. One shows the path of transformation of the physical from one level of consciousness to the next, the other the transformation of the spiritual from the blinkered to the fully aware. In my book *The Shining Paths,* this road took the reader through the process of being remodeled and proved to be a path that changed almost everyone who read it.

The lightning flash on its descent down the Tree of Life strikes downwards from Geburah. For those who have struggled to reach certain levels in their Mystery work, this can often cause great tests. The Geburic power strips away all that is familiar and safe and just when you thought you were doing nicely it all goes wrong, seemingly. What it is really doing is acting as a potent Lamed, thrusting you into situations for which you feel unprepared. Remember, Tiphereth is where sacrifices are made.

Lamed can also be a good friend who urges you on and helps to bring out the best in you. Long ago when I began to write I showed some chapters to a good friend and a writer of repute. He blasted the work and me. He told me in no uncertain terms that what I had written was bad and worse than bad and that it was in me to do much better. I was devastated; I had thought it was good, but I gritted my teeth and went through the work, looking at it with his words in mind. He was right, it was bad. He was honest enough and loved me enough to tell me the truth because he knew I could do better. He was my Lamed and continues to be so to this day. If you have a friend like this, you have a treasure.

Meditations

First Meditation

Sit down and think, really think, about a task you dislike doing, and I mean *dislike.* Scrubbing floors? Mowing the lawn? Ironing? Flying? Taking your mother-in-law out for a day? Make a list and go over it carefully. Choose one and then do it. *But* do it with a determination to do it well and with good grace. Find just one thing you can enjoy about it. Do it to the best of your ability and think about it while you are doing it, making the action into a physical meditation.

SECOND MEDITATION

Make another list, this time of three or four things you have always intended to do but never seem to get around to doing: paint the spare room, go to an art gallery, visit a place of interest, try your hand at painting, clear out the attic and have a yard sale, etc. The time for just thinking about it is past. Now you *do it* and within seven days. Before you begin, write down what you intend doing, or going, or seeing, and how you feel about it. After you have done it, write how you feel about it now, what you have learned from it. The idea is that you need that ox goad to get you started. Lamed implies progress, the first step on a journey, an end to inertia. Meditation does not always mean sitting comfortably and thinking nice thoughts.

THIRD MEDITATION

Consider the Lamed as a combination of the hand and the nail equaling the Kaph and the Vav. If you are a Christian the usual thought will be of the crucifixion. However, think laterally this time. Think of a hand hammering the nail into the hand of a person you love.

Pathworking

Settle into a light trance and begin to build a desert landscape from astral matter. Build in the atmosphere: hot, dry, no shade from a burning sun, tinder-dry scrub and sand under your feet. You wear leather sandals and a coarse cotton robe that comes to your mid calf and is tied with rope. Another piece of cloth is tied around your head and hangs down your back. You have a waterskin half full and nothing else.

You are walking through the desert toward a range of mountains with some low foothills before them. You know there is someone behind you but you are unable to turn round and face whoever it is. All you know is that you must keep going. The heat is growing, the sweat is running down your face and you can taste the salt of it on your dry, cracked lips. Your feet ache from the rough terrain and your legs ache from the effort of putting one foot in front of the other. From behind you comes a voice, insistent and almost harsh.

"There is no time to rest, you must reach the foothills before night falls. It is dangerous to be in the desert at night. Keep going. You are not as thirsty as you think you are, you are not as tired as you feel. Keep going, do not rest."

You want to shout at whoever it is to shut up and let you take a few minutes to rest and have a drink of water. But when you try to stop, a hand in the middle of your back pushes you on and that voice goads you to keep walking. You know you are here for a purpose but you can't seem to remember what that purpose is.

The foothills are nearer now and the sun is beginning to lose some of its heat. You can hardly keep your balance now and you drink the last of the water as you trudge on. It is important that you reach your goal.

"You are stronger than you know, there is untouched strength within you. You know it is true. The spark of the Creator lies deep within you. You can endure, you can reach the foothills, you are a child of Light, draw on the power within you."

The voice seems familiar and there is a sense of déjà vu; you struggle to remember just what it is. Then the sun touches the hills and twilight races across the desert toward you. You turn and there is the Lamed. It appears to you as a twisting column of indigo light intermixed with particles of silver. Memory fills you up like rare wine and the twilight envelops you, wrapping you round with purple shadows, and for a moment you lose your astral consciousness.

You struggle toward a light, reaching as if to a loved one, but it remains beyond your reach. Despair, loneliness, and sorrow fill your heart and mind. The light retreats from you and you struggle desperately to remain as close as possible. You know it is important for you to remain in the light but apart from that one narrow band the rest is shadowy darkness that takes on forms and shapes that make you fearful.

Behind you speaks a voice full of a strength that is almost austere, almost military, yet supportive. "Life, listen to me: you have the Light within you, use the Light within to carry you to the Light without. Shadow cannot abide the Light, use it, you have the right to use it. This is not the time to give in, it is the time to fight and win."

You can feel pressure building up inside you as lava builds within a volcano. You feel it surge upward from the solar plexus, the heat radiating outward, driving the shadows back into the darkness from which they came. The Light above seems brighter and nearer and you stretch out a hand, but that is no good.

"Reach with the heart, Life," comes the whisper. "Lift the Light from the belly to the heart, lift the Light."

You try to visualize the Light streaming out from your heart; for a minute nothing happens and then, just as you are about to give up, a crimson flame bursts outward and you feel yourself lifted up to the Light above. Now you know what to do and you bring the inner Light up to the throat center and let it out in a blaze of silver beams; you force it up again to the third eye and again it follows your command and like a shaft of sunlight the last of the shadows flees. You are almost there.

"Once more, Life, once more," encourages the Lamed.

You open the lotus center and like a firework display the Light emerges in a multicolored display to join with the Light above. You gaze upward, lost in the brilliance, and the power begins to flow back.

It fills you, shakes you, takes you apart and puts you back together again. It fills you with fire, then with ice, turns you into a nova and annihilates you only to re-birth you from within itself. You simply allow it to take control and follow the Light.

A long time later you emerge as from a deep sleep, knowing only that you have experienced something totally wonderful. Beside you the Lamed waits.

"You see, Life, all the things you think you do not have—endurance, strength, willpower, knowledge, courage, wisdom—are all within, waiting to be awakened. It only needs the right incentive, and that is dedication. One day I will stand with you as you make the unreserved dedication. When that day comes, all the letters of the Aleph-Beth will be beside you, sharing your joy and your coming of age. Forgive me that I was harsh with you, but only those who are ready to try their strength are tested. The teachers never subject the truly weak to such extremes. You will go far, Life, and now I too must go. My blessing upon you and your species, we shall meet again."

The Lamed lengthens and becomes a comet that streaks across the astral sky and disappears. You watch it until you can see it no more and for a moment you wonder what will happen next. Then you straighten your shoulders. Whatever it is, you will be ready for it, for the strength of the One lies within you. The inner Light shines brightly, like the lantern of the Hermit, like the light of the Star. You sink down into sleep and awaken in your own world.

The Hound of Heaven (excerpts)

I fled Him, down the nights and down the days;

I fled Him, down the arches of the years;

I fled Him, down the labyrinthine ways

Of my own mind; and in the mist of tears

I hid from Him, and under running laughter,

up vistaed hopes, I sped; and shot, precipitated,

down Titanic glooms of chasmed fears.

From those strong Feet that followed, followed after

Naked I wait Thy love's uplifted stroke.

My harness piece by piece Thou hast hewn from me,

And smitten me to my knees, I am defenseless utterly.

I slept, methinks, and woke,

And, slowly gazing find me stripped in sleep.

That Voice is round me like a bursting sea:

"And is thy earth so marred, shattered in shard on shard?

Lo, all things fly thee, for thou fliest me.

Strange piteous, futile thing.

Whom wilt thou find to love ignoble thee,

Save Me, save only Me."

Halts by me that footfall; Is my gloom after all

The shade of His hand outstretched caressingly?

"Ah fondest, blindest, weakest, I am He whom thou seekest

Thou drovest love from thee, who drovest Me."

—FRANCIS THOMPSON (1859–1907)

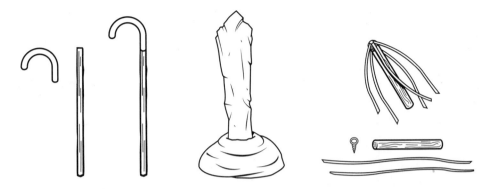

MAGICAL TOOLS, FROM LEFT: CROOK, STONE, AND SCOURGE

Ritual

You need four magical tools that can be used as a Lamed. In the south a scourge, in the west a shepherd's crook, in the north a slender stone about five or six inches high and, like a standing stone, this should be set into a clay base to hold it steady on the altar, and in the east a dagger. The scourge is a ten-inch piece of wood about twice the thickness of your thumb, sanded to smoothness and polished. Obtain six leather shoelaces. Fix a loop screw into the top of the wood, then fix the leather strips to the loop and let them hang loose. The crook can be made from a piece of wood with the actual crook made from clay. If you have the skill, carve it from wood and glue or screw it together. Prepare the usual altar with a cloth and center light.

Begin by cleansing the temple with salt and water, then with flame, and finally with incense. Then light the center light and begin with an invocation.

"Blessed Spirit of the altar, look with favor upon the work about to be undertaken. Strengthen me that I may give of my best, bless me that I may work with a pure heart, imbue me with wisdom that I may work with intent, fill me with love that love may fill this ritual and overflow into the world about me. *Face east and make a pentagram.* Ye high and mighty Spirits of the east, come forth from the lands of the dawn and assist me in this rite. Open my mind and my eyes to the glory of the universe around me and grant me the power to achieve my desire. I hereby state that this desire is to overcome the inertia that binds me to the lower levels of energy. I ask for the energy to work with enthusiasm both in the everyday world and on the spiritual levels."

Take up the dagger. "Let this dagger be the Lamed that urges me on to the achievement of my goal. Let it be to me as a spur is to a horse. Fill me with the determination needed to accomplish my tasks in the worlds above and below. This is my desire, let it be so."

Replace the dagger. Go to the south, take up the scourge, face south and draw the pentagram. "Ye high and mighty Spirits of the south. Come forth from the lands of the noonday sun and assist me in this rite. Open my heart and my belly to the glory of the universe around me and grant me the power to achieve my desire. I hereby state that this desire is to overcome the listlessness that drains me of endurance. I ask for the courage and skill to work at the lowest of tasks and the highest of aspirations both in the everyday world and on the spiritual levels. Let me tread joyfully on both the black and the white squares of life's carpet. Help me to find enjoyment of the smallest task and the ability to do it well. Help me to serve with love no matter what is asked of me. Let this scourge be the Lamed that urges me on to the completion of my destiny in this life. Let it be a symbol of the driving force that lies behind the whole of Creation. Fill me with the wonder of life and an appreciation of the power of love that sustains it. This is my desire, let it be so."

Replace the scourge. Go to the west, take up the crook, face west and draw the pentagram. "Ye high and mighty Spirits of the west. Come forth from the realms of the setting sun and assist me in this rite. Open the sacred center and core of my creative abilities and grant me the power to achieve my desire. I hereby state that this desire is to increase the creative powers within me that I may emulate that which created me and all things. I understand that I am just a pale shadow of my Creator, yet I also know that I am made in the same image and that the same powers on a smaller scale have been secreted within me. It is my task to search for these powers and, having found them, to train myself to use them for the Light.

"I ask for the powers of discernment and discretion that I may live my life in service to the Light and that I may, in a small way, be a beacon for others who are still searching. Help me to face the Lord of Justice when the time comes. Let this scourge be the Lamed that urges me on to the completion of my destiny in this life.

"Let it be a symbol of the driving force that lies behind the whole of Creation. Fill me with the wonder of life and an appreciation of the power of love that sustains it. This is my desire, let it be so." *Replace the crook, go to the north. Take up the stone, face north and draw a pentagram.*

"Ye high and mighty Spirits of the north, come forth from the realms of the sun at midnight to assist me in this rite. Open beneath my feet that center that connects me to the Earth Mother and grant me the power to achieve my desire. I hereby state that this desire is to stimulate my spiritual growth in the upper worlds and to build within me the power to endure in the lower worlds. Open in me the ability to see every living thing as a holder of life and thus being worthy of the love and care of our mutual Creator. Teach me to care for others as I would care for myself. Sustain me as I move through the years of my life; if I am given a long life and health, I give thanks for that grace. If I am destined for tasks and burdens that will try my strength, then I ask for the understanding to accept them and the endurance to bear them. I ask for the gift of knowledge and the power to pass it on to others. I ask for the blessing of good friends and companions to lighten my days. I will try as far as I may be able to give what I can to those who have less. I will strive to be a good neighbor and a steadfast friend. Let this stone be the Lamed that acts as a signpost, pointing the way to the worlds above. Let it be a symbol of the ancient ways, reaching out to the wonders that are to come. At the end of my life, let me know that I have done the best I could do and pass into the Light in perfect love and perfect trust." *Replace the stone and return to the east, facing the altar.*

"Gather about me, ye spirits of the mighty elements; come close, ye holy creatures; draw near, ye regents of the quarters, and join with me. I am a child of the Creator, made in the sacred image. Let us give praise to that which is known by many names. I call forth from my heart the holy letters of the Aleph-Beth. With love and with humility I ask them to make of themselves a hymn of praise to the Creator of all life. Every prayer, every song of joy, every plea for forgiveness consists of the holy letters. Sing for me, my dear companions, and let there be music in paradise."

Allow some minutes to pass, or play some music, then close down and depart.

MEM

Mother of Life, thirst-quencher, rain-giver,
How sweet thou art upon my tongue.
In the desert and in the mountains
thou art my sustenance.
The music of the rain was my first lullaby.
The onward surge of the great waters
fills my dreams and washes the
deserted beaches of my soul.
On thy face so many moods can be seen.
Sometimes strong and dangerous,
then soft and caressing.
Deep in thy mothering belly
lie the hulls of drowned ships.
A silent tomb for those
who rest and dream in them.
But on land the tall trees and blossom-filled meadows
suckle from thee, sweet mother.
Thou art Mem, thou art water, thou art the cradle of life.
I praise thee unceasingly for thy caring.

Image: Water
Symbol: מ
Path on the Tree of Life: 23
Numerical Value: 40

Prayer

In the desert countries a cup of cool, sweet water is a precious gift. In those countries where water is plentiful we are much more careless of it. We waste it and pollute it with little thought of how it would affect us if it became scarce. The prayer is at once a song of love and an invocation to the Great Mother as the giver of life, for all life comes from her.

Without water of course we cannot survive. We carry the primeval ocean within us, in the salt of our blood and in the very makeup of our body, which is largely made up of water. In the wanderings of the Hebrews in the desert, thirst became a torment. Then Moses struck the rock with his staff and water was provided for both human and beast, as manna was provided for food.

It is a sobering thought that every drop of water on this planet is already here; there is no more, just what we have. It is constantly filtered through the oceans, through the atmosphere, through rock and marsh and meadow. But if we continue to pollute and waste it, if we continue to increase the population of the world, there will very shortly be a serious shortage of water. This means not just for humanity but all animal and plant life as well.

The prayer is a hymn of praise for the ocean from which all life emerged. It speaks of the sound of the sea being a lullaby, a dream catcher, and a deep, quiet tomb for those who die by the Ocean Mother's hand. The sea can be dangerous and merciless, and one offends the Ocean Mother at one's peril. The storms that claim many lives each year remind us the Mother brooks no interference. The fittest will survive; all others will return to Her womb to await rebirth. We have created deserts and wastelands by our neglect, greed, and selfishness. It is almost too late.

The Letter

Mem consists of a Kaph with a Vav on its left-hand side, the Vav being joined to it at the top. We can play around with numbers here for although Mem has the value of forty, as it is made from three Vavs valued at six each (two head-to-head to make the Kaph, and the third added at the side), it can also make eighteen. This added together makes nine, the number of completion before beginning a new phase.

The number forty is well represented in the Bible. Moses spent forty days on Mount Sinai communing with his deity. Noah and his family weathered the flood resulting from forty days and nights of rain. It is said that a man should reach the age of forty and be married and have children before studying the Qabalah. It is also said that one really begins to live at age forty having, presumably, raised one's family and established oneself in the community and therefore having time to spare for study and leisure. In the shape of the letter one can see an older person bent over, supporting themselves by a staff. This bent posture is also assumed during prayer or when entering the presence of the King (Melech) or of God.

The letter Mem has two forms: one is open at the top מ and the other, used only when it ends a word, is closed ם. The open Mem can be used anywhere in a word; because of this it represents the overall rulership of God. It openly displays the wonders of God's creation around us of which water is surely the greatest. Water is the Mother, the cradle of life. From this source all life came forth at the command of the One. The closed Mem symbolizes the hidden part of God's law.

We might at this point look back toward the first letter Aleph and again make note of the fact that the two Yods show two different aspects of the hand of God, that which blesses and that which directs. In the same way the two aspects of Mem, the open and the closed, tell us that while some knowledge is openly given, there is a withdrawn knowledge that is hidden from us until we prove ourselves worthy of it. Mem begins the words *maggid* (wise teacher or spiritual guide), *Malkuth* (manifestation in matter), and *Malech* (angelic messenger).

Path 23 on the Tree of Life connects the spheres of Hod and Geburah. The element of water is applied to Hod along with the spheres of Binah and Chesed. When separated from the rest of the Tree, they form the Power of Water triangle, just as the spheres of Geburah, Chokmah, and Netzach form the Power of Fire triangle. This interlacing of the spheres and elements is an important part of the study of the Tree of Life and of ritual magic. The link between a water sphere and a fire sphere appears to be contradictory but, as Gareth Knight says in his *Practical Guide to Qabalistic Symbolism*, "There is in Geburah an aspect much akin to the action of water . . . it achieves its effect by the wearing away of accretions over a period of time [as] dripping water wears away a stone."

Hod, on the other hand, being a sphere of both water and communication, offers a means whereby we may see images, knowledge, and ideas reflected in its watery surface from the supernal spheres beyond the abyss. As children we look into a wood or coal fire and see images of dragons and castles in the glowing flames. In water or in a mirror the adult with a trained mind can see into the inner world of the spirit. In many ways this is a path of mirror magic and the closed form of Mem can be taken as a frame around the mirror of the mind.

When we rely on physical sight we see "in a glass darkly," but by looking into the pool in the water temple of Hod we can see more clearly, as you will find in the pathworking that follows this discussion. The Tarot card of Path 23 is that of the Hanged Man, and once again we come across the hidden keyword of this chapter, which is *reflection*. The figure is suspended over an abyss, held safely only by a fragile link. Though he may seem to be a sacrifice, it is a willing one, for he has understood the meaning of "that which is above is the same as that which lies below." Here the sacrifice has mirrored himself in the two triangles of arms and legs. He looks up toward Binah, the Great Mother, and the Great Sea, the source of all water both actual and spiritual. The two forms of Mem reflect the dual kingship of temporal and spiritual power. This applies also to humanity, though on a much lower scale. We can exercise kingship over our personal physical kingdom of the body, and spiritual kingship over our higher self. In fact, the two forms of Mem illustrate perfectly the "as above, so below" maxim.

Jesus of Nazareth used the open and closed forms of teaching through the parables. The open communication spoke to the simple folk who gathered around Him, but the closed form spoke to the disciples and those close to Him. This way of teaching in levels can be seen even today when we read fairy tales, myths, and legends; we can choose to read them for amusement or as concealed teachings.

When entering school a new student is like an open Mem. Such a student expects things to be easy, that all will be revealed and the secrets of the universe will soon belong to them. After a while it becomes apparent that hard work and long hours of study and dedication are required, and many leave to seek a school that is less demanding! Those who stay and adapt to the requirements will one day become like the closed Mem, the guardian of secrets. In ancient Egypt there was a level of the priesthood named the Keeper of Secrets. You can choose which kind of student you want to be.

The importance of the numerical value of Mem, forty, is seen throughout the Old Testament. Besides the two already mentioned (Moses' stay of forty days on Mount Sinai and the duration of the flood), Solomon fasted for forty days before writing the Book of Proverbs, the wanderings in the desert lasted for forty years, and so on. It is worth tracking some of these events down as they explain a great deal in terms of the open and closed forms of the letter. As always I recommend Rabbi Michael Munk's *The Wisdom in the Hebrew Alphabet* (Mesorah Publications, 1986) for further study.

Meditations

First Meditation

Take any one of the parables and explore its meaning, first as a simple tale explaining a simple law or fact. Then examine it further and ask yourself what deeper meaning a more educated person would glean from this. Finally go over it a third time and put yourself in the place of the disciples and try to see what it would have taught them. Try this with a different parable for several days. You can also use any story from the Bible in this way, and some will reveal ideas and connections you have never thought of before.

Second Meditation

This is liable to be more difficult. Put yourself in the place of the Hanged Man (not literally, I hasten to add). Simply imagine yourself looking down at the sphere of Hod, seeing it as a pool of crystal clear water in which you can see yourself. Contemplate your image for a few minutes, then reverse the process and look up at the sphere of Geburah, a glowing ball of fire, and try to see forms and shapes in the flames. Then reverse it again, look down for a few minutes, and then again look up. This is a technique that can be used with all the paths, which can give you some very precise realizations.

THIRD MEDITATION

Contemplate the letter Mem in both its forms. See how many images you can recall in which the open and closed idea can be connected with water. Example: Faucets—open and water flows easily to give you a drink, fill a vase of flowers, fill a washing machine, etc.; closed it will cut off the flow of a burst pipe, stop water overfilling a receptacle, etc. Just contemplate these seemingly simple images. The constant opening and closing off of the element of water not only offers images that tie in with it, but it will strengthen your ability to open and close the psychic centers, for psychism is a fluid talent connected to water in all its forms.

Pathworking

Sit for a while in contemplation; feel the air around you on your hands and face. Notice your breath as it enters and leaves your lungs. Listen to the sounds around you, identify them, then give them passage through your consciousness. If you resist sound, it increases; if you accept it, it will pass through the conscious mind and leave little trace. Now begin to withdraw step by step. Block out feeling, scent, and touch. Turn your sight inward and focus on a dull-gray surface. Gradually withdraw attention from sound, then rest and know nothing for a while. You begin to be aware of a rocking motion and the sound of water lapping against wood and you realize that you are in a boat. It is quite small and has a turquoise sail on which is painted the card of the Hanged Man. In the stern of the boat sits a presence of Light. You know immediately that it is the letter Mem. Its colors are sea green and silver and its emanation is feminine. You ponder the fact that you always see the letters simply as more or less human-shaped forms of Light distinguished only by color and by feeling. You feel at ease with the letters now and greet the newcomer with quiet joy.

"I am happy to be with you, Mem. May I ask a question?"

"What would you like to know?"

"Why do I see you and your companions as a sort of human-shaped light, and never just as letters?"

"In reality we are neither forms, we are as we are; if your body vibrated more quickly, a lot more quickly, you would be able to see us as we are. Do not be impatient; the point in space where this will happen is already ordained and moving toward you."

"I don't understand—do you mean time?"

"No, time does not exist for us; it exists for you only because you have been conditioned to acknowledge it. Thought knows no time, it is instantaneous. Think of us as visible thought. Does that help?"

"Not a great deal."

"Then you must have patience and wait for the point of knowing to arrive, Life. Do you see that island on the horizon? That is where we are going and where I will show you something of myself and my power."

The boat skims over the water toward a sun that is slowly setting amid a riot of gold, purple, red, and saffron-colored clouds. You can see on either side the heads and tails of white seahorses as they race toward the island. You watch, fascinated, as they change form again and again. Then the boat touches the sand and you have arrived. Eagerly you climb out and splash through the surf to the beach.

The island is full of trees and shrubs and the air is heavy with the scent of blossoms. Overhead the sky is alight with color and the sun is touching the sea. Together you walk along a path toward a wood where the leaves of the trees give off a spicy aroma. Entering the wood you plunge into a world of green and gold as the last of the sunlight filters through the leaves. A stream runs into a pool and enters a small lake. A wooden causeway gives access to a temple of white marble built in the center of the lake.

With the Mem you cross the causeway and enter the temple. Inside six high-backed chairs stand in a semicircle around an altar of sea-green glass. In each sits a presence of Light wearing a crown of gold. On the altar is a cloth of white linen edged with pearls. Above hangs a lamp burning a sweet-smelling oil. A light in a crystal bowl stands on the altar and beside it is a pair of soft leather sandals. The way to the altar is blocked by a carpet of thorns and here Mem stops you.

"Life, this is the path of the willing sacrifice. The sandals are yours to wear as you walk the rest of the paths of the Aleph-Beth. To get to them you must walk the path of thorns. You do not have to do this yet. You can wait and return to this path; no shame will be yours if you choose not to walk. It means you have not arrived at the point where the sandals can be yours. You can try again."

Here you must make a choice. If you choose not to take the sandals this time, go to each of the crowned presences and ask for a blessing. Then you may leave the temple and walk back to the boat with the Mem.

If you want the sandals, set your bare feet on the carpet and walk to the altar. It will hurt as much as you think it will. Your feet will bleed. You take the sandals and return to the Mem. She invites you to sit on a small stool by the side of the door, then she bathes your feet by touching them and the water that is a living part of her letter falls from her touch, healing and soothing them. She places the sandals on your feet and raises you.

You go to each presence and each blesses you and gives you a word; each word will begin or end with the letter Mem. Try to remember them. When you come before the altar again, the carpet of thorns has gone. On the altar is a cup of water. Drink it down.

Mem leads you from the water temple over the causeway to the boat. Silently you climb into it and set sail for the distant shore. It is now night and the stars are brilliant overhead. A light breeze becomes a forceful wind that in turn grows to a full storm. You cling to the side of the boat and, as you do, it begins to melt into the water, becoming water itself. Mem turns and takes you in her arms and together you sink into her element.

Holding you, she melts into the sea. You become part of what is within you, the ocean that gave you life. You and the Mem are one with the ocean around you and everything in it. You are conscious of flinging yourself against the white beaches of the South Pacific, but at the same time you know the coldness of being an arctic berg floating in the sea at the top of the world. The voice of the Mem speaks within you.

"Life, you are mine, as I am yours; all life comes from me and to me it will return in time, for I am the sea of space as well as the oceans of Earth. In time you will cross the vastness of space and visit the shores of unknown planets, and I will be there with you. Of all the letters I am the one who lives within you; I am the salt in your blood, the rushing of the waters in your inner ear. This, this is my power, Life—you are my power, all life is my power."

There is a mighty surge beneath you and you are thrown up onto the shore, breathless and stunned by the awesome strength of the sea. You lie there trying to take it all in and there, resting against the sand, you slide into sleep to wake in your own world.

Deep Sea Soundings

Mariner, what of the deep? This of the deep.
Twilight is there and solemn changeless calm.
Beauty is there, and tender healing balm.
Balm with no root in earth or air or sea,
Poised by the finger of God it floateth free,
And, as it threads the waves, the sound doth rise,
Hither shall come no further sacrifice.
Never again the anguished clutch at life,
Never again great Love and Death in strife;
He who hath suffered all need fear no more,
Quiet his portion now, for evermore.
Mariner, what of the deep? This of the deep.
Though we have traveled past the line of day.
Glory of night doth light us on our way,
Radiance that comes we know not how or whence.
Rainbows without the rain, past duller sense.
Music of hidden reefs and waves long past,
Thunderous organ tones from far off blast.
Harmony, victrix, throned in state sublime,
Couched on the wrecks begrimed with pearls of time.
Never a wreck but brings some beauty here,
Down where the waves are stilled the sea shines clear.
Deeper than life the plan of life doth lie.
He who knows all, fears naught, Great Death shall die.

—SARAH WILLIAMS (1841–1868)

Ritual

You will need a central altar with a blue or sea-green cloth; a blue or green bowl holding a blue or sea-green candle for the center light; four bowls (glass or china) in yellow, red, blue, and green; a thurible or bowl of burning incense (I suggest lavender, oak moss, a touch of camphor, and a grain or two of myrrh); a glass chalice; salt and water. Prepare four small altars in the quarters with cloths and candles to match the quarter colors. In the east, a small glass jug of water with a few drops of yellow food coloring in it; same in the south, only use red coloring; repeat in the west with blue coloring, and again in the north with green coloring.

Come to the central altar and bow. Take the thurible and make a circle of sacred space. Repeat circle with salt and water. At the altar, state your intent and offer an invocation.

"I praise the Light of Lights and state that the intent of this ritual is to contact the powers of the letter Mem in the four quarters and align it to the elements. For my purpose I invoke the presence of the spiritual being that is the essence of Mem. Rest upon my altar and be welcome in this place. *Bow, cense center altar with thurible, bow again, and replace the incense. Go to the eastern altar and light the candle.* I invoke the presence of Paralda, elemental king of air. I open the gate of elemental Air with the sign of the spiral, symbolizing the encircling of earth by this element. Come to my call and let there be peace between us. *Pause.* I welcome thee with the breath of my body. *Blow into the east, and take up the jug of water.* I offer to thee the element of water and ask that it be blessed by you making it water enclosing the element of air. One within the other, together yet apart. I strengthen the bond with my breath. *Blow into the jug.* I here present the element of air enclosed and empowered by the element of water." *Turn and present the jug to the south, the west, and the north. Take it to the central altar and pour about one inch of water into the chalice. Return to the east, and replace the jug. Go to the southern altar and light the candle.*

"I invoke the presence of Djinn, elemental king of fire. I open the gate of elemental fire with the sign of the spiral, symbolizing the encircling of earth by this element. Come to my call and let there be peace between us. *Pause.* I welcome thee with the breath of my body. *Blow into the south, and take up the jug of water.* I offer to thee the element of water and ask that it be blessed by you, making it water enclosing the element of fire. One within the other, together yet apart. I strengthen the bond with my action. *Douse the candle flame in the jug.* I here present the element of fire enclosed and empowered by the element of water." *Turn and present jug to the south, the west, and the north. Take it to the central altar and pour a little into the chalice; return to the south, replace jug, and go on to the west. At the western altar, light the candle.*

"I invoke the presence of Nixsa, elemental king of water. I open the gate of elemental water with the sign of the spiral, symbolizing the encircling of Earth by this element. Come to my call and let there be peace between us. *Pause.* I welcome thee with the breath of my body. *Blow into the west, and take up the jug of water.* I offer to thee the element of water and ask that it be blessed by you making it Water enclosing the element of water. One within the other, together yet apart. I strengthen the bond with the fluid of my body. *Lick your finger and lightly brush the rim of the jug.* I here present the element of water enclosed and empowered by the element of water." *Turn and present the jug to the north, the east, and the south. Take it to the central altar and pour about one inch of water into the chalice. Return to the west, replace the jug, and go to the north. At the northern altar, light the candle.*

"I invoke the presence of Ghob, elemental king of earth. I open the gate of elemental earth with the sign of the spiral, symbolizing the encircling of earth by this element. Come to my call and let there be peace between us. *Pause.* I welcome thee with the breath of my body. *Blow into the north.* I offer to thee the element of water and ask that it be blessed by you, making it water enclosing the element of earth. One within the other, together yet apart. I strengthen the bond with a part of myself. *Take a single hair and dip it into the jug.* I here present the element of earth enclosed and empowered by the element of water." *Present the jug to the east, the south, and the west. Take it to the central altar and pour a little water into the chalice. Return to the east, replace the jug, and go to the central altar.*

"I here invoke the attention of the four regents of the quarters, the four kings, and the four elements. Let this be a time of blending the four elements with the spirit of the children of Earth. I salute you, mighty unseen ones. I call upon you to join me at the altar of Light. *Drink from the chalice.* Praise to the regent of air for your strength and devotion. Praise to Paralda for your grace and beauty. Praise to the element for its obedience to the will of the One.

"Praise to the regent of fire for your strength and devotion. Praise to Djinn for your power and beauty. Praise to the element for its obedience to the will of the One.

"Praise to the regent of water for your strength and devotion. Praise to Nixsa for your strength and beauty. Praise to the element for its obedience to the will of the One.

"Praise to the regent of earth for your strength and devotion. Praise to Ghob for your abundance and beauty. Praise to the element for its obedience to the will of the One. May we exist and grow in peace and harmony together."

Bow to the altar, snuff out the candles, and depart.

NUN

How like thy image art thou.

A gleaming silver fish darting here and there.

A thought, a word, a promise

slipping between the ripples of my mind.

Sometimes I catch and hold thee,

and you lie trembling in my hands.

I feel the surging life within thee,

beating in tune with my own heart.

Tenderly I replace thee in the life-giving water

and watch thee dart away.

So fragile is life and yet how tenacious,

so loving of breath.

Life and death together in one tiny form.

Let me touch thee, silver Nun.

Give me of thy knowledge

for I desire thee as I desire life and fear death.

He, the Wise One, knew of your wisdom

and fed you unto His flocks.

Let me feast upon thee and give thee unto others.

Though it be after another fashion.

Image: Fish
Symbol:]
Path on the Tree of Life: 24
Numerical Value: 50

Prayer

First the water, then the fish to swim in it. There is so much symbology in this letter that it will be difficult to choose what to include. But first we begin with the prayer. This is more of a reverie, a spiritual quietness that even in the worst time of one's life gives one a moment in which to breathe, pray, and hope. This was written during one of those times.

Fish are slippery at the best of times, and our thoughts and especially our dreams have a habit of slipping through our fingers before we can get a firm grip on them. But when you do get hold of one it is very like holding on to a live fish. One can feel the life and the strength within; it gasps and struggles and begs with limpid eyes to be set free into its own world.

The world of thoughts and dreams is full of "fish." They dart about and hide under the rocks of everyday work and chores, and peer shyly at us as we try to seek them out. The best way is to sprinkle new thoughts on top of the water of the thought world and lure them up to feed on them.

The more time we give to thinking and dreaming, the more they will trust us and seek to show themselves. Of course it has to be balanced; too much dreaming is as bad as not enough. We should all set aside a time each day in which we can feed our dreams—then, one day, sitting quietly with our feet in the water of the world of Yesod, we will find them swimming close to us and waiting to communicate.

This prayer seeks to know the Nun as the giver of wisdom, for their species has always been seen as the guardian of knowledge. Indeed we are often told that fish is a brain food. It recalls the miracle of the feeding of the five thousand with five loaves and two fishes. If we look at this story with understanding we see that Yeshua was born in Beth-Lechem, meaning the House of Bread. He, of Himself, was the bread with which He fed so many. The fishes were His thoughts, knowledge, and wisdom. All this was made clear in the upper room at the Last Supper. Born in the Age of the Twin Fishes, as the aeon of that age He was destined to bring a new understanding of older truths into the world. That it was corrupted by men who desired power over others is a risk all sacrificed Godforms run, no matter in what age they appear.

The Letter

Nun is made up of a Zayin and a Vav. The top half is the Zayin and the bottom half is an upside-down Vav. It is almost as though the Creator loved the shapes of the letters so much He wanted to keep using them over and over again to create other letters. Its value is fifty, but we also have to look at the gematria of the combined letters. Zayin is seven and Vav is six. Put them together and we get thirteen—the twelve Apostles plus Yeshua.

Fifty, on the other hand, reminds us of the fifty gates of Binah. The seven spheres from Malkuth to Chesed are those that affect us most because they are below the abyss, separating us from the supernals, and each sphere is a gate. There is a complete tree in every sephira so if in those seven internal trees we count the gates from Malkuth to Chesed, we get seven times seven equaling forty-nine, with Binah herself as the final and fiftieth gate.

In the Jewish calendar every seventh year is a Shimittah year, and seven such years make forty-nine, with the fiftieth year being that of Yovel or Jubilee. This is a very important and special time.

The letter Nun has two forms, the bent ‭נ‬ and the straight ‭ן‬. Rabbi Munk tells us that the bent Nun symbolizes Hashem sitting on his throne, while the straight or elongated letter represents the angels standing before Him. Nun stands for faithfulness in two ways: Hashem's faithfulness to his creation and the faithfulness of those who look to Him as their Creator. As a fish is faithful to the ocean in which it swims safely, so the ocean supports, feeds, and gives life to the fish. Life may serve like the bent and humble Nun, or like the straight Nun, proud to serve. When a Jew recites the Shema each day, he is reminding himself of the faithfulness of Hashem to His creation.

When we think of our higher self, we cannot do better than to think of it as a candle flame lighting up the darkest recesses of our life and making them visible to us. In this way we can adjust our way of thinking and acting if it is needed. The words of Osios R' Akiva come to mind: "At times the soul is withdrawn and resigned like the resting Nun, and at times active and upright like the erect Nun. When a person is inactive and immobile, his soul lies fallow. When he is vibrant and motivated his soul draws itself upright to its full height."

The path of this letter is that of Netzach to Tiphereth, on which we find the Tarot card of Death. It is also linked to the astrological sign of Scorpio. It is interesting to note that this path continues over into the path from Tiphereth to Geburah, on which we find the card of Justice. These paths form the journey of the Duat.

The card of Death is not to be feared, for it has an opposite meaning. It points the way to regeneration and rebirth. In the SOL Tarot deck, Death is seated in a boat that floats on the ocean (Mem) and the white goddess, the Mother, sits in the boat with Death, for it is She who gives us rebirth. The boat sails toward the setting sun and Amenti in the west, where life is restored to us. It is a card of hope and joy and trust.

Scorpio is often looked down on as an astrological sign but it, like the card, is really a sign of regeneration. Unlike other signs, Scorpio has many incarnations. It can be seen as a snake (Teth), as a scorpion (Nun), and as an eagle (one of the Four Holy Creatures), and in its final triumphant form as the phoenix, the soul in excelsis. It is a difficult sign to live with and deal with. The natives of this sign are demanding in their need to achieve, voracious in their desire to know all there is to know. They seem secretive and sharp of wit and not someone you would want for an enemy. They may be persuaded to forgive, but they will never forget.

The upright Nun can be seen as the silver pillar of the temple, the pillar of force, as the black pillar is the pillar of form. It stands straight and carries the weight set upon it with fortitude and endurance.

In an earlier chapter we spoke of the letter Kaph and the crown of the good name. The person who is like an upright Nun will find the weight of such a crown easy to bear because it is theirs and has been earned by right.

Gareth Knight remarks that "All the paths moving into Tiphereth are paths of sacrifice." This does not always mean martyrdom or a great and tragic loss but simply that sometimes one has to be prepared to give up something in order to have something better. All too often we cling to things we don't really need but to which we are attached by habit. If we can make the break and endure the momentary pain we often find there is something much more rewarding in the offing.

Let us not forget the story of Jonah and the whale, a mighty fish if there ever was one. First let us consider what type of fish it might have been. I may be wrong but I doubt if many whales can be found in the Mediterranean! Dolphins, yes, and porpoises, but whales, no. What is more, although we are familiar with the story of Jonah and the whale, the Bible does not actually tell us what kind of fish it was. On top of this, Jonah was a willing sacrifice, for he offered to be thrown into the sea.

The story is obviously an allegory for an initiation. The fish itself had been prepared by God for this purpose and so must represent something other than what it purports to be. It might represent a sacred place where such initiations took place, or a vault, such as the Egyptians used. Whatever and wherever it was, the ocean symbolism tells us that it was to bring about the rebirth of Jonah. Like the Egyptian form of the rite, he was incarcerated for three days and nights. However, strangely enough, it did not seem to do him much good, for according to the Bible story he seemed very ungrateful afterwards.

Finally we must mention the teacher from the sea. The greatest of these was said to have emerged from the sea, showing himself to the fishermen working by the shore and their families. Each day the stranger came and sat with them, teaching them many things. In the evening he returned to the sea. He used the name of Oannes and it is said that his flesh was like that of a fish and he had scales on his skin. He came for many weeks and then as suddenly as he had appeared he left and came no more. I do not propose to make suggestions as to who or what he may or may not have been, but the emphasis laid on the words "skin like the scales of a fish" seem fairly significant. It remains a mystery upon which to speculate.

Meditations

FIRST MEDITATION

Not all meditations need to be done sitting in a chair with your eyes closed. If you have an aquarium near you, pay it a visit and sit for a while just looking at the fish. Watch their movements and observe their suppleness; see how perfectly adapted they are to their environment. Allow their silent dance to soothe you as you contemplate the beauty of their world. If significant thoughts arise, write them down. Think of the water world as a mind and the fish as the thoughts swimming around in it. If there is no aquarium, maybe a friend has a fish tank, or use a National Geographic video.

SECOND MEDITATION

Sit quietly and imagine that you are now the fish and you are doing all the things you saw them doing the other day. When you are used to this, think of yourself as a thought swimming in the universal mind. What kind of thought are you? Are you a thought or are you being thought about? How can you make yourself known to the outside world?

THIRD MEDITATION

Contemplate the word *faithfulness*. Have you been faithful to yourself, to your beliefs, to your friends, family, partner, country, race, etc.? Have they been faithful to you? How do you define this word? Is there anything you would be faithful to through thick or thin?

EXTRA MEDITATION

Stand upright like the straight Nun. Imagine yourself as a pillar of the temple, bearing part of the weight of the great roof overhead. Keep yourself straight, though not rigid; try to imagine the ceremonies going on in the temple below you. You are a part of it all, for you were built to endure. Remember, nothing is inanimate; all things have a sense of self, no matter how dim it may be.

Pathworking

Slip into a light trance and build up the image of a seashore. It is just past dawn and there is a cool breeze. The salty tang of the sea is pleasant and the feel of the sand under your feet is cool. Soon when the sun comes up it will get hotter and you will long for the coolness you now enjoy.

You sit on a rock and look out to sea. Far out you can see ripples on the water; they come nearer and nearer and you wonder what it can be. Then from the water rises a shining oval of light, gleaming silver in the early morning sun. It rises until it is as tall as a tall man. It stands before you and speaks. "It would have been very like this, Life, on that far-off morning when the stranger came to the fishermen. They would have been frightened at first and probably ran away, but when they saw that the stranger returned each day they gradually lost their fear and came near. You are more knowledgeable than they were and you are not afraid, but it is good for you to imagine what it would have been like. Shall we walk and talk a little while?"

You rise and smile at the Nun and together you walk—at least you walk, the Nun glides across the sand a little above it. The sunlight seems to shine right through it and this makes it sparkle as if it were made of tiny diamonds. For a while there is silence, then the Nun speaks. "Life, I wish to speak about the concept of faith. That is a part of my power—I am the epitome of faith. I represent it, I underline it, I channel the faith of the One to humankind. But do you *know* what faith is and what it means to you as a human being? Tell me."

You must try to explain to the Nun what you have found in your meditations.

"Thank you for sharing this with me, Life. I have heard much about you from my companions. Tell me, what have you found most important in your dealings with my kind? Have you found it easy to speak and be with us? Some find our presence disturbing, others find our auric differences make it hard for them to breathe. You must understand that it is seldom we have the opportunity to be close to humankind. It is as much a learning process for us as it is for you."

You can tell the Nun how you feel about the letters, and what you have found most interesting. You may ask questions; you may even get answers. Now the Nun stops walking and turns to you. "Life, do you know the story of Jonah and the fish?

Ah, I see you do. Tell me, do you think you could endure what Jonah endured? If so, will you?"

Think about this. Do you think you could endure three days and nights in the belly of a fish? Is this what you are being asked to do? Or is there another meaning involved?

You ask the questions that are in your mind. The Nun explains.

"What I am asking you, Life, is could you endure solitude and little light and fast on just water and bread for three days? Your only comfort would be communication with me and those of my brethren you have already met. If so, the test would be the next part of your learning process."

Think about this for a while. What the Nun means is that the ritual for this letter would entail a three-day fast, living in one room with little light, no human company of any kind, talking to no one. If you cannot, say so. If you can, then accept. The Nun speaks again.

"We have agreed, my brothers and I, that it would be unfair to ask three days of you, for this is not your way of living, nor would it be right to ask one of your time to undergo such a task. I ask this instead. For just one day and two nights, will you undertake to live and sleep in sacred space with just water to drink and bread to eat? During this time, Aleph through Nun will be with you, surrounding you and supporting you. Contemplate us and we will be there."

There is no compromise on this; either you do or you don't. If you don't, but want to do it in the future, you must continue to the end of the work with the letters and then go through the work again until you reach this point and then take the test. It will not work if done out of context.

If you are willing to do this, if it is possible to do this, then bless the Nun and return to your own time. Pass on to the ritual, which will embody this test; otherwise continue on to the next letter.

Genesis 8

And God remembered Noah and every living thing

and all the cattle that were with him in the ark;

and God made a wind to pass over the earth and the waters were assuaged.

The fountains also of the deep and the windows of heaven

were stopped and the rain from heaven was restrained.

And the waters returned from off the earth continually:

and the waters were abated.

And the ark rested on the seventh month on the seventeenth day

upon the mountains of Ararat.

And the waters decreased continually until the tenth month.

In the tenth month on the first day of the month,

the tops of the mountains were seen.

And it came to pass that at the end of forty days

Noah opened the window of the ark he had made

and he sent forth a raven which went to and fro

until the waters were dried up from off the earth.

Also he sent forth a dove from him

to see if the waters were abated from off the face of the ground.

But the dove found no rest for the sole of her foot

and she returned unto him in the ark

for the waters were on the face of the whole earth.

∾

Ritual

You will need to make arrangements to be on your own for thirty-six hours. Make sure no one will call and unplug the telephone. The room you will be using should be as uncluttered as possible: no books, papers, TV, phones, or anything that might disturb you during this time. You will need a small altar with a white cloth, a center candle (white and several of them), some incense sticks, matches, a mattress, a small pillow, a sheet, a blanket, a chair in which to meditate, a suitable picture to contemplate, four-inch copies of the Aleph-Beth from Aleph to Nun, three two-liter bottles of water, and three large loaves of bread, preferably homemade.

The only time you may leave the room is to use the toilet and to wash your hands and face three times during the day. If there are other people in the house, make sure you are not seen. Prepare everything the night before. Take out of the room anything that might distract you or could be used to amuse or entertain you. No cigarettes, no alcohol, no tea, no coffee, no soft drinks. No paper and no pens. Bathe and wash your hair; put on clean nightwear or a robe if you prefer. Cleanse the room with salt and water, light the center candle, open the quarters with a pentagram, and invoke the archangels to watch over you during this time.

Your time will begin at midnight; as far as possible divide your time into meditation, contemplation, rest, sleep, and gentle exercises that stretch limbs and muscles. Yoga exercises are ideal. Here are some things you can do.

PRACTICING THE PRESENCE OF GOD

1) This is a contemplation exercise; sit comfortably and allow yourself to drift into a light trance. Imagine yourself out in space and move outward, leaving the solar system behind. Just keep going—you will not get lost, so don't panic. Go until you feel you cannot go any further. At the edge of space you see a light and you go toward it. It grows in intensity until it is so bright you can hardly bear it. Stop here and build up the sense of a great presence. Feel the love and the compassion that comes from it. Allow it to wash over you and heal you. Open your heart center and allow the love to enter. You may feel moved to tears; if so, let them fall—this is as it should be. Allow the energies of the letters you have worked with to build up around you. Use them to praise the presence and ask for its blessing. Then allow the letters to bring you back so you do not have to make an effort. This can be a very moving experience, so do it only once.

2) Meditate on your own name, repeating it every few seconds until it becomes a mantra. Then stop and allow the vibration of the name to fill your mind and thoughts.

3) Call on the letters you have met so far, either singly or collectively. Interact with them and try to go deeper into their powers and the essence that is at the core of their meaning.

4) Call the letters to you and ask them to dance for you. Ask them to make words for you and then try to understand the words and why they were chosen.

5) Meditate on what you actually believe in. This is harder than you might think. We all say we believe in things, but can you actually define it?

6) Simply sit and look out of the window and observe.

7) Sit and give thanks for what you have had in your life so far.

8) Look into the candle flame and see its separate parts. The black and red wick, the bluish aura between the wick and the yellow flame, the point where the flame rises to a thin wisp and then becomes a shimmer of energy. Try to go beyond the flame into the radiation of the flame itself.

   Try not to sleep in order to pass the time, remain active and alert as far as possible. Take in with you a homemade rosary with a bead for every hour you will spend alone. At the beginning of each hour create a prayer for one of the beads.

   Use your time to search your heart, mind, and soul. You may find this very hard as the things you will remember or which will surface are going to be the things you have been trying to forget. Face them and cleanse them from your mind. This is not an easy thing to do; if you can do it, you will reap rewards that will amaze you.

SAMECH

Thou art the foundation of my house of life.

I lean upon thee when weary of toil at eventide.

Thou art the rod and the staff,

a comfort for the lame and the halt.

Thou art the axis of the universe,

the tie beam of the vault of heaven,

the buttress that defies the pressure of time.

Because of thee the temple of Solomon

sprang up from the earth at the command of the King.

Thou art the Spine of God, the Djed of Osiris,

the trunk of the World Tree.

Thy roots straddle the cosmos.

Thou art the Divine Inner that fills my heart

and in thee I store my memories of joy and sorrow.

Behold the hand of God upholdeth thee,

and the Earth supporteth thee.

Mighty art thou, Samech, and mighty is

the One you serve.

Image: Crutch or Staff
Symbol: ס
Path on the Tree of Life: 25
Numerical Value: 60

Prayer

The powers of Samech are varied and many and, like its magical image of the crutch or staff, it supports us when we have need of it. The word *support* is the core of the inner meaning of this letter. As I worked with the Aleph-Beth over the years I came to look upon them first as teachers, then as friends, and finally as members of my spiritual family. I love the self-effacing Aleph and the stroppy little Yod, the slightly pompous but lovable Heh, gentle Mem, and her companion Nun. All of them have given and continue to give love and advice and support.

Samech is like a large older brother who keeps an eye on us and when we fall down, it picks us up and dusts us down and tells us to observe where we are going! This letter is like the shaft around which the axis of the universe revolves, or like the axle of a wheel shaft. Its center is the "empty inner" of the Buddhists—everything depends on it at some time or another.

In a very old building the roof will have something called a tie beam; this particular piece of wood takes the initial strain of the whole roof and then directs it down through the other beams and finally the walls. Samech is in many ways the tie beam of heaven. By the same token it is the Djed and the trunk of Yggdrasil. Where Samech is, there one will find inner strength and an outward support.

The Letter

Samech is formed by a Kaph and sealed completely by a Vav (כו). As a letter its value is sixty, but if taken as separate letters then Vav is six and Kaph is twenty, which added gives twenty-six, the same number as the Name of God. This tells us we can as safely lean on God as we can upon a crutch or support.

Support, protection, and memory mean different things until you begin to reason them out. Support speaks for itself. Protection is a different kind of support but when one is being bullied, slandered, or demeaned in any way, protection from the perpetrators is a very welcome kind of support. Memory as a support can be found in the idea of *siman,* which translates as a "mark, symbol, or mnemonic." Simanim (plural) are often used in the study of the Torah, Talmud, and other books of the Jewish religion. A rosary is a mnemonic for a prayer cycle and so is also part of the work and power of the letter Samech.

Acronyms are another form of memory training, as are parables and folktales that carry traditions and cultural behavior patterns over the generations. Tarot cards can be classed among them, as can the mark of Cain that served to remind people and, indeed, Cain himself, of what had been done. Catch phrases and the use of locus or locations are all memory aids.

The use of gematria in the Aleph-Beth is an example where numbers are used instead of letters and vice versa. To give an example of gematria, God is seen as being one and thus indivisible, but the gematria of One is אחד or thirteen. א is one, ח is eight, and ד is four, in total thirteen, reminding the devout Jew that God manifests thirteen aspects of divine love or mercy. It is also a reminder of the twelve apostles and the one teacher, Yeshua.

"Samech" comes from *Somech,* meaning "to rely on," and is a constant reminder that we are not alone, that we are being looked after even when it seems that everything is going wrong. This is where another part of the Samech's power comes in, that of abundance. Because its number is sixty, which is over and above the halfway mark of fifty, it is seen as forecasting the unending and overflowing power of nature to heal and provide. No matter what happens there is an abundance of love on which to rely.

The shape of the letter is round and closed like the final Mem, but this is the only regular letter that is so totally enclosed. Many years ago when I was writing an essay as part of my work on the Inner Light course, I began it in this way:

"It is only when one turns away from God that one begins to approach Him. For He is at once the central core and the periphery of existence. After travelling away from the center one meets Him at the edge of the created universe, you turn back and He is there at the center. Like Frances Thompson's poem 'The Hound of Heaven,' one cannot outrun Him."

When I began to work on this letter I found in my research this sentence: "Both the completely empty inner area of the Samech and its outer enclosure are interpreted in Qabalistic literature as symbols of God" (quoted from Rabbi Michael Munk's *The Wisdom in the Hebrew Alphabet*, page 160). All those years ago I was writing nothing new—it was already known to many—but I had just discovered it for myself. We are all capable of such inner realizations and heart-lifting truths, and the letters of the Aleph-Beth are more than willing to be our guides.

Every walled city in ancient times had a sacred center where its heart lay. We can see the "empty inner" in every sacred place, be it a synagogue, a temple, a church, or a Wiccan glade. It is the altar with the Light of Lights burning, it was the Holy of Holies in the temple of Solomon. It resided in the Ark of the Covenant in the simple tent in the desert. It is the throne of the Shekinah in every home. This is the power of the Samech.

Path 25 leads from Yesod to Tiphereth. Its Tarot card is Temperance. This is a path for those inclined to the mystic way and will invariably lead to a dark night of the soul in one way or another. Indeed, one often feels the need of support and the strength of Samech when treading this road. However, remember as you set out that you travel from one of the great lights (the moon) toward the second (the sun), and so you will always be aware of the Light around and within you, even though you cannot always see it.

The card of Temperance shows an angel pouring the essence of Life from a golden vessel into one of silver. It symbolizes the life force moving toward matter, passing through the moon sphere and the astral level as it does so. The higher self leaves the golden realm of Tiphereth for that of Yesod and incarnates for another life of instruction and experience. It will make the return journey as it goes through physical life in the form of tests and trials, some greater than others. But there is always help to be had—the soul can be cheered and strengthened as it struggles toward the Light if it remembers that the power of the divine inner light can never be extinguished. There is the added comfort of knowing that we are not the only ones who go through this, that Yeshua took this same path when He struggled with His destiny during His forty days and nights in the wilderness.

Sagittarius is the astrological sign here, the double life-form that shows both our human and animal side aims for the highest point with its arrows—perhaps those of which Blake sang:

Bring me my bow of burning gold, bring me my arrows of desire.

Bring me my spear, O clouds unfold, bring me my chariot of fire.

All the more significant when we remember the Merkaba, the chariot of fire in which Elijah ascended into heaven to be transmuted from human flesh into the form of Sandalphon, the archangel of Earth.

Samech has another symbolic meaning, a deeper, older, and for our times more meaningful symbology. In the allegorical story of Adam and Eve we hear that God took a rib (in this day and age of cloning, might we presume He used Adam's DNA?) and from it fashioned a woman to be his companion and spiritual support, or Samech. We can look at this in many ways. Feminists, please bear with me, I am not decrying womanhood, nor am I arguing about which gender came first. I want to give a possible explanation for the animosity of the Christian Church toward women in early medieval times and up to the twentieth century.

When the new religion began, its main source of historical information came from the Old Testament. At this time the ability to read and write was confined to a few. The majority of Christian converts were poor people—ex-slaves, farmers, and shepherds who had little use for such refinements. Those who could read and write were few and far between and though most could speak Aramaic/Hebrew and a little Greek or Latin beside their native language, an understanding of the finer points was not available. Even today the translation of important documents from one language to another requires a special kind of talent; it is not enough to substitute one word for another, the whole nuance and subtlety of meaning must be considered.

Such skills were not available when the Old Testament was first translated. Some words were mistranslated entirely, the meanings of others were a matter of substitution of intent rather than accuracy. Please keep this in mind as we go on.

According to the Kol HaTorah, woman was intended to be a complement to man, "neither his shadow nor his servant, but his other Self." It says, "to bring this about the woman must be ready to act as his opponent, she must support him (his Samech) and also oppose him when the need is there." The wise men said, "If a man is worthy, woman is his support/equal; if he is not, she is his adversary, making him aware of his weaknesses, for it is difficult to admit one's faults."

The word *adversary* is important here, for it is the meaning of the word Satan, the angel whose God-given task was to oppose and tempt humanity so the gift of free will could be exercised. Satan was the prosecutor, the recorder of sins. In the hands of unskilled and biased translators, the word become synonymous with woman as the tempter of man. She became the evil one, the corrupter and temptress of men. The supportive role, the Samech she should have been, was denied her.

◯ and 𝕎 are often pronounced in the same way and this can cause confusion, but the Samech is pronounced with a plain *sss* sound while the Shin is more of a *shhh*, hence the different spelling of Satan and Shaitan. In conversations with fellow author Herbie Brennan over the finer points of the above theory, he pointed out that Lucifer (the Light Bringer and equated with Satan) is called the Morning Star. The Morning Star is Venus (Aphrodite, the goddess of beauty and sexual desire, woman). Don't you love it when things fit together?

Meditations

FIRST MEDITATION

You will need a mirror for this, one about eight to ten inches square. On thick paper (the kind you use for sketching or watercolors) and with a thick black felt pen, draw the letter Samech large enough to be cut out and act as a frame around the mirror. Place the mirror and frame on a table where you can see your face comfortably. Look into the mirror and contemplate your face surrounded by the support of the Creator. Allow your thoughts to drift up into the conscious mind and record them. Now think of the face in the mirror as a part of the Creator looking back at you. Lastly think of yourself, made in the image of the Creator, looking through the supporting frame of the Samech to your physical self, and pour love and strength into the reflection.

SECOND MEDITATION

Sit down with a pen and paper and think of how many ways you could be a support to others, or they to you. When you have a list ask yourself how many of those ways have you actually used to help others, what you can do in the future, or what you are prepared to do. How many kinds of support have you received? List how many times you have been helped in a seemingly divine way.

Third Meditation

The letter begins with a Samech (support) and ends with a Heh (window). The Heh as a final letter has double the creative power of Heh as a first letter. This means that by using the power of the Samech you can expect twice as much support from the spiritual world. Think about this and try to find a way to apply it. How would you use it and for what? Try to be specific.

Pathworking

Close your eyes on the physical world and open them on the astral; allow yourself time to adjust to the difference. When you are ready, begin to build a landscape from the astral proto matter. Before you is a long winding track. On the right side there are paths that lead off toward the foothills of a mountain range. In the distance you can see a river winding its way down through the hills into a large lake. On the left are woods and trees interspersed with fields of wheat and barley.

Behind you the road looks the same. You wear a light woolen tunic of brown and trousers of the same material in a lighter shade. You wear leather sandals and a belt but you have nothing else with you. You begin to walk. The sun is just rising and there is a light breeze so you enjoy looking around you as you go. But as the sun climbs higher it gets hot and soon you take off the tunic and wear just the cotton undergarment beneath. You come to a point where the track gets very rough and broken and you have to go slowly. Your sandals are not very strong and suddenly one of the leather ties snaps. You sit down to rest and look at the damage. What you need is a piece of leather or strong string to hold it on your foot, but this will be impossible in this lonely place.

Wearily you get to your feet and walk on, carrying the broken sandal. You see the lake quite clearly now, so at least you will be able to drink, wash, and cool off. As you walk along you see something in the middle of the path and at first it looks like a snake, but as you get closer you see it is a strip of leather. What luck! Hastily you mend your sandal and go on toward the lake.

The track leads across the river and then on to the lake itself. The trouble is that the middle part of the bridge has collapsed. You walk along the bank looking for a shallow place to cross but the river is fairly wide and swift running. Then, tucked away under an overhanging bush, you see a raft. It looks a little flimsy, but with luck you might manage to get across on it. It looks even worse close up, but you think it will get you across. A little pushing, pulling, and untangling from the weeds and you are ready to go. You find a branch that can act as a pole and with a little trepidation you kneel on the raft and begin to push your way across the river. You are most of the way across before it begins to sink, and all the way across just as it slips under the water. Wading ashore, you strip off and lay your clothes out in the sun to dry; the air is still and full of the scent of wildflowers. The water is clear and fresh and you quench your thirst.

This side of the river is much nicer, with grass and flowers and close by is an old ruined farmhouse. You go to explore and find one room that is quite watertight and even has an old broken sofa. You collect bits and pieces of wood and stack them against the evening when you might need a fire. You also find an old, badly broken mirror; before the sun loses its strength you go outside and with dried grass and slivers of wood you manage to get a small fire going.

You feel well pleased with yourself. Although you are in a strange place you have water, shelter, and a fire. Exploring further you find the remains of a vegetable patch and scavenge some carrots and turnips, two tomatoes past their best but edible, some beans, and a squash. Further on, you find some fruit trees; like the farm, they are old and gnarled, but there are still a few apples for your dessert.

This is turning into an adventure and you take your finds back to the house. More rummaging around the house brings a very battered pan to light and this you take to the river and scour out with sand and stones and fill with water; you wash the vegetables as well and take everything back to the house. The stew is put on the fire to cook slowly and you take an apple and go to sit outside where the sun is beginning to set.

You feel content and happy; you know that all this is happening in a different dimension and that time is passing much more quickly here, but you feel calm. You also know that soon someone will come; you are expecting the letter Samech. The shadows are lengthening so you go inside and put more wood on the fire. Supper is almost ready.

Then you notice on the hearth a flat stone and on it a small heap of white crystals. It is salt, the one thing you need to make supper taste even better. You also know that salt is a highly prized gift in small countries. There is a prickling sensation on the back of your neck. Quietly you say: "Shalom, Samech, my friend. I have been waiting for you. Thank you for the gift of salt. Be welcome in my tent in the desert."

"Shalom, Life, friend and companion of the Aleph-Beth." You have done well, it seems. You smile and turn to see the shining oval of rose-colored light that is the holy letter.

"I suspect that is because you have been with me all the time, helping me and directing me. Is that not so, my friend?"

"It is so. I have supported you from the beginning, long before this adventure. I have been beside you when you found the work hard and unrewarding. I have entered your dreams and filled you with new strength, rejoiced with you when you were happy, and kept vigil when you were sad. This is one of my duties that I do with love. I support those who undertake journeys and tasks that will lead them into the ways of knowledge and understanding. I have many gifts to share, among them memory and the ability to correlate what you already know with what you are learning."

You think about this as you eat your supper. Samech waits until you are ready to speak. You think back to the time you have spent with the other letters and then ahead to those still to come. The shadows deepen and the moon rises, sending slanting beams of light through the broken window, and finally you rouse from your thoughts. "I am sorry to keep you waiting, Samech, I was lost in my thoughts."

"There is no need to be sorry. I do not exist within your concept of time, Life, for me there is no sense of time passing, the word 'waiting' holds no meaning for me. I am here, you are here, you thought deeply so I remained within the moment until you were ready to speak. I exist within the eternal circle of God's presence, as do you, Life, but after another fashion. It is difficult to explain, just accept that I do not 'wait', I exist."

You look out over the lake bathed in moonlight. Your life has been enriched by the letters and there is a desire in you to do something for them in return.

"Samech, you and the other letters have given me so much and opened my eyes to things I never knew existed. What can I do in return to show my love for you all?"

"Ah, Life, you have already given back as much as we have given to you. You have used us to express yourself and to pass knowledge of us on to others. To be used as we were meant to be used, to raise the consciousness of Life in all its forms, it was for this we were created. We exist to serve and to teach, to praise and, above all, to love."

"Then, Samech, please tell the other letters—especially those that are yet to come—that I love them all. I love to use them in my daily life and I will try to use them well. Also I would ask a favor of you. I am very tired and want to return home; can you take me, please?"

The Samech quivers and its brightness becomes brilliant as it flashes through the colors of the physical plane spectrum.

"Life, I am a gateway to all the dimensions. I enclose them as they enclose me at their center. I will be a door between this world and yours; you can return at any time if you summon me with love."

It enlarges until it stands as tall as the chimney and as wide as the wall behind it. You pass through and open your eyes on your own world.

Psalm 1

Blessed is the man that walketh not in the
council of the ungodly,
nor standeth in the way of sinners,
nor sitteth in the seat of the scornful,
but his delight is in the law of the Lord.
And in his law doth he meditate day and night.
And he shall be like a tree planted by the rivers of water
that bringeth forth his fruits in his season.
His leaf shall not wither,
and whatsoever he doeth he shall prosper.

The ungodly are not so, but are like the chaff

driven by the wind.

Therefore the ungodly shall not stand in the judgment

nor sinner in the congregation of the righteous.

For the Lord knoweth the way of the righteous,

but the way of the ungodly shall perish.

◦∽

Ritual

This is a very simple ritual, but do not be deceived by its simplicity. You will need a bit of space for it so you might have to move furniture around a bit. Your other needs will be for twenty-two tealights and saucers or small plates on which to stand them. Because of the quantity you need to be extra careful about the fire risk. Clear the center of the room and place the unlit tealights in a circle large enough to accommodate you either sitting on a cushion or on a chair if that is better for you. You will also need a small table on which to put a glass of water, your papers, matches, a large candle in a holder, some incense sticks, salt and water, and a complete set of the Aleph-Beth letters on cards. These need not be large, about four by four inches. Light one candle before all the others, as you will be putting out the main room light before you begin.

Begin the ritual at midnight, but thirty minutes before that, go for a walk; try to do this ritual on a night with no clouds so you can see the stars. As you walk, look up at them and try to feel the ties that bind you all together. Invite the spirits of the stars to join you in your ritual. Invite the tree spirits and the garden nature spirits. Build within you a feeling of joy.

On your return, put on a robe and enter the temple. Bless and cleanse it with salt and water, circle the room with the lit candle, and then hallow the room with incense. Seal the door with the sign of infinity (a horizontal 8). From a position by the door, read the following invocation and then put out the main light.

"I greet all who are present, seen and unseen. If you be of the Light, join with me; if not, depart hence and come to this place no more. The intent of this ritual is to align my higher self with the unseen worlds and with the powers of the holy letters. I now seal this earthly room with the most Holy Name ה ו ה י." *With an incense stick, draw a pentagram as you address the four quarters.*

At the east, say: "Guardian of the eastern gate, I greet you and welcome you to my sacred space. Your presence is my rod of mercy. Empower this quarter with the healing presence of the Winged Man that I may be filled with its love and light. ה ו ה י."

At the south, say: "Guardian of the southern gate, I greet you and welcome you to my sacred space. Your power is my sword of might and defense. Empower this quarter with the strength and majesty of the Winged Lion that I may be filled with its love and loyalty. ה ו ה י."

At the west, say: "Guardian of the western gate, I greet you and welcome you to my sacred space. Your grace is my chalice of inner sight and intuition. Empower this quarter with the joy and knowledge of the Eagle that I may be filled with its spirituality. ה ו ה י."

At the north, say: "Guardian of the northern gate, I greet you and welcome you to my sacred space. Your strength is my bread and salt and my sustenance on Earth. Empower this quarter with the power of growth and regeneration of the Winged Bull that I may be filled with its ability to endure. ה ו ה י.

"I call on the seen and unseen guests to join me in praise of the holy letters created by God that Life could be brought into being and given the means to express its feelings, love, power, and beliefs.

"Creator of all things, we give thanks for what we have received in the way of life, intelligence, this rich earth and all it contains. We also give thanks for the gift of the holy letters with which you created this universe. You gave us the priceless gift of language, of letters, of memory, and the power to create with them the many wonders of knowledge and mental growth. In ancient Egypt the rite of Opening the Mouth was of great importance, but you were the initiator of that rite, for you gave to us the power of speech. We offer our thanks, our praise, and our love to those beings with whom we humans fashion every word we utter, and ask you to bless them in your Holy Name. *In the center of the circle, begin the rite.* I welcome Aleph, the One. Your image is that of the strong ox and upon your strength the whole of the Aleph-Beth rests. I bless and thank you for your companionship." *Light the first tealight on your right and place the Aleph before it.*

"I welcome Beth, the second letter, who begins the word of blessing. Your image is that of a house, the house of God, the house of the family. I bless and thank you for your companionship." *Light the second light and place the Beth card before it.*

"I welcome Gimel, the third letter, whose image is that of the patient camel and whose power is kindness. I bless and thank you for your companionship." *Light the next tealight on your right and place the Gimel card before it.*

"I welcome Daleth, the fourth letter. Your image is the door to life, to death, and to the higher worlds. I bless and thank you for your companionship." *Light the next light on your right and place the Daleth card before it.*

"I welcome Heh, the fifth letter. You hold the boundless power of creativity and your image is the open window. I bless and thank you for your companionship." *Light the next tealight on the right and place the Heh card before it.*

"I welcome Vav, the sixth letter. Your image is that of a nail and your power is to bind things together that were apart. I bless and thank you for your companionship." *Light the next tealight and place the Vav card before it.*

"I welcome Zayin, the seventh letter. You show the sword of both justice and mercy. I bless and thank you for your companionship." *Light the next tealight and put the Zayin card before it.*

"I welcome Cheth, the eighth letter. You are the fence that teaches us discipline and self-restraint. I bless and thank you for your companionship." *Light the next tealight and put the Cheth card before it.*

"I welcome Teth, the ninth letter. Your image is the serpent and you hide your real self from all but the Wise Ones. I bless and thank you for your companionship." *Light the next tealight and place the Teth card before it.*

"I welcome Yod, the tenth letter. You are the hand, the worker, the accomplisher. I bless and thank you for your companionship." *Light the next tealight and put the Yod card before it.*

"I welcome Kaph, the eleventh letter. You are the palm of the hand outstretched in welcome. I bless and thank you for your companionship." *Light the next tealight and place the Kaph card before it.*

"I welcome Lamed, the twelfth letter. You are the ox goad that drives us toward perfection. I bless and thank you for your companionship." *Light the next tealight and place the Lamed card before it.*

"I welcome Mem, the thirteenth letter and the water image from which we all emerged. I bless and thank you for your companionship." *Light the next tealight and place the Mem card before it.*

"I welcome Nun, the fourteenth letter. You are the fish, symbol of the thoughts and feelings that swim in the ocean of the mind. I bless and thank you for your companionship." *Light the next tealight and place the Nun card before it.*

"I welcome Samech, the fifteenth letter. You are the crutch, the support that helps us when we are weary. I bless and thank you for your companionship." *Light the next tealight and place the Samech card before it.*

"I welcome Ayin, the sixteenth letter and the eye by which we see clearly, or by which we can be deceived. I bless and thank you for your companionship." *Light the next tealight and place the Ayin card before it.*

"I welcome Peh, the seventeenth letter and the mouth with which we can say thank you. I bless and thank you for your companionship." *Light the next tealight and place the Peh card before it.*

"I welcome Tzaddi, the eighteenth letter. You are the hook with which we catch the fish of the Nun and draw it forth from the ocean of the Mem. I bless and thank you for your companionship." *Light the next tealight and place the Tzaddi card before it.*

"I welcome Qoph, the nineteenth letter. Your image is that of the head with which we think and act. I bless and thank you for your companionship." *Light the next tealight and place the Qoph card before it.*

"I welcome Resh, the twentieth letter. You show the back of the head to remind us that we come and go with equal ease. I bless and thank you for your companionship." *Light the next tealight and place the Resh card before it.*

"I welcome Shin, the twenty-first letter. Your image is of a tooth, the most enduring part of the body, as the soul is the most enduring part of the spirit. I bless and thank you for your companionship." *Light the next tealight and place the Shin card before it.*

"I welcome Tau, the twenty-second letter and the last. With you all things end and come full circle. I bless and thank you for your companionship."

Light the next tealight and place the Tau card before it. Now walk around the circle of light and look at each letter, then bow to it and go to a chair and sit in meditation for as long as you wish. Then rise and give license to depart to the quarters, and bless and dismiss the seen and unseen guests, douse candles, unseal the door, and depart.

AYIN

You look forth upon
manifestation from the supernal triangle
by the command of God.
Thou art the Lord of the Horizon and
the Ruler of the twin Orbs of Light.
Thou art veiled by the curtain of illusion,
against the eye of the defiler.
Thou art the guardian of the tears of Isis,
weeping for her Lord,
the blood wept by Mary at the foot of the cross.
Thou art naked truth,
covered by the Mystery of Mysteries.
Show me thy beauty, look upon me
and see me as I am.
Behold me, I am that which suffers upon
the cross of illusion,
a cross of my own making, for I misunderstood
the words that said "Forgive them, Father."

Image: Eye
Symbol: ע
Path on the Tree of Life: 26
Numerical Value: 70

Prayer

The words of this prayer are heartfelt for they are accepting that some of the faults that cause trouble in our lives are self-inflicted. This is because we look out on the world and what goes on with the eye of illusion. The supernal eye sees the truth and easily separates one from the other. But we who are still encased in matter see through a dark glass, a veil of dust, a mist of illusion and self-deceit.

When we learn to lift our hearts, minds, and spirits above the world of illusion, then we can see clearly. But more often than not we can sustain such heights for short periods only, then we sink down again. But the more we try, the longer each time we spend in the Light will be. The letters of the Aleph were born into Light and have always existed in it. They cannot conceive of anything else. For them to descend into our world, even though they cannot because of their nature, is something that comes close to pain for them. Yet they do it, and do it for love.

To delude ourselves makes their task so much harder. The more we try to understand and the more we open ourselves to the right use of the letters in our words, deeds, and thoughts, the clearer our understanding will become.

We continually misuse words. Every time we lie we misuse and belittle them. Every time we say something good about someone they shine more brightly. Yet whatever we do, these first children of the One cannot be desecrated, they cannot be muddied or made less than they are. They are holy and remain so despite our human ways.

We really have no excuse because down through the ages we have had wise men and women who have tried to show and explain to the rest of us how things should be—we just don't listen. We prefer to see things as we wish to see them; it is more comfortable that way, at least for a short time.

Do we really "see" what was meant by the words "Father, forgive them"? It was not just a plea for the forgiveness of those who had physically hurt Him, but also for the whole of humanity as it was at that time, and on into the future. The words are still echoing through the universe. Every word that was ever spoken to this time is still echoing. Sound is self-perpetuating; it may diminish but it never entirely fades away. It is a vibration, the very basis of universal matter. It can change, but it won't disappear from the universe.

The Letter

Ayin is constructed from a Yod and a Zayin, a hand and a sword. Although the actual value of Ayin is seventy, its two separate parts (Yod is ten and Zayin is seven) add up to seventeen, the same number as for the word *tov*, or "good." If we look at the sword in the hand of the angels who drove the first parents from paradise, we understand that it was because they had seen truth in its original form and were dazzled by its power. They veiled their eyes and their bodies and, from this unwillingness to accept truth, began the descent into illusion. But illusion is all part of the divine plan; the moment we begin to seek out truth we also begin to take our first steps back to what we were always intended to be. Many illusions are placed before us deliberately to test our ability to see through the veil.

The illustration of an eye within the triangle shows us that within the area of the supernals the truth lies hidden and waiting. The eye, enclosed, is watchful and withdrawn; it sees without being seen and so can judge impartially. To reach real truth we must attain the purity of Chesed and then dare the crossing of the abyss. We often describe someone as having an evil eye, but there are those who have a pure eye, a clear-seeing eye as well.

Talking to a professional artist about how he looks at his subject was a revealing lesson. When painting a portrait he looks at the colors of a person. To an artist, each human being is a series of shades with an underlying main color; after that comes construction of the position aligned to lighting. The most difficult to paint are the hands and eyes. Sitters tend to put on a certain look that they think is needed. Best of all are those who sit and allow their thoughts to illuminate their face.

"The eyes are the windows of the soul." There used to be a belief that the last thing seen by the dying was imprinted on the lens of the eye; it was a belief that

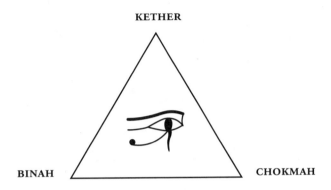

KETHER

BINAH   CHOKMAH

THE EYE OF HORUS WITHIN A TRIANGLE

was held for many hundreds of years. The eye of Horus and the eye of Ra were symbols and talismanic forms that carried much power in ancient Egypt, and still do today.

We tend to use expressions in everyday conversation that link the eye to intelligence and understanding. "I *see* what you mean." "You do *see* what I'm saying, don't you?" "*Seeing* is believing." "*See* what you have done now?" "I came, I *saw*, I conquered." "It opened my *eyes*." The list is endless. In the mundane world of beauty products, women have been using cosmetics to enhance their eyes since the earliest times. Ask men and women what they notice most about another person and a good percentage will say their eyes.

To look kindly upon one's neighbors and not to make judgments in haste is considered to be a great virtue, one we could all benefit from at one time or another. For to judge a neighbor harshly means that inevitably you will be judged in the same way.

Ayin refers also to the inner or spiritual sight as well as the physical, so it symbolizes the intuitive and clairvoyant areas of the brain. The third eye and the limbic or midbrain system have a part to play here. The pineal gland, situated just above and between the eyebrows and deep within the cortex, has traditionally been the seat of inner vision.

The eye as the letter Ayin enlightens us to the hidden truths standing behind the everyday aspects of the world about us. It is said that every word of the Torah or indeed that comes from the ancient teachings of Light of any tradition has seventy hidden meanings. I can vouch for the fact that each letter, as I have worked with it, has opened my eyes to hidden depths of understanding. The Hebrew word *sod* means "mystery" or "secret," what we would call "occult." It has the same value of seventy, as does the word for wine (yayin), like the word Ayin, and if the seventy is taken down to its lowest denominator we have seven, which equals Zayin, the sword.

The eye, like the mirror, can become a magical implement, and the power of "the Look" that commands respect should not be underestimated. In the same way, it is by the Light of the Creator that we perceive the wonders about us. The eye is not only a window onto the world, it is an equally powerful window into the recesses of the soul within. To see this more clearly we need to return to the idea of yayin (wine) and its numerical twin sod (mystery or secret). In the Western Tradition we have a type of mystical revelation we describe as the Divine Inebriation. This occurs when one is "drunk" with the power of the divine inner wisdom. In the same way, wine holds the secret or sod of the grapevine. The lower, conscious, and higher selves come together in such a moment and, for a brief span of time, know each other perfectly.

Ayin has an elongated Yod on the right with its tail sloping to the left. The straight Zayin on the left represents the person who is good and just, while the curved Yod is the poor man who depends on the kindness of others. The two are joined showing that one's circumstances may change at any moment.

Path 26 goes from Hod to Tiphereth and it is symbolized by the Tarot card of the Devil. It is a path of changes—of heart, or image, ideals, or even loyalties—but it also changes the way one sees things. Dwell on the following: "When I was a child I thought as a child and understood as a child, but when I became a man I put away childish things." This is true. As a child we think about deity and its meaning in a childish way, and as we grow and gain deeper insights and understand more, we change our idea of God. This is fairly well known, but what is not so well known is that we change and our view of God changes. God also changes, for He grows also through our understanding of Him.

The mind's eye is a complex idea to discuss since it has no real place in the brain in the physical sense. Rather it is a combination of the faculty of imagination and the ability to conjure images both actual and fantastical within the brain itself. We humans are capable of building an entire universe of visual images, forms, landscapes, and events inside our heads.

They can be fleeting images or an accurate, highly detailed series of actions that come equipped with sensors. For some people this inner world can be more real than the one they live in. This can lead to aberrations that may require hospitalization. However for those who learn to control and polish their talent it opens up the higher levels of the inner sight. It has been said that if one desires to see God, look into the eyes of the person next to you.

The Western Tradition takes the view that the human body is a temple and if this is so then the eyes are the windows of that temple, and the final Heh through which the grace of the God Within may look out upon the world of manifestation.

When I began my magical training many years ago, I was taught to approach the Black Isis first and learned that by doing this she would turn into the White Isis as I drew closer to her. It is the same with the Tarot card of the Devil, for as one approaches, usually in fear and trembling, there is a moment of utter darkness, then blinding light as the Devil becomes the Son behind the sun. We must learn to see the card of the Devil as the goat-footed Pan, the god of nature and fertility, as the Horned Lord of the White Goddess. If one is looking for evil all the time, one will assuredly find it under every bush. If one looks for light under the same bush, it will be there. Keen observational power is the mark of the initiate. By looking we see, by seeing we understand, and by understanding we become wise.

Meditations

FIRST MEDITATION

Sit down and place a scarf or hood over your eyes, making sure you cannot see. Take a few moments to slow down your breathing and quiet the mind. Then begin to describe the room you are in, in the greatest detail you can manage. Not just a general outline but a correct description of each picture, its place and juxtaposition to others, each ornament, flowers in the vase, colors and number of cushions, patterns in carpets and rugs, styles of furniture, curtaining and wallpaper patterns. Do this methodically and then go over it to see if you have left anything out. Only then may you take off the blindfold and see how well, or how poorly (as the case may be), you have done. Do this in a different room each day for three days and see if you improve.

Second Meditation

Take a pad and a pen and go to an art museum. Find a picture you like; make it a reasonably complicated one. Look at it intently, noting as much detail as you can. Then begin to write down what you see, leaving out as little as possible. This will take you a couple of hours if you do it right. Do this once or twice a week for a month, then once a month, and you will find your ability to take in large amounts of detail in a few minutes will increase dramatically.

Third Meditation

Select a single flower and put it in a vase. Seat yourself as far away as you can and observe it. Write down what you can see in detail. Leave for a few hours, then go back and sit halfway to the flower and repeat the exercise. On the next day sit up close to the flower and repeat as before. A few hours later, return and take the flower in your hands and observe it with your eyes, nose, hands, heart, and mind. See how many new things you can see now. Write down as before. Look before you write, write before you speak, speak first with the head and then with the heart. These exercises may seem like pointless meditations, but you will learn that sitting with one's eyes closed is not always the best way to meditate. With eyes wide open one can see the stars.

Pathworking

Prepare yourself as usual with one exception: on a table before you, place a small vase of fresh flowers. Choose their shape, color, and type to please yourself. Put a crystal or semiprecious stone on one side, a glass of rainwater or any type of pure water on the other, and behind them a tall candle of any color you like. Spend about five to ten minutes looking at these things and enjoying them. Observe them and try to understand what they really are.

Now slowly close your eyes and begin to breathe slowly and deeply with a slight pause between breaths. Allow your mind to drift where it will for a while, then become aware that you are in a small white building with brilliant sunshine outside. It is a temple of some kind, for there is a white marble altar before you. On it you can see the four things you put on that table back home: flowers, a candle, a stone, and a glass of water.

Behind the altar is a column of the clearest, purest blue you have ever seen. It moves as if breathing and set into it near the top is a golden eye. You feel your heart leap within you and know that it is Ayin. You look and look, trying to absorb the sheer beauty of the color, the grace, and the power of the letter as it stands before you. A thought goes through your mind: How can something this beautiful be symbolized by the Trump of the Devil? Ayin's laugh rings through the temple.

"Life, dear Life, have we not taught you that nothing is what it seems to be? That what has been created by Hashem cannot be anything but beautiful or according to His plan, including the opposite of good? If you approach evil with Light in your heart, it will have to turn to goodness, it can do nothing else in the presence of Him. This is what the words of the psalm mean when they say, 'Yea though I walk through the valley of the shadow of death, I shall fear no evil for Thou art with me.' Cast fear from you, Life, replace it with trust and faith. I am the clear eye of God and if you look at the world through me you will see nothing but what is destined to be, and the underlying goodness of it—its real form."

The Ayin moves around the altar and comes to stand behind you, then it moves closer so that the outer edges of its brilliance envelop you. Its voice now sounds as if it comes from within you, and everything around you is tinged with its color.

"Look at the altar and tell me what you see now, Life."

You look. First at the flowers, they seem . . . alive . . . vibrant. The colors are intense and each bloom and leaf is outlined with a golden glow. The stone vibrates, gently expanding and contracting, its color getting brighter or dimmer as it does so. The water is dancing, its molecules swirling and moving up and down in an age-old rhythm, each particle shining like a star.

Then you look at the flame and see that it has many separate parts. You see the blackness of the wick with its glowing tip and understand its Binah connections through these colors. You see the golden flame as vortices of energy, the invisible space above it which is where the energy becomes heat, and the final aura of the whole candle flame that shimmers like a crown and becomes the Shin.

"You see, Life, this is how it really is. But there is more for me to show you. Close your eyes, dear one, and have no fear."

You do as you are told and close the astral eyes you have been using and feel yourself drawn into a spinning vortex of power. A moment of panic grips you, then you remember the Ayin's words and relax into what is happening. There is intense cold, equally intense heat, and a moment of pressure so great you lose your breath . . . then there is something solid under your feet.

"Life, you can open your eyes, but do it slowly. You exist in a higher level now and it will be very different to the astral, so be prepared."

You open your eyes halfway and squint through your lashes. The landscape, if it can be called that, is one of shifting colors, patterns, and eye-wrenching differences in spatial concepts.

You open your eyes fully and look around. You exist in a world of constant movement defined by colors, many of which you cannot describe because you have no name for them, and moving patterns that shift in and out of awareness, formations that you cannot hold on to long enough to understand. You feel giddy, unstable, and a little nauseous.

"Keep closing your eyes and resting them for a few moments, it will help. You are in the world of thought, the mental dimension. These colors, patterns, and movements are the thought processes of the universe. Not just your world and everything in it, but all worlds. Every thought that has ever existed anywhere in any galaxy at any time since it all began is here and will always be here. You are seeing through my Ayin, my eye, Life. If you were quick enough you could catch and listen to the thought of Abraham as he left Ur of the Chaldeans for the last time or the thought of Mark Antony seeing Cleopatra for the first time. The first white man to see the Pacific, the moment when Drake sighted the Armada, they are all here, Life. If you keep trying you will be able to touch them, if only for a second or two. Let me be your eye and I will show you the wonders of Creation. Look now upon the simple objects you chose."

You see before you the flower, the stone, the water, and the flame, but how they have changed! The flower radiates light and shimmers like a diamond, and each petal sings a note that accords with the whole. The stone also has a note, deep as the earth from which it came, and its age shows in its color, each million years a shade. The water praises its Maker in a high silver bell-like sound, and the flame is a radiating point of cosmic fire that has never been extinguished since time began.

"Does this please you, Life?"

Oh, yes, it does indeed please you. Ayin laughs and the sound appears as a rippling wave of color in front of you. You ask an eager question: "Is there more?"

"Life, Life, truly you are made in His image, you have such a love of knowledge. Yes, there is more, you will be able to exist within it for just a short time, but it will give you a taste of what is to come when you have traveled further on the road of evolution. Close your eyes and I will enclose you within myself to safeguard you. Do not move away from me."

You close your eyes and wait, tensed. There comes over you a feeling of warmth, love, but also something of a totally alien physiology that is not unpleasant, just a little startling. You are aware of moving and yet being in the same place. You think about this and come to the conclusion that you are not moving, but the dimensions are. You are feeling rather pleased that you can think in this way when everything becomes calm and still. Slowly, carefully you open your eyes.

It looks and feels as if you are within an infinite soap bubble. Everything is iridescent, translucent, and utterly still and silent. The faintly blue tinge to everything seems to be associated with the mental field of the Ayin. It is so different from what you expected. Perhaps more activity, color, sound, great sweeping choruses of voices. The odd winged figure maybe . . . but there is just silence. You wait. Pressure grows within you; there needs to be something happening, there needs to be some sound, there needs to be a presence.

The pressure within you becomes so great you feel you can no longer hold in what is there. You throw back your head, open your mouth, and out of it comes a sound. It is the sound of life being *lived*. It is the sound of your life, every second of it, the sound of every laugh and every tear. It is the sound of love and fear, pain and joy, good and bad; this is *you*.

Instantly around you everything comes alive and you realize that this space, far from being empty, is crowded with life from all dimensions. Life that has achieved its purpose to be able to exist here in this place. You have sounded your note of life and it has brought everything into focus. Around you the letters of the Aleph-Beth appear shining and beautiful and before you is . . . Something. Something so wonderful and so beautiful that you will never be able to describe it. You fall to your knees and bow, your heart unable to stand the power that radiates from it.

In the silence that follows something stirs deep within you, it rises to consciousness and fills your heart, eyes, and mind with itself. You rise, lift your head, and look as the God Within faces the God Without. Around it, winged like angels, you see the flower, the stone, the water, and the flame. Then it has all gone. In the silence and the darkness you weep, for you have already forgotten what it was you saw in that moment. Ayin surrounds you and comforts you.

"Life, do not weep, it is only the physical that has forgotten; the higher self remembers and it will all come back to you as you pass from the physical into the nominal world of light. That world, that dimension, that moment is eternal and yours. You will never be the same person you were before, you have been changed for the rest of this lifetime. That is the price you have paid. You have stood in the Presence, Life. Now, dear one, rest and let me take you back into your own world."

Like a child weary of play, you relax into the strength of the Ayin and dream as you are transported back into the world of the senses. You feel the chair beneath you and the faint sounds of Earth. Ayin leaves you with one last piece of knowledge.

"As you experience each letter it leaves its imprint within you, thus we are always with you. No matter how dark the world may become, or how events may overwhelm you, we are here within. I will be your third eye, Life, look through me when you wish to see truth. This gift is a terrible one that I give you, for you will see that you stand alone, yet I and my kind will be there to ease the burden. Farewell."

From An Essay On Man

All are but parts of one stupendous whole,
Whose body Nature is, and God the soul;
That, changed through all, and yet in all the same,
Great in the earth, as in the ethereal frame,
Warms in the sun, refreshes in the breeze,
Glows in the stars, and blossoms in the trees.

Lives through all life, extends through all extent,

Spreads undivided, operates unspent.

Breathes in our soul, informs our mortal part;

As full, as perfect, in a hair as heart.

As full, as perfect, in vile man that mourns,

As the rapt Seraphim that sings and burns.

To him no high, no low, no great, no small.

He fills, he bounds, he connects and equals all.

All nature is but art unknown to thee.

All chance direction, which thou canst not see.

All discord, harmony not understood,

All partial evil, universal good.

—ALEXANDER POPE (1688–1744)

≈

Ritual

You will need four small quarter altars, each with a small glass or chalice of wine and a candleholder of the appropriate color. In the center you will need something special that you will have to make. Take a sheet of white poster board and cut a circle that is two and a half feet across. Mark it with two circles in black felt tip, one just around the outside edge and the second circle about an inch farther in, and divide the inner circle into four equal parts, then paint the white areas blue.

In the south draw and color a sun, in the west a moon, in the north a quartered circle, and in the east a star. In the center draw an eye. Keep this after the ritual and use it in other rituals. Having prepared and robed as usual, enter the temple or room and seal the door with a spiral symbol. With salt and water, incense, and flame, cleanse, hallow, and defend the working area.

By now you should be well acquainted with this ceremony and able to use your own words. Stand on the circle where the star is depicted. With a wand, face the east and raise the power of that quarter. Work slowly and with deliberation, speaking with conviction. Remember, you are using one of the letters as a medium and focus of spiritual power.

"By my will and my desire, I open the gate of the east and summon forth the rose-winged presence of Raphael, the healing hand of God. Come in thy glory and in thy power and aid me in the celebration of this rite. I set upon thy brow the symbol of the divine letter Ayin that the eye of the One may shine through and heal what needs to be healed. *You may specify someone or something here but be realistic. "Healing the world" is not realistic.* I welcome the power of the Ayin; let the light of the primal stars fill this sacred space that all within may be healed. *Light the candle and circle the chalice with it.* Let this wine be filled with the power of the eye of God that I may be filled with wisdom and understanding.

"Heal me of my faults and look upon me with favor, help me to fulfill the destiny that was set out for me to the best of my ability. Grant me the opportunity to progress and to help others to do so. I offer my service to the Light through the medium of the eye of the Creator." *Drink the wine and stand in silence before the altar for a few minutes, then pass to the south.*

"By my will and my desire I open the gate of the south and summon forth the scarlet-winged presence of Michael, the warrior and shield of God. Come in thy glory and thy power and aid me in the celebration of this rite. I set upon thy brow the symbol of the divine letter Ayin that the eye of the One may shine through and fill my heart with courage and strength. I ask also that all those who need these powers of courage and strength may receive them through this intercession. *You may specify someone or something here.* I welcome the power of the Ayin; let the light of the solar logos fill this sacred space that all within may be healed and enlightened." *Light the candle and circle the chalice with it.*

"Let this wine be filled with the power of the eye of God that it may fill me with love for those less fortunate than myself. Heal me of my faults and look upon me with favor; help me to fulfill the tasks that were ordained for me to the best of my ability. Grant me the ability to control my anger, fears, and words. I offer my service to the Light through the medium of the eye of the Creator." *Drink the wine and stand in silence before the altar for a few minutes, then go to the west.*

"By my will and my desire I open the gate of the west and summon forth the azure presence of Gabriel, the messenger of God. Come in thy glory and in thy power and aid me in the celebration of this rite. I set upon thy brow the symbol of the divine letter Ayin that the eye of the One may shine through and fill me with the knowledge that is needful for my tasks. I ask that this gift may also be given to someone who is seeking with a good heart and has not yet found the way. *You may specify someone here.* I welcome the power of the Ayin; let the light of the lunar sphere of mystery and hidden words fill this sacred space that all within may be enlightened." *Light the candle and circle the chalice with it.*

"Let this wine be filled with the power of the eye of God that it may fill me with knowledge that I can use for others as well as for my own progress. Heal me of my faults and look upon me with favor; help me to fulfill the days of my life to the best of my ability. Grant me the opportunity to know and to serve. I offer my service to the Light through the medium of the eye of the Creator." *Drink the wine and stand in silence before the altar for a few minutes, then pass to the north.*

"By my will and my desire I open the gate of the north and summon forth the emerald-winged presence of Uriel, the sower of the seed of God. Come in thy glory and in thy power and aid me in the celebration of this rite. I set upon thy brow the symbol of the divine letter Ayin that the eye of the One may shine through and heal the Earth and the life upon it. *You may specify something here.* I welcome the power of the Ayin; let the light of Gaia the living Earth fill this sacred space that all may be made known and adjusted. *Light the candle and circle the chalice with it.* Let this wine be filled with the power of the eye of God that I may also be filled with the power to make a difference where the fate of Earth is concerned. Heal me of my faults and look on me with favor; help me to do what I can to help the Earth to heal. Grant me the opportunity to understand Earth's needs and to help others to do so. I offer my service to the Light through the medium of the eye of the Creator." *Drink the wine, stand in silence before the altar for a few minutes, and return to the east.*

"I, *(your name),* offer myself to be a chalice for the Light of the Creator. Let me do what I can according to my ability, my strength, and my understanding. I know that I am but one; I also know that I do not stand alone, that there are my brothers and sisters in the Light, all over the planet, that are with me as I begin my task. I know I am not the first, nor will I be the last crusader for the Light and for the Earth. I do not stand alone; the mighty ones of the spiritual worlds gather about me. On my right hand stands Michael, on my left hand stands Uriel. Before me stands Raphael and behind me stands Gabriel. Above me shines the six-rayed star of Tiphereth and below me is the living spirit of my Mother Earth. About me gather the Four Holy Creatures, the kings of the four elements, and surrounding this sacred space are the holy letters with which the universe was created. Hear me, ye mighty ones, the Earth has need of us all; gather your powers and your strengths. Let not the beauty of Earth be defiled by the greed of man. It was promised, 'Ask and ye shall receive.' I ask, in the name of the Most High, let work on the saving of the Earth and its creatures begin. Let it be so!"

Close and depart.

PEH

Through thee let me praise
the One True Creator,
the One who is above all
and by whom we are made manifest.
Be thou my way of speech.
Let my tongue be guided by thee
that my words may be fair to all.
Let me not speak evil of my neighbor
though he may harbor ill feelings toward me.
Let my companions know of my love for them.
In thy presence all things give voice,
each according to their way,
for thou art the Giver of Tongues.
Thou it was who spoke through the Apostles
at the feast of Pentecost,
who was heard in the voice of
John the Beloved.
Thou hast filled my mouth with the
power of thy letters
and my heart has been healed.
Walk with me through my life and be my truth.
Let me sing joyfully before thee,
for all that surrounds me is the work of thy hands.

Image: Mouth
Symbol: פ
Path on the Tree of Life: 27
Numerical Value: 80

Prayer

This prayer was written as I began to emerge from my dark night of the soul. I realized that, though battle scarred, I was still in one piece and my ability to believe in myself and my work was still intact. That realization brought a demand that I found difficult—to forgive. This is something we humans are asked to do many times during our time on Earth, and we often find it next to impossible to accomplish. To forget and to forgive go hand in hand; one can rarely be done without the other.

Knowing one does not have the unconditional love to do this by oneself, it is always best to begin by asking for help, for strength, and for understanding. Hand in hand with this goes the need to recognize that it always takes two—blame will often go two ways, so the starting point must be to look at oneself first.

Peh is the symbol for the mouth, the instrument with which so much pain and sorrow begins. Not for nothing does the story of Adam and Eve center around the taking of a bite of the apple. Maybe telepathy and no mouth would have been a better idea for human anatomy—at least with telepathy one cannot hide the truth!

Language has become a symbol of our place as an intelligent species, but our words have become swords and bullets. We speak of peace but use words to incite. Action and reaction erupt because of what is said and how it is said. In these days the arrival of the Internet has opened the world to a problem with two faces. On one side it gives us access to knowledge on a scale never before possible and it makes us neighbors no matter how far away we live. But it also offers a golden opportunity for the sharpest sword of all, malicious gossip.

The prayer asks for help in choosing words that do not harm others, and reflects back to the time of Pentecost and the granting of "tongues" to the apostles. Speech is a precious gift, but so is silence and if one cannot speak good, keep silence. Because we are human, it is impossible to promise to always tell the truth, or never to gossip harmfully, but we can strive to lessen this behavior by cultivating silence as well as speech.

To the pious Jew, slander is a very particular sin and one that is abhorred. A lie or harmful, spiteful words does not demean or corrupt the letters that form them, for they are holy and thus incorruptible. But it saddens them to be used in such ways. A few years ago I would not have believed this, but now I know better and understand more.

The Letter

Peh is one of the most interesting letters and the only one that holds within itself a second complete letter, for its shape outlines that of the letter Beth: פ ב. The mouth is an enclosed organ with a "door" that opens and closes, so the shape of the Beth or house is very appropriate. It is also an easy letter to recognize with its little "tongue" inside the mouth. This double image tells us that the mouth can be the house of truth or of lies.

Its value of eighty equals the number of days Moses spent on Mount Sinai in conversation with God. The letter itself is a combination of Kaph (twenty) and an inverted Vav (six), making twenty-six—the same gematria as the Tetragrammaton.

The symbol of the mouth reminds us of the word by which all things were created and of course that word consisted of the letters of the Aleph-Beth. We have yet to come to the letter Shin, which has the magical image of a tooth, but it is not too early to align these two letters and see that teeth can be likened to guardians ready to control words spoken in anger or haste. It has two forms, the bent appearing at the beginning or in the middle of a word פ, and the elongated used only as an ending ף.

Path 27 on the Tree of Life links Hod and Netzach, the sphere of the mind to the sphere of beauty. As do all the horizontal paths, it acts like a steel girder to brace the whole Tree, and therefore they all denote strength in one aspect or another. Here the strength is that of desire, the imagination, and creativity linked to thought, both active and passive. Between Geburah and Chesed the strength lies in the balance of justice and mercy, both of which lead to redemption and to the joy of knowing thyself. The path between Binah and Chokmah holds the strength to be found in the exact balance of male and female attributes.

Path 27 can be aligned to physical desire for a relationship and also to the mental desires that we call daydreams and fantasies. The Tarot card is that of the struck Tower; there are many who fall into self-destruction by overindulgence in fantasy. Why, then, do we place so much on pathworkings in occult training? Because dealt with under a strict regime it can teach self-control, and creative thought allied to control equals mastery.

The Tower can mean exactly what it shows or it can hold a meaning similar to the card of Death, a breaking down of the old preparatory to rebuilding anew. It is said that its original meaning was the Tower of Babel, a fitting symbol for the Peh if there ever was one. There is too much made of cards such as Death, the Tower, the Devil, etc. The cards cannot be generalized; they fit themselves to the moment and the person. In the same way Peh must be seen as a symbol or letter that must be interpreted in context with its use and who is using it. The Peh of a habitual liar will always be seen as suspect; that of one who wears the crown of the good name will be listened to with attention. The tongue of the Peh will need control; its planet is, after all, Mars!

All traditions have an oral foundation, for they begin by being passed "mouth to ear." This is still the case among some of them, especially in Africa, where the elders can recite the generations of their chiefs as well as the history and major events of the tribe going back hundreds of years.

Speech is linked to memory and to knowledge and in particular to the storing of knowledge. In the twenty-first century we have at our disposal the most sophisticated means yet devised as a memory aid, yet the finest computer of all is still the human brain. However, we could begin to lose our capacity for memory simply because we no longer have to rely on it. This is dangerous for if disaster were to wipe clear major computer libraries we could stand to lose as much knowledge as we did during the burning of the Alexandrian library. Books are eventually lost, destroyed, or they decay over the years; the more that is committed to memory and passed on, as in an oral tradition, the more will pass into the world memory via folklore and tales.

It is a pity that political correctness and biased minds are tampering with our folklore and fairy tales, for they are the basis of much of the old knowledge and ancient ways. We are going through a censorious age similar to that which drove the early church to destroy the papers and teachings of the ancient Mystery Schools and the Ottoman Empire to use what was left of the great library of Alexandria as fuel for their bathhouses.

We can use Peh in so many wonderful ways: to sing, to laugh, to praise, to say "I love you," to kiss and make up, to protest when we feel the need, to argue in debates and to discuss, to speak out against injustice and defend those weaker than ourselves. Sadly, true free speech, once the much-vaunted asset of the Western world, has become tied to red tape, political correctness, bias, and greed. The Peh has lost its "tongue"!

When we speak of, about, or to something or someone, we energize the subject and give it attention and therefore meaning. Neither the mineral nor the vegetable worlds can give tongue and though the younger brethren of the animal world can speak through sounds of varying pitch and tone and communicate between each other, only humans use words to formulate ideas and concepts.

Learning to speak is our first real accomplishment and we spend most of our formative years refining our command of language. It is with our mouths, our voices, and our tongues that we express our feelings, joys, fears, desires, and, above all, praise for our existence. Prayers, hymns, psalms, poetry, and song all come from within the house of speech, the mouth.

To speak of what you know and share it with others is a duty to be taken seriously. Teaching is a skill requiring a love of wisdom and of those to whom it is given. However one must also know when to be silent. Speech is silver but silence is golden, says the proverb.

Moses, it is said, was "afflicted in his speech," but this impediment became an advantage by increasing his intellectual gift. His mind and thoughts were turned inward instead, toward Hashem and the spiritual life, and he became God's human messenger.

The value of eighty denotes strength, both physical and spiritual, and Moses had both. Despite his speech problem he nevertheless became a great leader and prophet. This shows us that when we have something of importance to say, we should not let circumstances or intimidation hold us back—something many politicians and church leaders would do well to emulate.

There is one final point to make regarding the Peh that has nothing to do with words but simply with the mouth itself, or rather the lips. It was with a kiss that Yeshua was betrayed, the kiss of peace is exchanged between those meeting for a like purpose, the kiss of sexual love is given between lovers, the kiss of pure love is seen in that given by a mother to a child. We speak of the kiss of life and, equally, the kiss of death—there is more to Peh than the Ayin perceives!

Pathworking

When you open your inner eyes, you find yourself in a landscape of heat, dust, flies, and the smell of a lot of people gathered together. You are in a crowd that is all moving in one direction—men, women, and children plus the odd goat, donkey, and mule. Some walk on crutches and some are carried on rough litters but most walk. Their clothing, and yours, is of rough homespun cotton and wool. The men have knee-length robes and a longer piece of cloth that wraps around it plus a piece worn round or over the head and tied in place. Feet are bare or in simple sandals. The women wear longer robes with similar wraps but these are drawn over the head and often over the face to keep out the dust. The glint of gold and silver can be seen here and there in ears or around necks. The children are miniatures of their parents.

There seems to be a purpose in the movement of the crowd in the general direction of a hill some distance away. You notice that a river runs alongside the path and think longingly of dipping your dusty feet in it. But there is little chance of that, hemmed in as you are by the eager crowd.

Up ahead are some men who seem to be directing everyone toward the hill, which is slightly less dusty than the road and has a thin covering of bushes and grass. The sun is past noon now and less hot, but still enough to be uncomfortable. The crowd is sitting and talking among themselves, laughing and joking with good humor. There is a stirring in the crowd and from a small group of men, one emerges and begins to climb the hill.

He is of medium height with dark hair and beard, his complexion is lighter than those around him but not by much. He wears a robe of natural cream-colored wool with an earth-brown wrap over it. On his feet are plain leather sandals. He climbs the hill, greeting friends and stooping to bless the children. Everyone seems to know him. As he comes nearer, his dark eyes look this way and that and rest on you. The breath goes from your body. He comes right up to you and, bending low, places a finger on your mouth and smiles and nods his head. Then he climbs to the top of the hill and stands for a moment looking out over the land, and then over the crowd.

You see quite clearly standing behind him a clear green and violet oval of light and you know that the letter Peh is with him. The crowd goes quiet; even the children and the animals subside into silence as he begins to speak.

Blessed are the poor in spirit: for theirs is the kingdom of heaven.

Blessed are they that mourn: for they shall be comforted.

Blessed are the meek: for they shall inherit the earth.

Blessed are they who hunger and thirst after righteousness: for they shall be filled.

Blessed are the merciful: for they shall obtain mercy.

Blessed are the pure in heart: for they shall see God.

Blessed are the peacemakers: for they shall be called the children of God.

Blessed are they that are persecuted for righteousness' sake:

for theirs is the kingdom of heaven.

Blessed are ye when men shall revile you and persecute you and shall say

all manner of things against you falsely, for my sake.

Rejoice and be exceeding glad for great is your reward in heaven,

For so persecuted they the prophets which were before you.

Ye are the salt of the earth: but if the salt hath lost its savor,

wherewith shall it be salted?

It is thenceforth fit for nothing but to be cast out and

trodden under the foot of men.

The voice, deep and full of reassurance, goes on and on and behind him the brilliance of the Peh shines like a star. Amazingly, its voice is in your ear.

"Life, I hope you are listening, for each of these sayings comes from a time older than this. He learned of all this in his own training. What is being said is as much for your time as it is this one."

You acknowledge the presence of the Peh with a bow of your head. You do not think of asking how it speaks with you when it stands behind him at the same time.

"The reason is because I am in neither position but in both, but after another fashion. Dear Life, always curious, always seeking to know. I have brought you to this place and in this time because you need to understand the power of voice. You need to find this power within you and make it your servant. With it you can achieve great things, for the voice commands respect.

"You must understand that my power is that of the spoken word, the creative word. I am the mouthpiece of divinity. I attend Gabriel when that august presence bears a message from the Most High. I was there at the annunciation; through Gabriel I spoke with the magi and the shepherds. I stood beside Galileo at his trial, and eased the agony of the Maid of Orleans and Giordano Bruno in the midst of the flames.

"I am also the first word spoken by every child. I am there when lovers whisper and when a mother sings a lullaby. Every language, every syllable, every word ever spoken or song ever sung was within the power of Peh. Yet also, too, my great sorrow—all words of hate, of pain, of blame, every cry of horror, every unjust condemnation—is part of me. When Orpheus sang his last song, when Osiris cried out the name of his beloved Isis on his last breath, when Yeshua cried out upon His cross, I was a part of it all. Come with me, Life, and let me show you my ways."

Around you the scene fades—your last memory of him is his smile. Darkness rushes past you and a glimmer of light appears. It opens out onto a wide plain filled with tents, goats, and sheep. A vast gathering of people is before you and you are set down before a tent of black hide. Unseen by human eyes you enter and see a short thick-set man with black hair and beard streaked with grey. He speaks with a woman whose hair hangs to her waist in a thick black and silver braid. Sarah kneels before her husband Abraham and, weeping with joy, tells him she is with child after so many years of barrenness. They praise God for His gift and the Peh shares in their happiness.

The darkness falls again and when it recedes you are watching the ceremony of "Opening the Mouth" of a dead pharaoh and the Peh is standing beside the Anubis priest who presents a strangely shaped instrument to the mouth of the mummified king. We recognize the shape, for the instrument looks like an open or final Peh: ף.

Again we are swept from one time to another and we move through the ages seeing famous people, hearing them speak famous words that have changed the course of history. The Peh is always there, watching and empowering. We see Moses descend from the mount with the tablets of law, and listen to his words. We hear Elizabeth I speaking to her people before the Battle of the Armada, and the first public hearing of the Declaration of Independence. We listen to the first wireless signal and hear the first recording of a voice. Finally Peh brings us back to our own time and leaves us with a smile and a final word.

"Life, you were given a voice to use, use it well and with wisdom. Do not let it become a sword in your hand destined to hurt others. Use my power with discretion and discrimination. Farewell."

Meditations

FIRST EXERCISE

Find a poem, a long one. If you don't like poetry, then find a piece in the Bible, or the book of your particular religion or tradition, just so long as it runs to a couple of pages. Read it through several times until you begin to understand its meaning. Now look at the punctuation and mark the pauses with a red marker. Now you need to read it aloud, following your marks. After a few times, and after making any alterations you feel are needed, record it. Now listen to it. Chances are you are reading too fast. Record it again, but slower. Listen and adjust.

Work with it until you feel you cannot get it any better, then make a final recording. This may take the better part of a week but at the end of that week your voice should be 1) lower in pitch, 2) more resonant, 3) slower and richer in delivery, and 4) more compelling to listen to. The more you do this sort of training, the better your voice will become. To be a teacher, you need a good voice.

Second Exercise

Every room has a pitch—that is, a tonal point that makes everything in it vibrate. Every human being has the same kind of note. If you are lucky and have a strong middle-body note, you will be able to resonate with between 80 and 95 percent of all speaking venues. Most conference rooms are designed for good acoustics, but not all. If you are booked to speak, ask to see the room first. If it has a beam across the middle it will swallow every word you say and no one past the fourth row will hear more than one in three words.

Pitch your voice like a trumpet. Find a space out-of-doors and early in the morning take your poem or whatever you worked with and try speaking it out loud in the open air. It won't sound too good—you need a microphone to speak outside—but it will train your voice to carry. Do it for no more than ten minutes or you will strain your vocal chords. Don't shout, but speak with the intent of being heard. You'll probably pitch your voice too high in an effort to be heard; pitch it lower and keep your head up. Imagine throwing your voice out like a baseball. I want you to think about teaching because if you are reading this book and you understand it, you have the potential to teach . . . and you will need a good voice.

Third Exercise

Learn to think on your feet. Choose twelve subjects at random, including three or four about which you know next to nothing about, and write them on pieces of paper, fold them, and put them in a hat or box. Get your tape recorder ready and shake up the papers. Choose one. No matter what it is, you have to speak with reasonable efficiency and confidence on that subject for three minutes, then try for five. Out of fifty points, take off five points for every overly long pause, and three for every *er . . . ah . . .* and *umm.* Keep doing this until you have gone through all the subjects. Then do it with another twelve. You will soon learn to compensate for your lack of actual information by extending what you do know and repeating it in different ways. Public speaking is not easy and it requires a lot of practice.

Psalm 100

Make a joyful noise unto the Lord, all ye lands.

Serve the Lord with gladness

and come before His presence with singing.

Know ye that the Lord is God.

It is He that hath made us and not we ourselves.

We are His people and the sheep of His pasture.

Enter into His gates with thanksgiving

and into His courts with praise.

Be thankful unto Him and bless His name

for the Lord is good.

His mercy is everlasting

and His truth endureth to all generations

for the Lord commanded the blessing, and life forevermore.

Ritual

This is a ritual of movement and chant so you need to clear a space in which to move. At the quarters put small altars with room to walk around them during the rite. You will need two or three candles in the quarter colors with a small vase of flowers and an incense stick. In the center have a flat metal tray and four to five candles of varying heights in it as a centerpiece. You can use scented candles or three to four incense sticks in between the candles. You need a robe wide enough to give ease of movement, or use clean and comfortable clothing.

Cleanse your sacred space with salt and water as you have done before, invoking the power of Gabriel and Nixsa. With a candle, circle the room, invoking the protection of Michael and Djinn. Finally hallow the space with incense, invoking the help of Raphael and Paralda. When this has been done, light the center candles and invoke the presence and help of Uriel and Ghob as personal guardians. Use your own words for all of this; it is part of the empowering by the Peh that you

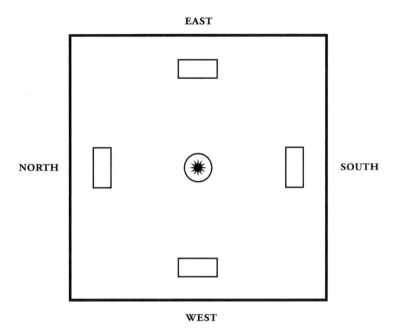

learn to compose such invocations. Seal the door and begin the rite. The layout of your space should look like the diagram above.

Light the candles and incense on the eastern altar with the flame from the center lights. Praise the power of the east. Speak slowly and with feeling:

"Hail and praise to the dawning day-star, the solar logos arises in glory. In thee we see the reflection of the Most High taking the throne of the east. Let the Earth sing the praises of her Maker, let the stones and the mountains, the hills and valleys hold up their heads and give thanks for the light of day. Let all growing things praise Adonai, for His strength and His purpose is in them. Let Life in all its forms praise the I AM, for in Him is their being."

EAST

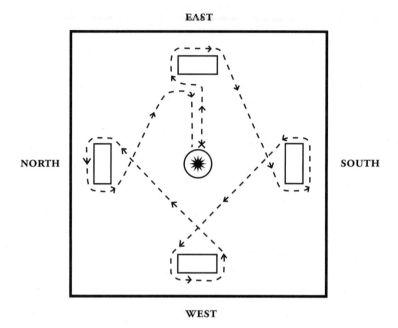

NORTH

SOUTH

WEST

The chant for this quarter is this: Kadosh, kadosh, kadosh Adonai Ha-aretz. Repeat as you move around the temple in the pattern shown above. Fold hands over your heart center and chant in a firm and joyful voice.

Continue in the same pattern until you arrive back in the east. Bow to the quarter and walk to the center, face south, and approach the southern altar and light candles and incense from the center flame. Slowly and with feeling, repeat the invocation.

"Praise be to the primal fire that gave by its sacrifice of self Life to the universe, the eternal, undying spark of that first fire lies within the heart of all life. I sing the praise of the love that offered itself that Life might become. The spark within me flames forth, desiring to return to its source. I give thanks to that One who supports, encourages, and sustains us all. In the midst of life's trials I praise Him, for they are my teachers, as the One is my primal Mother/Father."

EAST

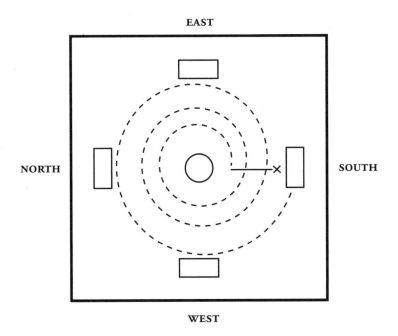

NORTH

SOUTH

WEST

The chant for this quarter is "Kadosh Shaddai el Chai, Kadosh Shaddai el Chai, Kadosh Shaddai el Chai." Repeat this as you move around the temple in the pattern shown above. Fold hands over your solar plexus as you walk. Continue in the same pattern until you arrive back in the south. Bow to the quarter, walk to the center, face west, approach the western altar, light candles and incense from center flame. Slowly and with feeling, repeat the invocation.

"I give praise to the Eternal Mother, the seat of intuition and the great feminine principle. The giver of both life and death, the holy Shekinah. The Great One whose kingdom lies in the Beth-El. Praise to the eternal woman, the comforter and sustainer of man. In Her glory She rises in the heart of Her children and they shall abide in Her love."

EAST

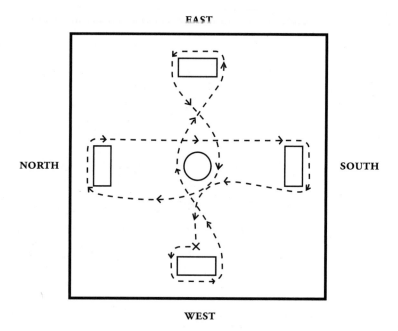

NORTH

SOUTH

WEST

The chant for this quarter is as follows: "Star-born Isis, Holy One, grant us peace, thy will be done." Repeat this as you move around the temple in the pattern shown above. Fold hands over your lunar center as you walk. Continue in the same pattern until you arrive back in the west. Bow to the quarter and walk to the center, face north and approach the northern altar, light candles and incense from center flame. Slowly and with feeling, repeat the invocation.

"Holy, holy, holy, art thou Gaia, Earth Mother, Corn Giver. From thy bounteous body we and all life on earth are fed. For our disregard of thy body we beg forgiveness and for our ill treatment of thee we plead guilty. We are but children and destruction is within us. Turn not thy face from us, but have patience, for we will learn to love thee as you love us."

EAST

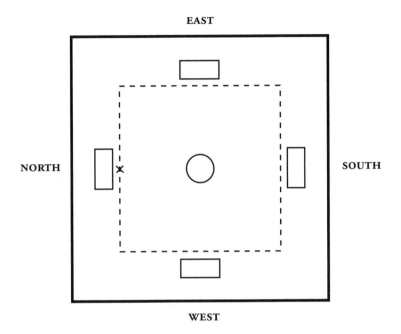

NORTH

SOUTH

WEST

The chant for this quarter is "Mother of Mercy, lead us to thee." Repeat this as you move in the set pattern around the temple with hands crossed on your breast.

Continue in this pattern until you return to the north quarter, then move to the east and bow to the center flames. Visualize Raphael, Michael, Gabriel, and Uriel standing around the center candles, and Paralda, Djinn, Nixsa, and Ghob standing in the quarters. Raise your hands, palms out, in blessing.

"Blessed be those who have come to my call. Blessed be the kings of the elements and the elements themselves. By the power of the Word spoken in the beginning, I bless you all. By the power of love that caused the universe to be, I bless you all. By the wisdom of the One in whom we trust, I bless you all. In the spoken word lies the wisdom of the world since it began. The Word lives within each fragment of life. Let the power of Peh be in my mouth that I may speak with purity. May I be worthy to receive the same blessing as I move through life to the mystery of death."

Meditate for a few minutes, close the quarters, put out the candles, unseal the door, and depart.

TZADDI

What is thy secret?

Is it hidden in the mists of time?

If so, how do I reach within and gain the prize?

I listen to thy silent voice and slowly understand.

Indivisible are the three Holy Beings.

First there must be that which can hold the secret,

then the secret itself to be contained within,

lastly there must be the means

by which the secret can be known and held.

Slowly I pull upon the unraveling thread.

Mem, thou art the womb, the tomb,

the chalice, and the sea,

the great encompassing cosmos, the source of all.

Thou art the Creator eternally making and remaking forms.

But in thy dark and silent depths I perceive a flash of silver.

The elusive life, the vital Nun swims here and there at random,

bringing life and giving death with equal largesse.

Ah . . . but I am the fisherman,

and with the Tzaddi of my mind I seek the prize.

I seek, I wait, I hope. I feel the tiny tug

and pull my immortality from the Sea of Time.

Image: Hook
Symbol: צ
Path on the Tree of Life: 28
Numerical Value: 90

Prayer

This is one of my favorite prayers because it brings together three amazing letters: Mem the sea, Nun the fish, and Tzaddi the hook with which one can catch the fish. For me these letters hold a secret that as yet I have not completely unraveled to my own satisfaction. I am still seeking something I know is there and which will reveal itself to me at the proper time.

The sea has always been a keeper of secrets: sunken treasure, ancient ships, lost islands, uncharted lands, everything from the Marie Celeste to the Flying Dutchman. Such secrets are like fish swimming in the depths of the world memory. Sometimes they rise to the surface and we catch a glimpse of them, then they are gone again.

We need to cast out a hook and line and bait it with dedication and determination; then if we are lucky we may pull in the slippery Nun. The prayer acknowledges that the sea, the ocean—whether it be the physical sea or that of time or of space—is the giver of life and death, the cause of change in individuals as well as the lands that border it.

We also have a sea within us, for we carry our inheritance of the primal ocean in the salt of our blood. Therefore we also have "fish" within . . . the thoughts, ideas, hopes, fears, and dreams that fill our minds with their presence. The mind itself is a sea of the knowledge we collect during our lifetime and fill with our experiences. The greater the experience, the deeper the realization, the bigger the fish.

The Apostles were chosen, drawn like fish from the Sea of Galilee by the Fisher of Men in the Age of the Twin Fishes. He was not the only teacher who came from the sea. Oannes the fish god also emerged from the waves to teach, inspire, and change those who were willing to listen.

Sometimes, when we are in great need, when we are starving for spiritual nourishment, in desperation we throw out a line and hook, hoping for the longed-for Fish of Knowledge. If the time is right, if we have learned the lessons that have gone before, then the Nun rises and allows itself to be drawn from the sea.

The Letter

The basis of the Tzaddi is (no prizes for guessing) the fishlike Nun with a Yod "hand" attached to its upper part. This really does seem like a parody of the old saying *A bird in the hand is worth two in the bush,* only this time it's a fish in the hand. The value of the letter itself is ninety, but the combination of the Nun and the Yod comes to sixty, the same number of letters in the blessing given in the synagogue. The little Yod faces upward as if looking toward its Creator, Hashem, while the Nun bends forward in homage.

While Tzaddi is the correct form, this letter is more often referred to as Tzaddik. The main form is that of the bent Tzaddi (symbolizing a righteous person) used at the beginning and in the middle of a word: צ. The erect form is used only at the end: ץ.

The word is also used to describe a person who is devout, upright, and seeks to live his or her life according to God's will. There are many Tzaddikim in the Old Testament worthy of this description. The supreme Tzaddi, of course, is the Creator Himself, but Abraham and Joseph and Joshua are all examples of earthly Tzaddik, as is Noah, who took on the task of renewing the world after the flood.

If you look at the letter you will see the humble and devout Nun bending forward; it seems to carry the smaller Yod on its back. We can see this as a symbol of one who wears the crown of the good name helping his neighbor, literally supporting him. Another interpretation is that the hand of Hashem is extended in blessing over the Tzaddik.

If we carry the symbolism on into other traditions, we can see St. Christopher carrying the Christ child on his back, or Hermes carrying the child Dionysius to Olympus. Or, indeed, Christ carrying the cross to Golgotha. We can even become the humble one, bending under the weight that has been placed upon us. If we bear it in fortitude the reward will be forthcoming, for in the end, like the final Tzaddi, we may stand straight and upright, rejoicing in the knowledge that we have done our best.

The shape of the letters can often lead the mind into very different but rewarding areas of understanding. Use whatever you can find to open up to those hidden meanings. That is why they are hidden, to coax you into the effort required to find them.

My Tzaddi is a hook that hopefully will bring the reader closer to the creative power of the words within them. If there is one thing I have learned from writing this book it is that the letters of the Aleph-Beth are *real*. They exist in a space and in a dimension that I do not understand, nor can I reach it. But they have reached out to me. I have felt their touch, heard their voices, seen fragments of their colors and forms. While I know I am not and can never be a Tzaddik, I know that for a short while I have been an instrument for them.

Path 28 leads from Yesod to Netzach, a path that has many sexual overtones, not the least of which is the fact that it is also the path of the Emperor Tarot card. After all, sex is nature's "hook" to keep the species reproducing, so this is always going to be a path of power—hidden power, but power nevertheless. How does this sit with the symbol of the humble Tzaddi?

There is a very interesting comment about the card of the Emperor; its esoteric title is "Son of the Morning, Chief among the Mighty." Lucifer was also know by the title of Son of the Morning, and he was the Chief or Principal of the angelic group to which he belonged. This linked to the sexual aspect, plus the fact that Lucifer was supposedly humbled by his Creator, makes interesting reading. Some traditional tales hold that Lucifer had sexual relations with Eve and by her had a son, Cain! Others say their son was Set(h), or Tubal Cain, chief among the Nephilim and, as a smith, one of the first magicians.

It is said "even one whose sins have caused him to forfeit a share in the world to come can regain his loss if he truly repents" (Rambam, Hil. Teshuvah 3:14). No one is beyond redemption, no one. We meet up with Lucifer again in the tale of Faust, a man driven by a lust for power, money, and a beautiful woman.

The magical image of Yesod is a beautiful naked man, while that of Netzach is of a beautiful naked woman—Adam and Eve, Ares and Aphrodite, the guardians of the world's desire. But we can also see on this path a mysterious conception of Godhood on the physical level. It has always puzzled me that while the mating of the sons of God with the daughters of men was seen as evil, and their children (the Nephilim who taught humanity the arts of weaving, smithing, and agriculture) were destroyed by humankind, the mating of the Godhead with a human woman was considered a divine event. Or have we perhaps been kept in the dark about certain things?

Humanity was commanded to go forth and multiply, which they did. Of late perhaps they have gone a little over the top and we are getting a mite crowded. *Tzniuss* beginning with a Tzaddi means "modesty," and though love and sex, passion and desire go together, modesty can still be observed. The Emperor is a title of power and it is easy to become overpowered by the glamor of this path, but as long as those who follow it remain humble and modest, they will come to no harm.

This is a letter and a path full of contradictions and images that metamorphose from one thing into its opposite. It hides more than it shows and carries in its heart a sacred symbol that can cleanse the soul, a chalice cut from a single emerald, one of three that fell from Lucifer's crown—the other two were the Emerald Tablets of Hermes Trismegistus.

Meditations

FIRST MEDITATION

Think about the burdens you have had to carry in your life. Ask yourself how you have coped with them and what solutions you have come up with. Have you solved them at all or are they still with you? Do you complain about them? If so, why have you not dealt with them? Can you deal with them now? Invoke the power of the Tzaddi and ask to be shown how to deal with these things.

SECOND MEDITATION

Look at your life in relation to your partnerships at home or at work. Do you work well with others? Do you have a good relationship with your partner? Have you ever failed to be supportive, in either case? Have they failed you? How do you relate to the opposite sex?

THIRD MEDITATION

Call up the image of the Emperor card and enter into it. Make it a meeting between you and the Emperor and ask him about things that concern you in your life.

Pathworking

As you pass into a light trance it seems as if you are waking up in another land. Your inner eyes open on a sunlit vista of woods and streams and a green plain stretching away into the distance. You sit up and look around you; the air is full of birdsong and a light cool breeze brings the scent of wildflowers. You sense a presence and turn, rising as you do so.

You already know who it is and, like a child greeting a well-loved parent, you open your arms and smile at the brilliant peacock-blue and silver being.

"Tzaddi, it is so good to see you. Am I late? Oh, I forgot, the letters do not wait, they just exist in the moment and let time pass them by." A peal of silvery laughter greets you.

"I see that you remember what we have taught you, Life, I will tell my brothers and sisters this, they will be happy. But come, we have much to do and you have a task ahead of you. We will follow the stream, farther on it becomes a river that is wide and fast running."

You walk along the banks of the stream in companionable silence, broken only by the gentle voice of the Tzaddi as it points out birds and animals drinking from the clear water. As you come over a slight rise you see the track now leads down to where the stream joins a much wider river with a strong current. You stop to drink.

"Tzaddi, do the letters eat and drink as we do?"

"No, Life, we are fed by the love of the Creator, we do not take in nourishment. Your species and those that share your planet need to do this in order to feed the cells of your bodies. We are not made that way. We are expressions rather than organisms. We do not bleed, we do not breathe, we have life of a less tangible kind than yours."

"You said there would be a task for me. What is it?" But the Tzaddi has gone, you are alone. You look around but there is no one there. A little hurt at the abrupt departure, you walk on around the corner and find a small boy sitting on the bank. He is about four years old, wet, cold, shivering, and tearful. You sit beside him and take off the woolen wrap you are wearing over your traveling robe. After removing his wet tunic you tuck your wrap around him and cuddle him close to warm him up. He cries for a while, then settles down and rests against you, enjoying the warmth of your body. You ask him where he is from, why he is here, and if his parents are near. He is lost, but he knows his parents live over the river but the bridge got washed away and he can't cross over on his own.

You look at the river; it is running quite fast. How deep is it? You get up and look along the bank for a long branch; there are several fallen branches nearby. Choosing the longest, you step down into the river, feeling your way with the branch. As far as you can tell, it goes no deeper than your hips. It should be no problem. The current, although you can feel its strength, is fairly easy to resist. You wade back to the bank.

You explain to the boy that you will carry him over to the other side, which is about fifty feet across at this point. He jumps up, eyes bright, and with a big smile throws his arms around you. His tunic is dry now and you use the wrap to tie him securely to your back. His arms round your neck, his legs round your waist, you step slowly and carefully into the water. As you do so, you see on the other side of the river a glowing column of blue and silver. The Tzaddi is waiting for you. You are already deep in the water when you realize that this is the task you have been given.

You try to turn your head to look at the boy, but you cannot; all your attention must be given to battling the current that now seems so much stronger than before, and deeper. It has reached your waist and the child is heavier than he looks. You feel for every step, carefully using the branch as a staff to steady yourself. With each moment the river seems deeper and the force of the water stronger. The child is still and silent but his weight is dragging you down. On the other side the Tzaddi stands, waiting.

At the midpoint your strength is failing but you are determined not to fail in your task. You are now almost certain of the identity of the child you bear and the knowledge is like an extra weight; you cannot fail now.

The water is now cold as well as deep and swift; every step is an effort that takes all your strength of mind and body. You look up at the opposite bank and see your friend waiting and make a decision. "Tzaddi, can I call on Samech and perhaps Mem for help?"

"You may call on any of the letters, Life, when the need is there." The image of Samech as a support builds up in your mind and the branch in your hand takes on a new form. The presence and the strength of the letter flows through you, giving you new hope. The image of Mem follows and the water around you becomes warmer, the speed of the current lessens, the footing becomes more secure.

It is still a struggle but you reach the other side and Tzaddi extends something close to being an arm to help you. For a moment you sit panting and shivering, then you remember the child. But the wrap is empty—there is no child. You look at the Tzaddi, your question in your eyes.

"Life, the child you carried was your own inner divinity. The child of God you bore was, is, and will eternally be you. It was your own experiences, faults, sins, sorrows, and wrongdoings that you bore, that weighed you down. You did well to get so far without help, and you were not too proud to ask for help when it was needed. For a little while you became a Tzaddik willingly bearing a burden."

The world around you fades as you begin to thank Samech and Mem for their help and you find yourself on a narrow cobbled street with crowds of people around. The noise is deafening and there seems to be some sort of procession.

First come soldiers, easily recognizable as Roman. After them comes a man staggering under the weight of a wooden cross twice his own height. Your heart contracts as the realization of what you are seeing strikes you. You are seeing another Tzaddik also willingly bearing a burden, like the small but weighty Yod on the back of the Nun. As He passes He raises his eyes to yours and smiles. Your impulse is to help, but the Tzaddi beside you keeps you back. It is a big broad-shouldered man who steps forward and takes up the cross.

"No, Life, this is something that has already happened, it cannot be changed, but you are here to see that burdens for others can be borne willingly. This is the meaning and the use of my power. To bear what must be with grace and humbleness and to accept that it has a purpose and a meaning. This knowledge can be applied to many areas of your life. All the sacrificed aeons of the ages must bear their burdens alone and for the world. Return now to your own place and with our blessing."

Aishah Shekinah

A shape like folded light, embodied air,
yet wreathed with flesh and warm.
All that of heaven is feminine and fair,
molded in visible form,
She stood, the Lady Shekinah, of Earth,
a chancel for the sky:
Where woke to breath and beauty, God's own birth,
for men to see Him by.
Round her, too pure to mingle with the day,
Light, that was Life, abode:
the link of boundless God.
So linked, so blended, that when with pulse fulfilled,
far, far away, his conscious Godhead thrilled.
And stars might understand.
Lo! Where they pause, with inter-gathering rest.
The Threefold and The One;
and lo, He binds them to her orient breast,
His manhood girded on.
The zone where two glad worlds forever meet.
Beneath that bosom ran;
deep in that womb the conquering Paraclete
smote Godhead on to Man.
Sole scene among the stars, where, yearning glide,
the Threefold and the One;
Her God upon Her lap, the Virgin Bride
her Awe-ful Child, Her Son.

—Robert Stephen Hawker (1803–1875)

∾

Ritual

Set an altar in the center with just the black cloth on it. In the middle place four candles, one in each quarter. Place a chair facing the altar in the east. Seal the temple as you have done before. Cleanse with salt and water, hallow with incense, and protect with flame. Then begin with the invocation of the archangels. Face east and draw a pentagram with an incense stick.

"I knock upon the door of the east and ask that it be opened to me. I offer as a key my sincerity in the Mysteries. *Picture the door opening and a shaft of gold-colored light shining through.* I humbly ask archangel Raphael to come forth and take your place in the east that your power of healing may fill my heart. I call upon the winged one, the inner power of air, to stand beside me during this ritual." *Move to the south and make a pentagram with the incense stick.*

"I knock upon the door of the south and ask that it be opened to me. I offer as a key my loyalty to the Mysteries. *Picture the door opening and a shaft of scarlet-colored light shining through.* I humbly ask the archangel Michael to come forth and take your place in the south that your power of love may fill my heart. I call upon the winged lion, the inner power of fire, to stand beside me during this ritual." *Move to the west and make a pentagram with the incense stick.*

"I knock upon the door of the west and ask that it be opened to me. I offer as a key my loyalty to the Mysteries. *Picture the door opening and a shaft of blue-colored light shining through.* I humbly ask the archangel Gabriel to come forth and take your place in the west that your power of clear sight may fill my heart. I call upon the eagle, inner power of water, to stand beside me during this ritual." *Move to the north and make a pentagram with the incense stick.*

"I knock upon the door of the north and ask that it be opened to me. I offer as a key my honor to the Mysteries. *Picture the door opening and a shaft of green-colored light shining through.* I humbly ask the archangel Uriel to come forth and take your place in the north that your power of regeneration may fill my heart. I call upon the winged bull, the inner power of earth, to stand beside me during this ritual." *Move to the east again and sit in a chair facing east of the altar.*

"Gather about me, mighty ones, lords of the quarters and regents of the elements. Let the Four Holy Creatures take their places beside me that I may know their strength and their comfort. I state the intent of this ritual to be the repentance of my wrongdoings. *Look to the candle of the east.*

"The east is the kingdom of the element of air, the place of speech, thought, and ideas. I will go back through my life and seek out those times when I have been uncharitable, rude, derogatory, and told lies. Help me, Raphael, by bringing to my mind those times." *Sit in meditation and think about these times. When anything comes to mind, write it down. Take about ten minutes, then turn to face the eastern door.* "These are the things I remember and that I now regret and for which I now hope to make reparation." *Speak what you have written aloud, elaborating where necessary. Do not attempt to explain circumstances or offer mitigating reasons. Simply acknowledge what has been said or thought.*

"Raphael, regent of air, winged one, I sincerely regret these things and I will try my best to control my speech and my thoughts in the future. Let an opportunity for me to make reparation come to me." *Move to the south and face the southern candle on the altar.*

"The south is the kingdom of the element of fire, the place of love, courage, and loyalty. I will go back through my life and seek out those times when I have been unloving, cowardly, and lacking in charity. Help me, Michael, by bringing to my mind those times." *Sit in meditation and think about these times. When anything comes to mind, write it down. Take about ten minutes, then turn to face the southern door.* "These are the things I remember and that I now regret. I will try harder in the future to be more courageous, to stand by friends and family when they need me, and to express my love more often both in word and in deed." *Speak what you have written aloud, elaborating where necessary. Do not attempt to explain circumstances or offer mitigating reasons. Simply acknowledge what has been said or thought.*

"Michael, regent of fire, winged one, I sincerely regret these things and I will try my best to work upon these flaws in my character in the future. Let an opportunity for me to make reparation come to me." *Move to the west and face the western candle on the altar.*

"The west is the kingdom of the element of water, the place of intuition, seership, and prophecy. I will go back through my life and seek out those times when I have been cruel, uncaring, and deaf to the inner voice within. Help me, Gabriel, by bringing to my mind those times." *Sit in meditation and think about these times. When anything comes to mind, write it down. Take about ten minutes, then turn to face the western door.* "These are the things I remember and that I now regret and for which I hope to make reparation." *Speak what you have written aloud. Do not attempt to explain circumstances or to offer mitigating reasons. Simply acknowledge what has been said or thought.*

"Gabriel, regent of water, winged one, I sincerely regret these things and I will try my best to see clearly and listen to the still, small voice within. May an opportunity for me to make reparation come to me." *Move to the north and face the northern candle on the altar.*

"The north is the kingdom of the element of earth, the place of growth, regeneration, and steadfastness. I will go back through my life and seek out those times when I have been uncaring of the Earth and its creatures, and when I have not cared for the environment. Help me, Uriel, by bringing to my mind those times." *Sit in meditation and think about these times. When anything comes to mind, write it down. Take about ten minutes, then turn to face the northern door.* "These are the things I remember and that I now regret." *Speak what you have written aloud, elaborating where necessary. Do not attempt to explain circumstances or offer mitigating reasons. Simply acknowledge what has been said or thought.*

"Uriel, regent of earth, winged one, I sincerely regret these things and I will try my best to be more caring in the future. Let an opportunity for me to make reparation come to me. *Move to the east and face the altar.* I thank those who have been with me and listened to me this day. I am but human and I know that I have many faults, but I will try, and I will keep on trying until I can face you all with an open heart without flinching.

"May you all be blessed to the amount you are able to receive, may the blessing of the Most High rest upon this place and upon all who sleep beneath this roof. Return to your own levels and let there be peace between us."

Snuff out each candle, unseal the temple, and depart.

QOPH

Thou art the giver of sweet sleep and
dreams of prophesy.
Thou art the angel that guards both the head
and the foot of the sleeping place.
At death thou art the candles lit to guide the soul
upon its journey.
Thou art Isis and Nephthys covering with outstretched wings
the body of Osiris in death.
Like Pisces, the Twin Nun, head to foot and back again to head,
you stand guard at the beginning of the higher paths.
Will you open the way for me?
I long to pass through.
I travel the road of dreams and walk
the corridors of Time.
Be my teacher, gentle Qoph,
open my inner eyes and let me see thee.
First among the teachers art thou.
In far-off days they named thee Narada.
Do you still weep for those who would not listen?
Golden Atlantis, how deep thy streets of marble have sunk,
and only the fish know where they lie.

Image: Back of the Head
Symbol: ק
Path on the Tree of Life: 29
Numerical Value: 100

Prayer

When I was working with this letter a few years ago, one of the gifts I received from it was an uninterrupted night's sleep. Every time I meditated on it, or path-worked it, I slept like a baby. It often came into my dreams as a kind of guardian. For reasons best known to my subconscious it seemed to equate with the Egyptian goddess Nephthys, known as the Lady of Hospitality.

It is aligned with the sign of Pisces, the dreamer, the psychic seer, so it was natural to see it as the guardian of the gates of the higher levels of consciousness. The letter also seemed to be akin to the twin gods Morpheus and Thanatos, and to be the bestower of visions, dreams, and fantasies.

The idea of Atlantis came much later and fit in well with the pre-diluvian information I was getting through. From there it was a short step to Narada, the menu or teacher of that time. There is also the fact that I was coming to the end of the first round of contact with the letters. Life was easier; I had rediscovered my spiritual path and felt ready to begin that part of my life again. I was to discover that there lay ahead a final test.

The Letter

This letter is sometimes spelled Kuf, but in the Western Tradition you will usually find it as Qoph. It is made from a Kaph and an elongated Nun or Nun poschut. These two add up to seventy, but the actual number of the letter itself is one hundred.

The Kaph, the main part of this letter, is of course the palm of the hand, while the Nun is the fish. How can we marry these two symbols together? To hold a live fish in your hand is similar to holding a bird—you can feel the life force pulsating in your hand and sending those pulses up the arm into your brain. They are saying, "I'm alive, like you; let me live."

The palm of the hand is the giver of benediction; the laying on of hands is a supreme blessing, as in an ordination, a marriage ceremony, or a baptism. Remember that service to one's God is a calling and this includes the fishermen who were drawn like fish from their simple lives to a life of service. They were held in the palm of God at that moment and their life force sent signals to the deity that they were indeed alive and willing to do the work chosen for them.

The back of the head is where the spine joins with the base of the brain, the medulla oblongata. It is a point where the entire nervous system comes together and proceeds toward the neocortex to spread its various messages to the whole brain. Damage at this point will lead to paralysis, coma, and eventually death. Humanity is a mirror image of God and is therefore essential to God. God is alone, a One, a solitary unit. In the beginning It could not behold or understand itself as It was, because It could not see Itself. Therefore humanity fulfills a unique purpose that no other species on this planet can do. It mirrors the image of God back to Itself. Humanity helps God to become conscious of Itself as God. One might go as far as to say that it was only when God created Adam that He looked upon Himself.

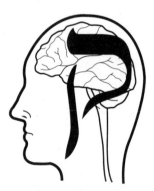

BRAIN WITH QOPH SUPERIMPOSED

Qoph or Kuf stands for *kedushah* or "holiness," specifically God's holiness. But humanity also takes part in this holiness, though not to the same extent. Nevertheless we can strive toward that state. This underlines the mirror image effect outlined in the previous paragraph.

In my workshops I often point out that when Kether reflects into Chokmah it creates a mirror image of itself. When Chokmah does the same in order to create Binah, the reversed image is reversed again. This makes Binah a true image of Kether. This is demonstrated in the Tarot card of the Lovers. The Angelic Being shines upon the man, the man looks across to the woman, who experiences the realization of the vision above her. In chapter nineteen of Leviticus (verse 2) God says to man, "Holy shall you be, for holy am I." What the deity promises, he delivers.

Qoph is a complex letter with an equally complex power network. It touches other symbols at a very deep level. Maybe this is why it is said to resemble the back of the head. It is here that we find the cerebellum, an area that controls much of our autonomous system without which we could not live. To achieve kedushah one should try to live a good, just, and fruitful life, but we are human and often find such demands irksome and restricting. What matters is that we keep trying.

Path 29 leads from Malkuth to Netzach, the sphere of Earth to the sphere of Venus, another link to Lucifer the Star of the Morning, who supposedly lost his kedushah because of pride. It is also a path that calls attention to the part sex plays in our lives. For some the living of a celibate life is a sacrifice. For others the thought of a life without physical love would be intolerable. Both viewpoints have their pros and cons. We speak of these two aspects as sacred and profane love. But don't take the word *profane* in the sense of being unclean and unspiritual. At the moment of complete union, man and woman are at their closest point to divinity.

Its Tarot card, the Moon, shows this duality very clearly in its symbolism with the wild wolf and the domesticated dog, the twin pillars flanking the misty road that can lead to both trials and rewards. The other side of the moon can be seen in those born under the sign of Pisces, for the dreamy, sensitive side of their natures can sometimes erupt into violent tempers when their dreams are shattered. A position of great holiness does not always mean the person in that position is holy themselves! A look at the history of the Papacy can tell us that. On the other side, that same seat has been occupied by men of great spiritual power. My late teacher and mentor once said, with his tongue firmly in cheek, "Some of the old saints could have done with a good psychiatrist." This is a path to tread carefully and with respect to the powers it embodies as a letter, as a Tarot card, and as a path on the Tree of Life. The word *holiness* implies self-discipline, the hardest discipline of all, but the most important in the work of the Mysteries.

While we are speaking of holiness, it might be as well to point out that this path leads to Netzach, whose Godform is that of Aphrodite. Linked to the letter Qoph, it is a reminder that physical love was given to us as both a pleasure and as a means of continuing our species. It is not to be despised; neither is it to be debased or perverted but to be seen as its goddess is seen, as both holy and beautiful.

In his *Practical Guide*, Gareth Knight recommends the reading of Lorca's lecture on "The Theory and Function of the Duende" for Path 29. I would add to this Algernon Blackwoods' book *The Centaur* (Wildside Press, 2002); at first it might not seem to have much to do with Qoph, but as an insight into the holiness of the Earth it is unequalled.

Beauty is said to lie in the eye of the beholder; the same may be said of the word *holiness*. The Shekinah is the holy aspect of the feminine and of conjugal love in its spiritual sense, in the same way we look to Eve as the mother of all living things, a human woman with faults and frailties, but capable of spiritual realizations, courage, love, and self-sacrifice—holiness, if you wish. In the shadows there stands another female form, one despised for thousands of years yet, according to ancient books, she was the original Shekinah, the Sophia of Wisdom who fell from grace. Her name is Lilith. You can read a similar story in Greek mythology about Hebe, the cup or grail bearer of Olympus. Hebe fell as she served the gods from her cup and in falling exposed herself. For this she was exiled to the world of men. There are many facets to the Qoph; as you work with it, the meanings will be revealed to you one by one. As you have discovered by now, each letter is different in the way that each human being is different. But all the letters are devoted to the spiritual growth of humanity.

Meditations

FIRST MEDITATION

This is a fact-finding journey. Your task is to visit places of worship in your area. Include a Christian church, a synagogue, a Buddhist temple or center, maybe a Hindu temple, a Shinto shrine, a mosque or any place used for worship. Enter and sit, pray, and steep yourself in the kedushah or holiness of the place. See if it differs from your idea of holiness; if so, how. Show respect, ask questions. Leave a donation, go home, and meditate on what you have learned.

SECOND MEDITATION

Read the fall of Hebe and meditate upon its symbolism. Write down your findings. Read the story of Lilith (*The Book of Lilith* by B. B. Koltuv [Nicholas Hays, 1986]) and do the same. Research the story of the Sophia of Wisdom and her fall from grace. Make all three the subject of one meditation, looking for the similarities and hidden symbolism in all three tales.

THIRD MEDITATION

Internalize the letter Qoph, placing it in a position that approximates the back of the head.

Pathworking

It is best if you approach this pathworking after fasting. Try to do it in middle to late evening after a day of fruit juice, water, and a small bowl of clear soup at lunch and dinner. Go to bed after the working and keep a pen and paper beside you. The effects may take twenty-four hours to reach you, so be prepared. Light a candle and some light, unobtrusive incense. Bathe and change into loose, comfortable clothing. Tune your mind away from the everyday world toward the letter Qoph. Consider its form and its inner power of holiness and righteousness. Become aware that you are standing on a darkened plain with just a few campfires here and there to show that other people are near. You are standing and waiting, but for what you do not know.

High in the night sky a red star glows; you watch it and wonder at its brightness. Then it begins to move, dropping down and crossing the sky as it does so.

A little above the horizon it changes direction again and comes toward you at a tremendous speed. Frozen to the spot, you can only stand and tremble as it hurtles toward you. Shouts from the direction of the campfires tell you that others have seen it, too. Red as blood but leaving a trail of golden light, the object drops down to within twice the height of a man and some sixty light years away. Now you can see it more clearly. It looks like a funnel of flames and emits a roaring sound, as if a hurricane was passing. A dark entry point opens up and the vehicle seems to be waiting for you to approach. Framed in the opening is an oval of white and gold light. It is the Qoph, and its voice sounds in your inner ear.

"Come, Life, have no fear—there is nothing here that can hurt you physically or spiritually. There are things for you to see and to try to understand."

Slowly you go toward the tunnel of fire; it costs you every bit of your courage, but you have learned to trust the letters and this seems to be of great importance. Qoph waits for you. As you reach the funnel you realize that far from being hot, it is cold. The funnel sucks you into itself and you tumble into darkness.

You rush through alternate levels of light and dark, of heat and cold, of dryness and moisture. The sound of thousands of wings beating the air fills your ears, then, abruptly, there is utter stillness and silence. You are suspended in a void that is somehow not a void because there is something else with you: Love.

Slowly, gradually, the void fills with friendly hands and voices. Aleph, Beth, Gimel, Daleth, Heh. The letters surround you, touch you, support you. The three still to come remain in the background; it is not yet time for you to touch their power, but they are there nonetheless. Then come the voices, the singing. So full of joy, so powerful, so majestic, your heart swells to hear it. There is a triumph to the theme and Aleph whispers to you, "Life, the song is for you, it is your music based on your body note, it tells of your sorrows and fears, your hopes and dreams."

You weep unashamedly for this show of love and the letters crowd closer.

Dawn comes; it is the only description that fits what is happening. Light in shades of turquoise, rose, gold, and blue seeps through the darkness, lifting and dispersing it. You are moving through clouds of color, the singing still sounding in your ears. The letters have made a chariot of themselves to carry you through the higher levels that you could not traverse unaided.

Through rifts in the colors you catch glimpses of great towering halls of crystal, aquamarine, topaz, sapphire, ruby, emerald, and finally one of pearl that glows with light. You are dazzled by the grace and beauty of the edifices and ask if you may go closer. Qoph answers: "No, Life, not yet can you approach the Seven Halls, but if you continue to develop your spiritual powers and strive to live a life of good intent, then one day you will enter them. It is enough at this time for you to know they are there, that they are real, that they are obtainable."

"But Qoph, what are they?"

"The dwelling places of the Most High, even Hashem the Everlasting Light, He of the many names of glory." The letters bow their heads in reverence.

"It is time for you to return, Life, it is not good for you to remain at this level for too long." Yod, as fussy as ever, begins to arrange the letters into a tight formation around you. Once more you are lifted and placed in your living chariot of letters. As you begin to move, a well-remembered voice whispers in your ear. It is the Heh.

"Look to your right as we descend, Life, and I will open the window of illumination for you, for that is my power and my gift to you."

Breathless with excitement, you look to the right as instructed just as you pass the gleaming towers and spires of the Hall of Sapphire. For one brief moment the walls become transparent and within the central hall you see a Presence: mighty, powerful, beautiful beyond belief. Clothed in silver and indigo, Gabriel, the messenger of God, sits in council.

The archangel raises its head and looks directly at you. Eyes of blue fire, deep as the oceans, burn into yours, and with the look comes words.

"You have done well; the Aleph-Beth speak well of you, child of Earth." Then you are into the tunnel once more, being whirled round and round. But your mind is clear. Was it like this for Elijah? No, it was more than this for him; you are a humble seeker of wisdom, Elijah was a master of wisdom. But you have begun the long journey that one day will bring you back to the Halls of the Hekaloth and the radiance that dwells at their center. You emerge breathless and dizzy from the tunnel, changed irrevocably by your journey, as you open your eyes on your own world.

Qoph

Glory be to Thee through all time and through all space.

Thou art the glory that was, is, and shall be unto eternity.

Thou art manifested in the everlasting universe of thyself,

and in the four directions shall the Holy Creatures declare thee

crowned by the Aleph-Beth, thy diadem is the Word.

Fiat, Fiat, Fiat.

Thou art One.

The pinpoint of Being, the word of utter loneliness.

Thou art Two.

The wisdom of otherness that suffers the torment of duality.

Thou art Three.

The understanding of the silence that precedes new birth.

Thou art Four.

The faces turn in each direction and give rise to the elements.

Thou art Five.

The destroyer who comes with a sword, but bearing seeds to scatter.

Thou art Six.

The mystical cadence that rules the rhythmic dance of creation.

Thou art Seven.

The chord of harmony that links together all life in a hymn of praise.

Thou art Eight.

The pattern of thought that turns in upon itself without ending.

Thou art Nine.

The bringer of dreams and nightmares, two sides of the same face.

Thou art Ten.

The completion of the One returning to its source.

～

Ritual

You will need space for this ritual, so clear as much as you can from the room you will be using. Prepare an altar with a white cloth; a central light; a white candle in a holder; a wand; a dagger; a chalice with wine; and a platter with bread and salt. You will also need either some palm leaves to spread on the floor around the altar or something like a mixture of bay leaves, rosemary, fresh sage, and pine. At the four quarters you will need the Four Holy Creatures. These can be either drawings of a winged lion, a winged bull, a winged man, and an eagle, or figures of a lion, a bull, an eagle, and a man. The animals can be purchased from a toy shop, the man can be an angel figure. Begin by cleansing the room with salt and water, as you have done before. Then hallow with incense, and finally protect with flame. Use the same procedure and words as given in other rituals. Light the central candle and lift the bowl and light up to eye level.

"Across time and space and through the dimensions of Light I send out a call to Raphael, archangel of the element of air. Open the doors of the east that I may look upon the sun as it rises, heralding the promise of a new day. I open the door of this temple to the Winged Human Being, to Paralda, elemental king of air, and to the sylphs of the air, his subjects. Be welcome, be at peace, be filled with grace." *Go to the south and stand with your arms open.*

"Across time and space and through the dimensions of Light I send out a call to Michael, archangel of the element of fire. Open the doors of the south to me that I may look upon the majesty of Light. I open the door of this temple to the winged lion, to Djinn, elemental king of fire, and to the salamanders of fire, his subjects. Be welcome, be at peace, be filled with grace." *Go to the west and stand with your arms open.*

"Across time and space and through the dimensions of Light I send out a call to Gabriel, archangel of the element of water. Open the doors of the west that I may look upon the setting sun in glory. I open the door of this temple to the eagle and to Nixsa, elemental king of water, and to the undines of the water, his subjects. Be welcome, be at peace, be filled with grace." *Go to the north and stand with your arms open.*

"Across time and space and through the dimensions of Light I send out a call to Uriel, archangel of the element of earth. Open the doors of the north to me that

I may look upon the sun at midnight. I open the door of the temple to the winged bull, to Ghob, elemental king of earth, and to the gnomes of the earth, his subjects. Be welcome, be at peace, be filled with grace." *Go to the east and take up the wand and hold it across your right arm. Walk clockwise around the altar seven times, invoking as you go.*

(First circle) "The wand is a symbol of wisdom and will. I invoke into this magical tool the wisdom of the five senses, sight, sound, touch, smell and taste."

(Second circle) "I invoke into this magical tool the wisdom of intent."

(Third circle) "I invoke into this magical tool the wisdom of patience."

(Fourth circle) "I invoke into this magical tool the wisdom of experience."

(Fifth circle) "I invoke into this magical tool the wisdom of the Light."

(Sixth circle) "I invoke into this magical tool the wisdom of the Word."

(Seventh circle) "I invoke into this magical tool the wisdom of Love." *At the altar, replace the wand. Go to the south and pick up the dagger. Holding its crosspiece upward, make seven circles clockwise around the altar.*

(First circle) "The dagger, like the sword, is a weapon for the brave and the true. I invoke into this magical tool the strength of self-discipline."

(Second circle) "I invoke into this magical tool the strength of actions."

(Third circle) "I invoke into this magical tool the strength of participation."

(Fourth circle) "I invoke into this magical tool the strength of will and leadership."

(Fifth circle) "I invoke into this magical tool the strength of the Light."

(Sixth circle) "I invoke into this magical tool the strength of true principles."

(Seventh circle) "I invoke into this magical tool the strength of love." *At the altar, replace the dagger, go to the west, and pick up the chalice. Holding it up, make seven circles clockwise around the altar.*

(First circle) "The chalice is a symbol of intuition and ability. I invoke into this magical tool the ability to see into the hearts of others."

(Second circle) "I invoke into this magical tool the ability to see the difference between truth and lies."

(Third circle) "I invoke into this magical tool the ability to make the right decisions."

(Fourth circle) "I invoke into this magical tool the ability to look into the Light."

(Fifth circle) "I invoke into this magical tool the ability to be discreet and exercise discretion."

(Sixth circle) "I invoke into this magical tool the ability to see true and clearly."

(Seventh circle) "I invoke into this magical tool the ability to love unconditionally." *At the altar, drink the wine, replace the chalice, go to the north and pick up the plate. Holding it up, make seven circles clockwise around the altar.*

(First circle) "The plate of bread symbolizes stability and growth. I invoke into this magical tool stability of action."

(Second circle) "I invoke into this magical tool the stability of thought."

(Third circle) "I invoke into this magical tool the stability of understanding."

(Fourth circle) "I invoke into this magical tool the stability of knowledge."

(Fifth circle) "I invoke into this magical tool the stability of the first Word."

(Sixth circle) "I invoke into this magical tool the stability of the first Light."

(Seventh circle) "I invoke into this magical tool the stability of love." *At the altar, eat a piece of bread, replace the plate. Go to the east and lift the light in the bowl.*

"I embed this light in my heart center that it may burn brightly from now until my last day in this incarnation. So mote it be."

Replace the light. Close the quarters and bless those who have been with you. Douse the lights and leave.

RESH

Thy countenance shines like the sun
and I draw near for warmth.
From thee I draw life and sustenance
and like unto the flowers of the field
I turn my face toward thee.
Thou art the Head that is above all,
endlessly holding the thought of creation.
I am one small part of that thought.
I hold Thee within my heart and my mind.
This is my treasure and my jewel,
my inheritance from Thee.
From life to life I have guarded it.
Now I offer it willingly and with love
to that which gave it.
Make of me a candle that will light
some small part of the darkness.
Though it be imperfect,
yet it will not shine for itself alone
but for those still in darkness.
I will stand steadfast for the Light,
like the wick for the Lamp of Melchisedek.
My light will reach out into the darkness
and defeat it.

Image: Head
Symbol: ר
Path on the Tree of Life: 30
Numerical Value: 200

Prayer

This is a prayer of realization, the moment when one makes the connection between what you thought you were and what you really are: a child of Light with embryonic powers that will one day make you fully conscious of yourself as a divine scion of the One.

We all have moments of full spiritual consciousness. British author Colin Wilson calls them "peak experiences," when we seem to live at a higher level and see a fuller sweep of our world and everything in it. Such times are rare, but they can be induced with training, patience, and self-discipline. We only need one such experience to understand that we spend most of our lives in a state of spiritual torpor.

Suddenly everything is brighter, clearer; we feel as if we could truly move a mountain. The mountain is our inertia and we *can* move it. We can train ourselves to expect these peaks of enlightenment and to look for them actively every day. You will find yourself waking each morning with a sense of excitement and anticipation. What will happen today that might change your life? Who will you meet, what can you do or achieve that as yet you have not succeeded in doing? Life becomes an adventure. We become as little children, seeing each day as a challenge and not as a prison sentence.

This is a heady feeling and one to which it is easy to become addicted, but after a while there comes an inner understanding that this exhilaration is not just for you. It has been given to you for a purpose. As a seeker you have two duties: first, to further your own spiritual awareness and second, to help others to reach the same goal. You have set your foot on the road leading to unreserved dedication.

To become a lamp for others to follow, you must first understand your own inner light. A lantern must be kept as clean as possible in order to shine brightly. We are human and have faults; we cannot hope to be as bright as we would wish. What we can do is to try our best. The faults, you can be sure, are known and allowances are made for them. To try, even if we succeed only partly, is enough; there are opportunities to improve in each life. Train yourself to be like the wick of a candle. The flame burns about it but it remains untouched and able to do its part. A thousand candles can be lit from one; if you kindle one extra flame, you will have done well. Think of yourself as a flame standing guard against the darkness.

The Letter

The Resh symbolizes the head, which can mean the will, and also stubbornness and pride. Resh stems from another word, *rush* or poor—poor in heart and in spirit as well as in riches. Before you can do anything along the lines of changing your life, you have to change your *attitude* to life. You must try to see things as others see them and weigh them against each other to find the best balance.

Following right after Qoph as it does, we see that pride and stubbornness can turn us away from the kedusha, or holiness, that Qoph represents. Whether Jewish or gentile, there are times when we should, indeed must, take time to review our life and see where improvements can be made, and see if we can right old wrongs or, equally important, forgive old wrongs that have been done to us. This is the more difficult of the two.

In the Servants of the Light School we train students to go over each day as they lie in bed, before sleeping. In this way they can nip certain tendencies in the bud before they get too big to handle comfortably. It is a simple exercise but an important one.

The value of Resh is two hundred, and if we reduce that to two we get Beth, the house; the head is the house of the brain and of the mind. It is where we, as a personality, live and work and interact with those around us. If the body is a temple, then the head is the adytum. As such it should be kept clean, tidy, and ready for the coming of the deity, for it is here that we greet and speak with our God, by whatever name you hold dear.

The head has always been held sacred, especially by the Celts. One only has to look at the names of the older pubs and inns in the British Isles to see this: The King's Head, The Queen's Head, The Nag's Head, The Horse's Head, Bran's Head, etc. We in England are or were a nation that revered the horse as a sacred animal (Epona the horse goddess) along with the cow (Mona of the Dark Isle) and Cerridwen (the white sow). Traitors were decapitated and their heads raised on a lance above Traitor's Gate in the Tower of London.

Kings and queens alike have been beheaded during our long and illustrious history. Alas, our history is now trampled on and derided as being "too nationalistic." Traitors are still among us, but the rule of the sacred head is far older than those who would like to see it fall, and they too may lose their "heads" in the end. Rulers are anointed and their heads crowned with gold and jewels in defiance of those who would cast them down, removing the image of the crown from currency and even the humble postage stamp.

The head contains knowledge and accumulated wisdom. The will decides if it will be used for good or bad. Train the will and you will train the head and make it worthy to wear a crown of gold, or even better, the crown of the good name (see the letter Kaph).

Resh is associated with the Tarot card of the Sun, which in turn is linked to Tiphereth (harmony), but the obverse side of this sphere has the vice of pride, the same flaw that led, so we are told, to the fall of Lucifer. We use words like "headstrong" to describe people who won't listen to reason, or we say they are going "headlong" into trouble. See what others you can find.

Referring back to Lucifer, we should look at the link between some of the ancient gods and the letter Resh with its symbolism of opposites, God or not-God, king or usurper, benefactor or thief. We are told that since God created everything, even those things that are diametrically opposite to Him must have some goodness in them, or some purpose for their being that way. We have already looked at the anomaly of a being called the Light Bringer, who was once the prosecutor in the council of God, now called Satan and Evil.

If we look at Orpheus, another of the many sacrificed gods, we see someone who tried to defy the law and bring his dead wife back to life. Prometheus stole fire from the gods to give to humanity and was punished most cruelly for it. Loki the mischievous Norse god did the same thing and, again, was punished for it. The raven stole fire and in carrying it back to earth was burned so severely that his once-white feathers turned black.

We must distinguish between positive evil and negative evil. Electricity provides many good things: light, heat, heart and lung machines, electric wheelchairs, and dialysis machines, all good and useful things. However, if an innocent child playing on the floor pokes a finger into an electrical socket, the child will die. Who do we blame? Not the socket, not the electrical current, yet it was the cause of death. Some things, some powers, are dangerous and when using them we need to make decisions.

There are many people who would say the use of "magical" power is evil . . . and yes, it can be. It can also be good and useful. It is not the power itself that is evil or good; it is the one who uses it and who chooses the purpose to which it will be put and how it will be used.

Resh is the head, so we must *think* when we use power and decide if that use will be good or bad. Those who rise to power are playing a dangerous game. They can become so entranced by their power that it becomes a drug. Nowhere do we see this more clearly than in governments. The mildest person can become a dictator riding roughshod over any who disagree with them.

Occult training can bring power into your life simply because it trains you to think, act, and work in a disciplined way, gives you knowledge of your own abilities and the confidence to use them. But it can also give you a taste for power and for hurting others, especially when they trust you. The choice is yours.

You can play safe and do nothing and remain in the shadow of others, never daring to try out your own ideas in case they go wrong. Chances are they will, at some time or another. But at least you will have learned something. We can only learn by experience and it is the mistakes we make that teach us the most.

Of one thing we can be sure—when we make a mistake and learn from it, it will have been worth it in the end. There is always a place for those who have taken the wrong road, retraced their steps and, having learned their lesson, tried again. This is how it must be: three steps forward and two back. Remember, a gradual advancement toward the Light is better than a headlong rush!

It is often the way that someone comes to power and through manipulation of the will of others establishes him- or herself in a position of trust. When that position is verified they begin to show their true colors. Against such a one, active force is almost always useless. The only solution is to allow the underlying force to achieve its full potential and then die away for lack of energy. "Give a false movement enough rope and it will hang itself," I was taught, and it is true. Falsity and pride will always overbalance in the end and bring about its own destruction.

If you struggle against it or use the same tactics, you will be drawn into the same headspace (to coin a phrase). Keep silence, have faith in the higher courts of justice. Allow them to handle it and you will not be tainted by it.

Path 30 runs from Yesod to Hod, from the sphere of the machinery of the universe to that of splendor. Hod is a mental sphere with obvious connections to the image of the head. Its title is the Collective Intelligence and that describes it exactly. The Tarot card of the Sun holds a position of power at the center of our solar system. It is paramount to our world as the Creator is paramount to our existence. It is also a path of love and warmth and joy, once we have learned our lessons. But too much heat can destroy and burn so we have to strike a balance in ourselves between our light and dark sides in order to achieve that balance.

This is a path that can hold the most important piece of knowledge we will ever learn: Know thyself. Sometimes knowing yourself can be a bitter disappointment, but if you can face it, you can also see where you need to change.

Meditations

First Meditation

In your meditation stand with a strong noonday sun behind you; allow it to illuminate everything before you. Allow certain aspects of your life to unfold before you and look at them in the full light of day. Ask yourself where you could have done better and how best to achieve new balance in your life.

Second Meditation

Read the myth of Prometheus and meditate on its symbolism, both as an example of suffering as a result of an act of compassion, and as a metaphor for a sacrificed God. Do the same with the myth of Loki.

Third Meditation

Meditate on the Egyptian Hall of Osiris and more precisely on the Weighing of the Heart. Imagine yourself going through this trial and meditate on the result.

Pathworking

If possible, do this pathworking out-of-doors, if not in a garden; if you have no garden, fill some vases with flowers and place them around the room. Allow the color and the scent to help you through the doorway into the inner levels. Before you is a gate of wrought ironwork, beautifully intricate and obviously the work of a skilled smith. The center is a tree in full leaf set in an oval of scrollwork. The four quarters represent trees of the four seasons: holly and spruce for winter, willow and catkins for spring, oak and maple for summer, copper beech and sycamore for autumn.

You open the gate and walk into a garden. For a moment you just stand and look; the quiet beauty and the atmosphere fill you with a sense of well-being. Before you is an old English herb garden set in traditional form with small geometric areas, each filled with fragrant herbs. You wander among lavender, rosemary, thyme, and sage. Chive and fennel and hyssop gather amid borders of old-fashioned box plants. Several kinds of mint spice the air, along with rose geraniums, poppies, and gentian.

You walk in and out of the borders, sometimes plucking a few leaves and inhaling the scent. Then you notice another gate; on opening it, you find it leads into another garden. This one is filled with bushes with variegated leaves. Though quieter in color and presentation, it is very peaceful, with the many shades of green and gold. Here there are wooden seats and you sit and look out over the richness of the plant life.

"Do you like my garden, Life? I have many of them and all are different. Often the seasons are different in them as well. I enjoy variety." The Resh stands before you. Like its garden it shimmers in a medley of greens and golds.

"I love your gardens, Resh, how many do you have?"

"As many as you wish to see, Life, but each garden has a purpose. You know by now that we all have something to teach you and to share with you. It is my turn now."

The Resh moves down a pathway toward a large bush of green and gold leaves and standing there is someone you know from your past. It is someone you have hurt or spoken ill of years ago. Resh turns to you and speaks gently.

"You have an opportunity to heal old wounds, Life, here and now, and then it will never worry you again. You will be free of it. Can you do that? If you do not feel you can right now, then you can return to this place when the time is right."

You have a few moments in which to decide, but it does not take long to say "I am sorry." The Resh takes you down another path and you hear voices. Ahead of you are two people having an argument; one of them is you. You search your memory and remember this time and what the consequences of the quarrel were.

"Do you wish to change what you are saying and doing, Life? You have a choice. Perhaps you do not wish to change what was said, just your understanding of the cause. That can often be the best way to understand situations when looking at them from a distance in time."

You come into the next garden. Resh indicates a door set into a wall. This is a garden full of old-fashioned flowers: goldenrod, pinks, sweet Williams, and hollyhocks. Sunflowers and lilac trees, fuchsia and geraniums, snapdragons and foxgloves jostle for places in the sun. You look around in delight. Then you look and see coming toward you someone who in the past has done you a great wrong. The person stops in front of you and waits. You feel you have to say something, but what?

"Sometimes, Life, actions are better than words."

You hold out your hand and it is taken and held. You feel you cannot yet do more than this; the hurt is deep. But a start has been made. You silently bless the person and move on. Round a corner of multicolored lupins you find a group of children playing. They are from your childhood. Old memories stir and make you smile and weep. You bless the children in that pocket of time, and go on.

Resh takes you into a rose garden ablaze with color and scent, almost too overpowering. You sit together on a bench and talk of your life. You spill out to the letter all your old fears, hurts, and imagined and real slights that you have endured. It listens, then speaks of the same thing from the opposite point of view, all the things you have done and said. It helps you to put things into perspective and to realize that holding on to all these old memories means tying up energy you could use for other, more important things.

"Life, you can come to me here at any time, you can use this garden and bring others to it. Fear, hatred, and bad thoughts have no place here. This has been built for peace of mind, body, and spirit and it is my gift to you. Come, there is someone you should meet." Resh takes you through the rose garden and into a meadow filled with wildflowers. A path leads to a stream with willows dipping green fingers into the water. A man sits by the stream feeding the birds with crumbs of bread. He looks up.

"Hello."

"Hello, can I feed them too?"

"Of course, here's some bread, just throw it on the ground and they will come to you; after a while they may eat from your hand."

"Resh said I should talk to you, but I don't know what about."

"Anything you want to say."

"Why is forgiving and being forgiven so important?"

"Hashem grows through our experience, good and bad. He gets to know what being human is like, what having a physical body is like, what loving and hating, quarreling and making up is like. But when you refuse to forgive and to be forgiven, you hold on to that experience and it cannot go to be taken into His understanding of human-ness. In not forgiving those you have hurt or accepting forgiveness from Hashem, you are being selfish." You think this over for a few minutes.

"Does He really care about us, about me—I mean, we are told He does but it is hard to see how He can, and . . . oh, it's just all so vague and so distant. How do I know He cares?"

"Because you are His child and you are loved." He holds out his hand and takes yours. There is a scar on the back of his hand. You look up into eyes that grow brighter and brighter until you can no longer see. The scent of flowers is all about you and when you open your eyes again you can see the flowers in front of you and know that you are back home.

Psalm 125

They that trust in the Lord shall be as Mount Zion,

which cannot be removed but which abideth forever.

As the mountains are round about Jerusalem,

so the Lord is round about His people

from henceforth even forever.

For the rid of the wicked shall not rest

upon the lot of the righteous,

lest the righteous put forth their hands into iniquity.

Do good, O Lord, unto those that be good,

and to them that art upright in their hearts.

As for such that turn aside unto their crooked ways,

the Lord shall lead them forth with the workers of iniquity,

but peace shall be upon Israel.

≈

Psalm 131

Lord, my heart is not haughty, nor mine eyes lofty,

neither do I exercise myself in great matters

or in things too high for me.

Surely I have behaved and quieted myself

as a child that is weaned of his mother.

My soul is even as a weaned child.

Let Israel hope in the Lord from henceforth

and forever.

≈

Ritual

This is a ritual of cleansing, so you will need certain herbs. You will need a central altar with a white cloth; a central bowl with a light; a candle in a holder in the south; a chalice with wine in the west; a plate of bread and salt in the north; and a bowl of incense and a bottle of oil of frankincense in the east. Prepare four bowls of water with a pinch of salt, one in each quarter, with the following mixtures:

East: Three drops of oil of frankincense, half a small bottle of Florida Water or any cologne, and some dried sage leaves.

South: Three drops of oil of sandalwood, the rest of the Florida Water or cologne, and dried thyme leaves.

West: Three drops of oil of lavender, lavender water, and some dried lavender.

North: Three drops of oil of lotus or neroli, half a small bottle of eau de cologne, and dried dittany of Crete.

You will also need four small towels, and something new to wear—a robe, slippers, a waist cord, or a white shawl to wear about your shoulders. Put this on a chair within reach. Bathe and wash your hair; ladies, put on a loose dressing gown, men, a towel wrapped around your waist. Light the altar candles and if you wish you can put quarter-colored candles in the quarters. Seal the door and spend a few minutes in prayer/invocation before the altar. State your intent to cleanse and reconsecrate yourself to the work of the Mysteries. Then, barefoot, walk around the altar seven times.

"I come before the Light of the World to be made clean and whole that I might be raised up and set my direction upon the higher worlds. I offer myself to the Light that I may add to its glory. I am conscious of my faults and I will do my best to control them and to increase my awareness of the spiritual paths before me.

"I desire to be made clean and whole and to live in the Light. I confess my faults and ask for forgiveness. If I have caused hurt or distress I ask for forgiveness, as I forgive those that have hurt me in the past. I am a child of the Creator and in His image I live my life upon the Earth." *Face east and invoke Raphael.*

"I call across the vast emptiness of time and space to the hall of Raphael, lord and regent of air. Come to me, be with me, bring me your healing presence and be welcome. I welcome Paralda, king of air, and the sylphs of the air that serve you. *Go to the bowl and wash your face.* With this prepared water I wash my face that I may look upon the world clean and whole. Bless me, Raphael, that I may be healed in body, mind, and spirit. *Sprinkle water over your head and dry off with a towel. Kneel and make an offering of yourself to the Light.* Let me be welcome in the courts of the morning, Raphael, that I may walk with you as my guide and my mentor." *Get up and walk to the south. Face the south and invoke Michael.*

"I call across the vast emptiness of time and space to the hall of Michael, lord and regent of fire. Come to me, be with me, bring me your strengthening presence and be welcome. I welcome Djinn, king of fire, and the salamanders of fire that serve you. *Go to the bowl and wash your hands.* With this prepared water I wash my hands that I may serve the Light and face the world clean and whole. Bless me, Michael, that I may be strong in body, mind, and spirit. *Sprinkle water over your torso and dry off with a towel. Kneel and make an offering of yourself to the Light.* Let me be welcome in the courts of the noonday sun, Michael, that I may walk with you as my guide and my mentor." *Get up and walk to the west. Face west and invoke Gabriel.*

"I call across the vast emptiness of time and space to the hall of Gabriel, lord and regent of water. Come to me, be with me, bring me your powers of communication and be welcome. I welcome Nixsa, king of water, and the undines of the sea that serve you. *Go to the bowl and wash your feet.* With this prepared water I wash my feet that I may walk in the world clean and whole. Bless me, Gabriel, that I may be untroubled in body, mind, and spirit. *Sprinkle water over your legs and dry off with a towel. Kneel and make an offering of yourself to the Light.* Let me be welcome in the courts of the setting sun, Gabriel, that I may walk with you as my guide and my mentor." *Get up and walk to the north, take off your towel or dressing gown and, naked, face north and invoke Uriel.*

"I call across the vast emptiness of time and space to the hall of Uriel, lord and regent of earth. Come to me, be with me, bring me your patient and steadfast presence and be welcome. I welcome Ghob, king of earth, and the gnomes of the earth that serve you. *Go to the bowl and wash your body down.* With this prepared water I wash my physical body and my spiritual self that I may look upon the world clean and whole.

"Bless me, Uriel, that I may be regenerated in body, mind, and spirit. *Dry off with a towel. Kneel and make an offering of yourself to the Light.* Let me be welcome in the courts of the midnight sun, Uriel, that I may walk with you as my guide and my mentor." *Get up and walk to the east. Dress in clean robe and slippers, spend a few minutes in prayer, then stand before each face of the altar in turn to receive the blessings of that quarter.*

East: "Bless me, Raphael, servant of the Most High. Heal my body, my heart, my mind, and my soul. Make me fit to follow the path of the Mysteries. Lift my prayers each day to the Creator in the astral form of three white roses to represent my physical, mental, and spiritual selves."

South: "Bless me, Michael, warrior of the Most High. Strengthen my resolve and make me strong to withstand the trials of life that I may faithfully follow the way of the Mysteries. Present my prayers each day to the Creator in the astral form of three scarlet candles to represent my devotion to that which created me."

West: "Bless me, Gabriel, messenger of the Most High. Speak with me when I have need of thy wisdom and let the knowledge I need find in me a willing pupil of the ancient Mysteries. Present my prayers each day to the Creator in the astral form of three white doves to represent my desire for perfection in His sight."

North: "Bless me, Uriel, sustainer of the world of humankind. Help me to overcome my inertia and to grow in knowledge, wisdom, and understanding that I may be patient with those who are yet young in spirit and that I may be a worthy teacher of the Mysteries. Present my prayers each day to the Creator in the astral form of three ripe apples to represent the ancient cause of the Fall and the gift of free will.

"I eat of the bread and salt and take into myself the food of earth. I drink the wine and fill myself with the blessing of the grape. I lift the Light and pass it over my head that I may receive the gift of a silver tongue in order to teach. I anoint my head with oil and offer myself to the Creator for whatever use is fitting. It is done. Selah."

Close down the temple, douse the lights, unseal the door, and depart.

SHIN

Triple-crowned glory of the Creator,

Flame of Flames,

holy, holy, holy art thou,

breath of the Divine One.

Give me Thy blessing and let me live in thy light.

Thou art the first Fire, the living flame

that issued forth at the beginning.

The darkness comprehended thee not.

The creative power of God is held in thee.

Tell me of that far-off first day.

Was it like some blazing star erupting at its zenith?

Would that mine own inner light could glow so bright.

Cleanse me, sweet Fire of Love, and fill me with thy self.

Each day I strive toward thee,

my soul yearns for thee.

Thou art the enduring energy of the One Creator.

Through thee I may glimpse Its glory.

Holy, holy, holy, Triple-Flamed One,

take my prayer to the One.

Be blessed for this.

Image: Tooth
Symbol: ש
Path on the Tree of Life: 31
Numerical Value: 300

Prayer

This is the penultimate letter and the whole mood is lighter, more confident, and shows less stress. It is a praise of thankfulness for what has been endured and learned over the course of a great trial.

It extols the birth of the first great fire and its power over darkness. As one of the four elements, symbolized by the winged lion, there is a feeling of majesty, power, and the ability to go forward into the future with total confidence.

There is also curiosity: "Tell me of that far-off first day." The question is enormous in its implication. What was it like, that first day? Was it really a big explosion of light, fire, sound, etc.? Or, being that there were no ears to hear it, was it a soundless burst of energy ripping space apart?

The prayer asks for that same power to be given to the inner light we all carry within. It asks to be cleansed by that fire and filled with its power. That primal fire is a living part of the Creator is made very clear, as is the longing to be a part of the One. Here the spirit has almost come to the end of its trials and looks forward to once more treading the path destined for it.

The Letter

The Shin stands very high in the hierarchy of the letters for it describes God as the master and as the peace giver. Its triple crown of tiny flames makes it easy to remember and to write. The prayer here is a chant of praise and admiration for its beauty and for being the first fire from which came the beginning of humanity's march toward civilization.

Added together its value of three hundred becomes three, the trinity, the triple Godhead. It is also the value of Gimel, the third letter and the one that can carry us across the wasteland to the world of the spirit. It is a journey that every seeker after truth must take sooner or later. Gimel's card is that of the High Priestess, and she is also the divine Shekinah who is the priestess of the hearth and home in the physical world and the teacher, guide, and mentor of the young in the spiritual world.

Shin, Kaph (poshut), and Resh together make up the word *sheker* or "lie." Each of these letters has a single point or foot and so are unable to support themselves; they have to lean on each other to stand. A lie needs support from other lies to make itself believable. The word *truth,* on the other hand, is built from Aleph, Mem, and Tav, all of which have firm bases on which to stand. The lesson here is tell a sheker and you will fall down; tell the truth and you can stand alone. Maybe it was the Shin that marked the forehead of Cain?

Looking at the shape of this letter, we can see many suggestions: the branches of a tree reaching up, the flames of a campfire in the evening, flowers in a vase, or the roots of a tooth, which is the meaning of the word *shin.* We can say the three stems remind us of faith, hope, and charity, or of the holy trinity. We can say it is a family group of father, mother, and child. It is a fan to cool you on a hot day or a road with three turnings, each of which will lead you in a different direction. When we raise our arms to heaven, the two arms and the head form a Shin. This can be a powerful stance in magical work; after all, it was this stance that Moses took during the battle with the Amalekites, for when he raised his hands the army of the Israelites prevailed. It can be the higher, lower, and physical selves, and there are many more.

We can see seven colors, but in actual fact they are made from the blending of just three primary colors, red, yellow, and blue. Shin begins the beautiful Song of Solomon with its rich description of the many aspects of love.

Shin and Samech sound very much alike and one has to be careful to make the right choice when spelling Hebrew words and pronouncing them. To do this incorrectly can change the whole meaning of a phrase.

Path 31 runs from Malkuth to Hod and is a path in which fire as an element plays a large part. In *The Shining Paths* (Thoth Publications, 1997) I used the symbol of campfires, family hearth fires, and the forge fire of the smith. Smiths have long been considered to be the first magicians, if only for their ability to take "earth" and make it into a sword or a ploughshare.

The path travels from the sphere of Earth itself to that of the mental sphere of Hod; the discovery of metals and the skill to forge weapons and utensils was a huge step forward in evolution. Fire has always been a creative element; it stimulates conversation and encourages speech and discussion—when this happens, the feedback between people begins to bring ideas to the surface. Once humans had learned to create, control, and use fire, they began to feel safer, live better (especially with regard to cooked food rather than eating it raw), and of course it extended their day by giving them light to work by and relax with. It raised their living standards and their consciousness at the same time.

The idea of a flame as something magical, and then sacred, became part of superstition, which in turn became religion. From the sacred flame of the vestal virgins to the sacrificial fires of Middle Eastern religions, the idea of fire as a God-given gift became paramount. This is where the earliest smiths came in: Tubal Cain, Vulcan, and Hephasteus were workers in metal and regarded as gods for their skills. The same idea is found in Celtic lands with Wayland the Smith and Govannon, his Welsh counterpart.

Shin as a symbol for a primal element is of great importance. In the Old Testament we find instances of fire being the cause of change and growth. Elijah's battle with the prophets of Baal (Kings 1:38) and his ascent into heaven in a fiery chariot (Kings 2:1) are just two of many.

The Tarot card of Judgement belongs to this path, and some see in the shape of Shin an indication of choice, neither left nor right, but the middle paths. This choice of three is seen in the card with two adults and a child between them. "Unless ye become as little children," said Yeshua. Shin is the letter that shows the primal spirit of the individual, the part of us that searches for the way back to our divine parent.

Meditations

FIRST MEDITATION

Take a pottery bowl and fill it with earth. Place on this three or four pieces of char-coal and light them. Allow them to burn through and then sprinkle with an incense of your own choice, though for preference a well-made kyphi would be advisable. Around the bowl place seven candles in small glass holders. These should be in the seven colors of the spectrum. When the incense is burning well, light the candles and contemplate the flames and the smoke and the scent. Allow the form of the Shin to rest lightly in your thoughts, allowing images to rise. Record any results.

SECOND MEDITATION

Build in the mind's eye the image of a column of light rays. These rays twist and spiral upward and each one is of a different color. At the top they form a lotus flower and from the center of the flower emerges a flame. Meditate on the symbol and record your thoughts.

THIRD MEDITATION

Sit within a circle of candles large enough for you to be comfortable within the space. With the light from the candles draw up a ray of light and bend it, linking it to a candle on the other side. Do this until you have a dome of light protecting you. Practice this diligently, it will be useful in the future.

Pathworking

When you open your eyes on the inner worlds, Shin is waiting for you. For the first time a letter appears in its symbolic form, three great towering columns of flames stemming from a single point. It is an uncompromising red-gold. It is sur-rounded by the roar of flames, but when you appear alarmed by its form and sound, the letter quickly tones down the roar to a soft whisper and the flames become spiraling shades of red, gold, and orange.

"My apologies, Life, sometimes I forget to modify my forms; it is seldom we get to deal with you and your kind. The regent of fire, Michael, the warrior general of the Most High, requests that I escort you on your journey." The letter sounds very formal, almost military. You reflect that this must be normal if it is connected to Michael the warrior.

"Come, Life, there is much to show you and it will be better if I carry you. Are you still afraid of my element or will you trust me?" You hesitate for only a moment, then step forward confidently. The triple flames brighten and then advance toward you, enveloping you within their aura. It is warm and soft within the fire and you feel yourself lifted and transported. Like a child you nestle into the softness and relax. The Shin talks as you go.

"I want to show you fire in its many forms, Life. It has been one of the greatest influences upon humanity, both a blessing and a curse. Some things would be too painful to show you as they really were; my element has been sadly misused and the King of Fire, even the great Djinn himself, has wept to see his salamanders used so horrifically. Fire happens in nature also, but that is according to the will of the One who has set up laws that are always obeyed. Even He, may His name be blessed, cannot go against those laws. If He did (the Shin chuckles), Yod would remind him. You have met with Yod, I think?"

There is a silence and then the warmth is withdrawn and you are standing on a high rocky outcrop with the Shin at your side. Before you is a stark, primitive landscape with volcanoes and great smoking rifts covering miles and miles.

"This is how it all began," Shin tells you. "Fire is still there in the very heart of the Earth. You know this, of course, for you still have active volcanic ranges in your own time. Fire can be destructive, but it also fertilizes the earth. You can see this still, for where the lava flows the earth becomes rich and crops grow well. Some plants require fire to help them germinate." It wraps round you again and you move on.

The next stop is better; there are now plants and trees and there is evidence of fire being used by humans. You see a fire at a cave mouth and food being roasted over it. A small group of people gather round it, some sit and wait, others are busy carving bone into hooks with sharp stones and making rough clay pots and baskets. They are not Neanderthals, but Cro-Magnon, the higher species. They wear rough fur and hide clothing and have flint-tipped spears. Shin urges you toward the cave mouth.

"They cannot see you. Come, I want you to see them as they paint the walls of their caves." You enter the cave and follow behind the Shin, whose glowing light makes it easy to see the way. You come eventually into a much larger cave where men are working by the light of tiny flickering oil lamps filled with smelly animal fat and wicks made of twisted fur and plant fibers. The pictures are breathtakingly beautiful and amazingly skilled.

"But look at the tiny lamps, Life, see how little light they give. These people will never see the full beauty of what they are creating. They do it on faith alone; it is enough that it is done and they leave something behind to speak of them and their way of life."

You look and marvel at the skill and the dedication. How can one speak of such people as "primitive"? Shin envelops you again within its warmth and you feel the rush of wind against your face as you travel through time. It becomes a series of vignettes of history: you watch a potter in ancient Egypt arranging his ware in a kiln . . . a smith forging Roman short swords . . . a Japanese master swordmaker heating, folding, and beating the metal that will become a samurai sword for a shogun. You watch brushwood piled high to prepare for the burning of Giordano Bruno, but the Shin will not let you see the sentence carried out.

"You do not need to carry that in your memory, Life, it happened many times and degraded the element of fire as well as those who ordered it. Those who endured it were helped, and have since found the strength to forgive. Let me show you something better. This is a campfire and these young people are from many countries and many religions. See how they sit together to laugh and sing and talk about themselves and their hopes and dreams.

"This is my power, Life, the power to bring people together, to talk, to exchange their views, to give warmth to the cold, food to the hungry, and safety to the oppressed. My element can be degraded and misused, it is true, but I can offer the heights of the spirit to those that are strong enough to stand the tests. I am power itself, Life—like my symbol, the tooth, I grind down those that misuse me. Let me fill you with the inner fire of the spirit as my gift to you."

You turn to the Shin, trusting and ready for whatever comes. The triple light turns once more to flame and opens itself to you. You walk into it and stretch out your arms to it. You breathe in the spiritual fire and feel it fill you from head to toe. You bless the Shin for its gift and all the letters of the Aleph-Beth, and send a prayer of thanks up to the very throne of the Most High for what you have received. You become part of the fire itself and there is lit within you three flames that will never, ever go out. One flame lights in the brain, one in the heart, and one in the genitals; one for thought, one for love, and one for creativity. The Shin steps away and for a moment you feel cold and bereft; then the flames within you flare up and you laugh, for you know that you will never really be apart from now on. Your own world envelops you and you wake full of energy.

Pentecost
ACTS OF THE APOSTLES 2–1

And when the day of Pentecost was fully come,

they were all with one accord in one place.

And suddenly there came a sound from heaven as of a rushing mighty wind,

and it filled all the house where they were sitting.

And there appeared unto them cloven tongues like as of fire,

and it sat upon each of them.

And they were filled with the Holy Ghost,

and began to speak with other tongues,

as the Spirit gave them utterance.

And there were, dwelling at Jerusalem, Jews, devout men

out of every nation under heaven.

Now when this was noised abroad, the multitude came together,

and were confounded because every man heard them speak in his own tongue.

And they were amazed and marveled, saying one to another,

Behold, are not all these that speak Galileans?

And how hear we every man in our own tongue

wherein we were born?

Ritual

You need an altar with a white cloth; a wand; a sword; a cup; a platter; and four small drawings of the letter Shin. Make the drawings of the letter on edible rice paper or on a sacrament wafer, using food coloring as ink. Each quarter has a table holding a bowl of burning charcoal in the south, a chalice of wine and a lit candle in the west, a bowl of earth and some seeds or bulbs in the north, and an incense burner and incense in the east.

Facing east, draw the symbol of Shin in the air. "Raphael, bright-faced Son of the Morning, regent of air. Brush away the clouds of night and reveal the sun. Come forth from the unutterable brightness of the Presence of God; I call to thee from beyond the bright realms of the spirit. I invoke thy presence in this place prepared for thee. Come forth, thou healer of the wounded heart. Bless me with thy peace and healing." *Visualize the opening of the eastern doors and the coming of Raphael, the winged aeon, Paralda, and the sylphs. Go to the south.*

"Michael, captain of the warriors of God, raise thy sword in protection that I may rest in peace. Come forth, thou wielder of the sword of the sun. I call to thee from the darkness of despair and pain; I invoke thy presence that the children of the Earth may have hope. Be present in this place prepared for thee and bless me with courage and love." *Visualize the opening of the southern doors and the coming of Michael, the winged lion, Djinn, and the salamanders. Go to the west.*

"Gabriel, bright regent of the element of water, spread thy wings of violet and silver and come forth from the cave of the moon. I call to thee from across the sea of time and space; I invoke thy presence in this place prepared for thee. Come forth, thou messenger of the One Creator, and bless me with thy presence." *Visualize the opening of the western doors and the coming of Gabriel, the eagle, Nixsa, and the undines. Go to the north.*

"Uriel, dark-browed regent of the element of earth, unfold thy star-studded cloak of night and come forth from the realm of Persephone. I call to thee from the depths of my heart and soul; I invoke thy presence in this place prepared for thee. Come forth, thou gardener of the One Creator, and bless me with thy presence." *Visualize the opening of the northern doors and the coming of Uriel, the bull, Ghob, and the gnomes. Return to the east and lift the incense.*

"I bless the element of air and fill it with the power of Shin that its powers of communication may be made even greater. *Take one of the letters and drop it onto the incense. When it has turned to ashes, lift the bowl again and present it to the east.* I offer the combined power of air and fire to the Most High. Let my words be made powerful with love and grace. Let me speak words of comfort to the lonely and give them warmth of heart. Let me share my knowledge with those of like mind that they may know the fire of the spirit that burns within me. Let me pray humbly to the One Creator and let the fire of love burn within me."

Go to the south and lift the bowl of charcoal. "I bless the element of fire and infuse it with the power of itself that its strength may be multiplied. *Take one letter and drop it onto the charcoal. When it has fully burned, offer it to the south.* I offer the doubly empowered fire with fire to the Most High. Let my strength be the strength of many. May I be a protection for the weak. Fill me with courage that I do not shrink from the trials destined for me. I offer my love to the One Creator unconditionally."

Go to the west and lift the chalice. Take one of the letters and light it with the candle. Let the ashes drop into the chalice and drink it down. Present the chalice to the west. "I bless the element of water enriched with the power of the Shin that its power of intuition and clear sight may be made brighter and clearer. Let my inner sight be made clear and true that I may be a pure channel for the Light. Let my powers of empathy be increased that I may be of use to those in need. I offer such powers as I have to the One Creator and dedicate myself to the Light."

Go to the north and take the last letter and bury it in the earth, then plant the bulbs or seeds firmly over it. "I bless the element of earth and revitalize it with the power of the Shin that its powers of growth be multiplied and that it may be healed of the scars inflicted by humanity. I offer it to the Most High. Let my spiritual growth advance, let my physical growth be strong and healthy for my work. Let my powers of patience and self-discipline be increased that I may be of use to the One Creator." *Go to the east and raise your right hand.*

"I salute the east. Protect me, thou Prince of Air, star of the morning, eastern reeve. Healing angel, heed my call. Let your singing breezes send me word. I thank thee, Raphael, bright thane of air, earl of morning, eastern reeve. Angelic healer, give me peace. Keep me safe as the circle fades." *Close quarter and go to the south.*

"I salute the south. Protect me, thou Prince of Fire, the sun's bright warrior, southern reeve. Fierce defender's glowing sword *(trace the circle)*, guard me well. Send me word. I thank thee, Michael, bright thane of fire, the sun's high earl, eastern reeve. Defending angels, arcane power, keep me safe as the circle fades." *Go to the west.*

"I salute the west. Protect me, thou Prince of Water, star of the waning day, western reeve. Herald of the heavenly voice, send me word. I thank thee, Gabriel, bright thane of water, waning day's earl, western reeve. Words of goodness, guiding voice, keep me safe as the circle fades." *Go to the north.*

"Protect me, thou Prince of Earth, giver of dreams, northern reeve, deep earth watcher, guard our souls safe from death. Send me word. I thank thee, Uriel, bright thane of earth, earl of nighttime, northern reeve. The dying light leaves me filled. Keep me safe as the circle fades. Wind and fire, water and earth, quarter lords, leave me not. Holy warriors, through the night keep my peace and guard my dreams. So mote it be."

TAU

I hang suspended above the Earth, impaled,
held fast to thy form by the Vav.
My hands out flung on either side
are clenched against my agony.
Lama a' sabbathani?
The Spear of Adversity pierces my side,
and my blood feeds the earth beneath.
Below me my enemies rejoice in my pain.
Could they but know, they have given me the key
to spiritual freedom, and the glory
to be found in forgiveness.
My mouth crack'd dry with pain yet murmurs,
help me to forgive.
Crucifixion now sets free my soul and I rejoice,
for my pain is the saving of those who revile me.
Slowly I spin at the center of the cosmos
and become One with my God.

Image: Cross
Symbol: ת
Path on the Tree of Life: 32
Numerical Value: 400

Prayer

This is the final prayer, the final test, the last painful realization. It begins with the bitter knowledge of where you are, and of your own part in what has happened to you. Sometimes leniency is not the answer and a few sharp words in the very beginning can mean less trouble later on. Turning the other cheek is not always the only option. The spite and envy of others can be anticipated if we are observant enough and it is dealt with there and then.

But it can be that a particular lesson must be learned at that time and we have to go through it and endure the pain. Like Yeshua, though on a vastly smaller scale, we come to that point when we ask: "Why have you forsaken me, what did I do to deserve this pain?"

Hard though it is to ignore the hurts and betrayals, it can and must be done and the prayer sets out the hardest lesson of all: "Could they but know, they have given me the key to spiritual freedom." If one asks for help it will be given; that I have proven to myself.

What was once seen as a struck Tower becomes an equal-armed cross, not so much a crucifixion as an equalizing of cause and effect that has finally been balanced within. At such a point one becomes the center of that balance and the center of the inner universe at peace with itself. The pressure of the God within becomes equaled by the pressure of the God without.

The Letter

The Tau or Tav is made from a Daleth and a Vav so although its own number is four hundred that of the combined letters is ten. Ten symbolizes the new beginning that emerges from the completion of one through nine. Thus the Ten Commandments constituted a new set of rules to live by and a new beginning for those to whom they were given.

Like the Nun that is the front part of the letter Tzaddi, the Vav here is bent, showing a willingness to obey the rules that have been laid down. Unless we learn to live by certain rules and are willing to accept laws made for the good of all, we cannot expect to make a success of life. There are some who cannot abide law or restrictions of any kind. They are unhappy people who lead unhappy lives and often have unhappy endings.

אמת, Aleph Mem Tau, is the Hebrew word for *truth*. It is spelled with three important letters of the Aleph-Beth, the first letter, the middle letter, and the last letter. Truth is a strange thing: it holds enormous power, it can change everything, but it never changes itself. Truth remains truth forever. It can be covered, it can be hidden, it can be disguised, but underneath it remains the truth. Falsehood is spelled שקר and the great teachers are quick to point out that these letters have no firm support, all ending as they do in a single foot. Rabbi Munk points out that even when a falsehood is at first taken as truth, it has a limited stability, and, like the false prophets, will inevitably fall.

With its foot pushed forward as if taking the weight, the letter Tau looks like a traveler setting out on a long journey, or maybe we could see it as the prodigal son returning home to the father's welcome. We might also, if well versed in symbology, see in this attribute the strange tradition that almost every sacrificed god is lame in one foot, usually unable to put the heel of the left foot on the ground. Those who are interested should read Robert Graves' book *King Jesus* (Farrar Straus & Giroux, 1981). We might also look at the card of the High Priestess with one foot set upon the crescent moon, or think back to the legend that the beautiful and wise Queen of Sheba was said to have a club or deformed foot. Hephasteus, the creative smith god, was flung out of heaven by his mother Hera and fell for three days and three nights to earth, and was lamed in the fall. I was once told a long time ago that it was customary in ancient times to deliberately lame an apprentice smith. It was presumed that they, being essential to a tribe, could not then run away.

When I began work on this book I was assured that the letters of the Aleph-Beth were divine and thus could not be desecrated or harmed. They were incorruptible. By the same token so is the Tau, for it is an integral part of truth. Truth is perfect and totally unique; it always will be.

Path 32 goes from Malkuth to Yesod, from the manifested world to that of the formative astral level, called the Treasure House of Images, wherein is found the machinery of the universe. Its ruler is said to be Saturn or Time, the disciplinarian, the teacher, and the mentor. It is known as the Great One of the Night of Time, but the Greeks called him Chronus. It is a path that can be made of dreams or nightmares, and we create both ourselves.

The Tarot card of the World is given to this path, for the world depends on dreams for its existence. If we could not dream the things we dream, we could not build the things we build. This path marks the first signpost on our way back to the Tau of perfection and truth. When we take our first step on this path we begin the long journey back to Eden.

When we set out, as the Fool, to seek our fortune in the world of manifestation, we do so in a state of naiveté. Each path along the way is signposted by symbols, letters, signs, and portents, and we ignore them at our peril. These paths must be trodden again and again, backwards and forwards, until we have thoroughly learned the lesson each one contains. The letters of the Aleph-Beth, being a living part of the spiritual world at the level of creation, can guide us through the dark times and rejoice with us in the good times.

The Tau cross has only three arms and is the masculine part of the *Crux Ansata* or ankh. There are many forms of the cross and much can be intuited by a study of the various forms. In *Practical Guide to Qabalistic Symbolism,* Gareth Knight writes at length upon this path and I can do no better than to direct your attention to what he says:

"We began with the letter Aleph, the first breath of God before uttering the WORD. It seems to me that that WORD would contain all the letters so that a piece of each one of them would exist in the same moment and with the same power to create, albeit in different ways and with different consequences. It ends with Perfection, Tau. There is nothing more to say concerning it, for it speaks for itself."

Meditations

First Meditation

Imagine yourself spread-eagled on an equal-armed cross, spinning slowly in space. Watch the stars and planets as they move past you in their stately dance around the sun. This meditation gives a sense of the passing of enormous passages of time. Record your thoughts and visions.

Second Meditation

Meditate on standing at the gate of the sphere of Chesed knowing that you have lived your last incarnation on the Earth and you will soon pass beyond the sphere of manifestation. What will you miss about never again having a physical body? What will you miss most about Earth? Make a list. Imagine yourself saying farewell to Earth in the sense of becoming a purely spiritual being.

Third Meditation

Meditate on the word *truth*, then on the concept of truth, and finally on the definition of truth.

Pathworking

As your mind drifts gently into an altered state, you begin to discern a huge gate set into a wall. As the picture becomes clearer you find yourself walking in a city that is just waking up. Dawn light is filtering through the gates of a walled city and you are walking toward the gates. Two sleepy guards wave you through into the countryside beyond.

The road ahead is fairly wide, certainly wide enough for carts and wagons to pass each other. But, as yet, the traffic is light and you are soon beyond the few early travelers and alone on the road. At first you swing along at a good pace, but as the sun rises and the day gets hotter you begin to flag. Your feet hurt and you really need to find water and some shade.

Much more slowly now you climb a hill and see, in the middle distance, a few shade trees. The sight spurs you on. When you get there you find a small and rather muddy stream as well. It is clear enough to drink, however, and cool enough to bathe your aching feet. Feeling better, you lean back against a tree and reflect on the letters.

What you really need is Samech. The support that letter gives would be good to have on this road. You ask yourself if it would be a good idea to call on that letter for help. Almost at once you hear the voice of Samech in your head.

"Life, this is not my path, but my brother letter Tau will be with you soon. It will provide the help you need on this path." You acknowledge the message and wait. A long, low, golden note of sound fills the air. This has never happened before and it startles you. It comes again, nearer, and you feel your body begin to vibrate in response. Then from the center of the sound comes a voice, the same timbre as the note, almost a continuation of it.

"Life, you have asked for help? I am here, make use of me." You turn and see before you an oval shape of deep amethyst edged with silver. It pulsates with sound, lower now and less intense.

"I am Tau. I have come to help you on this, the last part of your journey with us—at least, the last part at this level. There are other, higher levels where I and my companions can teach you even more. Are you ready to go on?"

You rise to your feet, smiling and ready to go forward in the company of the beautiful Tau. You take to the road and notice that the afternoon is drawing to a close and the sun is dipping into the west. The long shadows of early evening appear and the sky turns to a pale turquoise, filled with clouds turned to rose and amber by the setting sun.

The road now becomes steeper and you begin to feel the ache in your muscles. The surface of the road is rougher, no longer smooth but pitted here and there with potholes. The Tau journeys beside you, speaking rarely but always aware of your discomfort. You realize that until you ask for help, Tau will not offer. You are determined to go on unaided for as long as you can.

Your body seems to become heavier and heavier, as if you are carrying a weight far greater than just your own. You bend forward, trying to force yourself to make step after step. You pause and look back, and see your shadow behind you—is it your shadow? It looks different; it looks as if you are carrying something—as if you are hauling a heavy shape . . . a Tau shape.

"Tau, I thought you were going to help me. Why are you adding to my burden?"

"Because that is my power, Life. I am Truth, and truth is always a burden to bear. I change all things, but I am never changed myself. You are carrying with you the truth of your life and your existence to this moment. Soon will come the time when I will carry you, Life; then you will understand a great truth—that because of what you are, a soul who has been awakened by the desire to know in order to serve, you have to carry others of your species who are, as yet, unable to carry their own truth."

"Tau, I don't think I can do this."

"You can, Life, if you let me carry you. But if I do, it will be even more painful than before. But it will only be for a short while."

You look back at the shadow and at the shape of what you carry. A feeling of déjà vu comes over you but you cannot put it into words.

The Tau comes toward you and envelops you in an amethyst cloud. You are lifted up, but instead of comfort an excruciating pain flares through your body. Before your inner eyes images appear and pass before you, some you recognize, others you do not know. Osiris in his white shroud, holding the crook and flail . . . Orpheus with a golden lyre . . . a young man in a rough tunic carrying a bow . . . a tall man wearing a leather apron and carrying a smith's hammer . . . another with a face full of sorrow and bearing the sign of the Tau seared into his forehead. Right at the end, just before the pain becomes too much to bear, you see two forms walking together. One is so brilliant you cannot actually see what or who it is, the other is shorter, olive-skinned and dark-haired with a smiling mouth and gentle eyes. His hands and feet are both badly scarred. The voice of the Tau is soft with tears.

"Ah, Life, this is truth. That those who are aware are also those who must suffer the burdens of those who still sleep. These are the sacrificed ones who bore the weight of truth for you. Osiris and Orpheus, Tammuz and Adonis, Hephasteus and Cain, and many others; but remember what happened in the garden, Life. Remember who was willing to be separated from his kind in order to become the derided one, the outcast, so humanity would have the priceless gift of choice. He who once wore an emerald crown walks with the last of the sacrificed ones.

"Rest now, Life, rest and sleep, your last trial is over. You have accepted me, for I am Truth. You are the prodigal child who is now on the road back home. I have many forms, Life, the Tau cross is just one of them."

You are surrounded with golden sound, filled with love, and clothed in a myriad of colors. The Aleph-Beth, complete now, fill your ears with their song of joy. They are all around you, a part of you, as you will be forever a part of them. They bear you upward into a sky full of stars and into sleep, to wake in your own time.

The Disciplines

In the church-quiet hours of the morning I arise

before the wild sweet clarion of the lark

and tune my restless, seeking soul

toward the Light, away from doubt and dark.

Toward that inmost shrine wherein I dwell

safe, hidden from the jeering eyes of men

to draw on hidden stores of faith

to stay me 'ere the night shall come again.

When noon's bright sun above me hangs God high,

and blesses all the earth with warmth and light,

I stand with hands uplifted, praising Him,

a quiet pool of thought amid days' strife.

A space of time eternal seconds long,

when angels bow their heads and fold their hands,

and I, unnoticed, join the silent throng.

When day has gone and night, cat-footed, stalks the moon,

alone I learn the lessons of the day.

Was all my work the best that I could do?

Have I incurred a debt that I must pay?

As sleep sets free a prisoner long held,

and joyously my soul takes upward flight,

I seem to burst the barriers of earth,

and leap from bondage to another Light.

—©1974, Dolores Ashcroft-Nowicki

Ritual

This is the only ritual that requires help from a friend, and then it is merely to act as a guardian and timekeeper. Set your altar with a plain white cloth and a center light in a blue bowl. This is your contact light. In the east, place a thurible with a mixture of frankincense and myrrh on hot charcoal. In the south, place a red candle, lit. In the west, place a chalice of wine and water, mixed. In the north, place a bowl of seeds. Have a small pillow at hand. By the door, place a chair for your helper and provide him or her with a bell. The bell should have a silvery sound, not harsh or strident.

The ritual should be done in the evening and after a day of fasting, with just water or tea to drink. Bathe thoroughly and put on a fresh robe, preferably black or white, though any dark color will do. Your feet are bare. Outside the temple room place a tray with a flask of hot tea or milk (not coffee) and something substantial to eat—sandwiches, fruit, and a small piece of chocolate for energy. Throughout the day, keep turning your mind toward the image of the Tau. Spend the day quietly; do not allow yourself to become excited, angry, or anxious.

When you feel ready, enter with your helper and take your place in the east, standing before the altar. Take up the thurible and circle deosil around the altar. Replace the thurible and step back, raising your arms upward. Speak:

"With perfumed air I open the gate of the east and call upon Raphael, the healing hand of God, to support me in my endeavor to raise my soul to the spiritual realm of Atziluth (pronounced *at-zee-loot*). I invoke the elemental king of air, Paralda, that I may speak with the Holy Ones and know their wisdom. Grant me understanding that I may fulfill my task on Earth."

Move to the south and, with the lit candle, circle the altar. Replace the candle and step back, raising your arms upward.

"With flame I open the gate of the south and call upon Michael, the warrior of God, to support me in my endeavor to raise my soul to the spiritual realm of Atziluth. I invoke the elemental king of fire, Djinn, that I may display the courage of those guardians of the Light who have gone before me. Grant me strength that I may fulfill my task on Earth."

Move to the west and, with the chalice, circle the altar, sprinkling wine and water. Replace the chalice and step back, raising your arms upward.

"With wine and water I open the gate of the west and call upon Gabriel, the messenger of God, to support me in my endeavor to raise my soul to the spiritual realm of Atziluth. I invoke the elemental king of water, Nixsa. Show me how to make contact with the inner realms and gain entry to the hidden temples of the mind. Grant me intuition that I may fulfill my task on Earth."

Move to the north and, with the bowl of seeds, circle the altar, scattering them. Replace the bowl and step back, raising your arms upward.

"With deeds I open the gate of the west and call upon Uriel, the peacemaker of God, to support me in my endeavor to raise my soul to the spiritual realm of Atziluth. I invoke the elemental king of earth, Ghob. Grant me compassion that I may make contact with all forms of life and be a true initiator of the younger brethren. Grant me the power of love that I may fulfill my task on Earth."

Move to the east and for five minutes contemplate a mental image of Raphael as the healer facing you with arms outstretched to the side in the form of the Tau. (The bell sounds at the end of the five minutes.) Change the image to one of Paralda in the same stance and hear with the inner ear the word Ehehieh (eh-heh-ee-yeh). When the bell sounds at the end of five minutes, take up the same stance in the form of the Tau and maintain it for five minutes or as long as you can, contemplating the discomfort of the position. When the bell sounds again, lie facedown, head to the altar, with your arms outstretched, using the pillow to protect your face. Contemplate the meaning of the Tau and the loneliness of the willing sacrifice for five minutes.

When the bell sounds again, move to the south and for five minutes contemplate a mental image of Michael as the warrior facing you with arms outstretched to the side in the form of the Tau. (The bell sounds at the end of the five minutes.) Change the image to one of Djinn in the same stance and hear with the inner ear the words Elohim Gibor (el-o-him geeb-or). When the bell sounds after five minutes, take up the same stance in the form of the Tau and maintain it for five minutes or as long as you can, contemplating the discomfort of the position. When the bell sounds again, lie facedown, head to the altar, with your arms outstretched, using the pillow to protect your face. Contemplate the meaning of the Tau and the courage of the willing sacrifice.

When the bell sounds after five minutes, move to the west and for five minutes contemplate a mental image of Gabriel as the messenger facing you with arms outstretched to the side in the form of the Tau. When the bell sounds at the end of the five minutes, change the image to one of Nixsa in the same stance and hear with the inner ear the word Shaddai el chai (shad-i el high). When the bell sounds again, take up the same stance in the form of the Tau and maintain it for five minutes or as long as you can, contemplating the discomfort of the position. When the bell sounds again, lie facedown, head to the altar, with your arms outstretched, using the pillow to protect your face. Contemplate the meaning of the Tau and the dedication of the willing sacrifice.

When the bell sounds, move to the north and for five minutes contemplate a mental image of Uriel as the peacemaker facing you with arms outstretched to the side in the form of the Tau. When the bell sounds at the end of the five minutes, change the image to one of Ghob ("Gob" as in go) in the same stance and hear with the inner ear the word Adonai (Ad-don-eye). When the bell sounds again, take up the same stance in the form of the Tau and maintain it for five minutes or as long as you can, contemplating the discomfort of the position. When the bell sounds again, lie facedown, head to the altar, with your arms outstretched, using the pillow to protect your face. Contemplate the meaning of the Tau and the endurance of the willing sacrifice.

When the bell sounds for the last time, stand and walk to the east.

"I give thanks for the understanding I have gained, for the guidance of Raphael and the inspiration of Paralda. I now understand a little more of the inner meaning of this letter and the loneliness of those who undertake the task of guarding the Light. Let the gate of the east be closed; there is a blessing on all who serve."

Pass to the south. "I give thanks for the courage I have now found within me, for the guidance of Michael and the strength of Djinn. I feel I now have the will to walk the path of Light and I have seen the courage of those who fully accept the will of God. Let the gate of the south be closed; there is a blessing on all who serve."

Pass to the west. "I give thanks for the ability to see beyond the veil, for the guidance of Gabriel and the generosity of Nixsa. I have gained new knowledge of the inner worlds and will strive to use it in the right way. I hope I can match the dedication of those who have gone before me. Let the gate of the west be closed; there is a blessing on all who serve."

Pass to the north. "I give thanks for the health and strength within me, for the guidance of Uriel and the loving-kindness of Ghob. I have touched the soul of the world and now understand my place in the wholeness of things. I will strive to be worthy of what has been given to me. Let the gate of the north be closed; there is a blessing on all who serve."

Douse all lights and depart.

Aleph-Beth Pathworking

Before you begin this working, spend an hour or two designing a lamen (pendant). It must be of gold on a gold chain. Draw your design with care and make the engraving or symbol in the center as beautiful and as meaningful as you can. When you have designed it, sit and create it in astral matter and then duplicate it twenty-two times. On the back of each lamen put one of the letters. I ask you to create them well for they are to be your gifts to the letters of the Aleph-Beth, a token of the bond between you. In the coming days, months, and years, you will forget some of what you have learned, but the bond will always be there. Remember what one letter told you: "We do not have your concept of time, so we do not wait; we exist in the moment."

So no matter how much time flows between you, when you need them, they will be there. It will be as if you have never parted. When you are ready, we will begin.

Put flowers around you, use your favorite incense, have a picture or statue of your deity close by. Remember what you have learned, the One Creator is the foundation of all gods of Light. He is just wearing a different face and answering to a different name.

Sit quietly and establish a slow breathing pattern. Close your eyes and begin to feel your body lighten in weight. Aim for a floating-on-air feeling. As your altered state gets deeper, let go of the earth level and rise up to the Light.

Before you is a building of white marble veined with gold that glows in the light of a spectacular sunset. Clouds of songbirds fill the air with their music and the path before you is lined with beings from the upper levels; the path itself is scattered with flowers and fragrant herbs. You look down at yourself and find you are dressed in a shabby and badly stained robe, torn at the hem. Your feet are bare, callused, and dirty, yet it seems as if you are expected and you are urged along the path to the entrance of the building. The sound of voices cheering is augmented by the notes of an organ deep inside the building.

You come to the entrance, and the doors open. There is someone there to guide you to a room where you find a sunken bath, oils, towels, and fresh, clean clothing. You bathe.

When you have bathed, put on your deep-blue robe and matching slippers. The helper offers you a small glass of wine, then conducts you back to the main hall, where you are asked to stand before two magnificent bronze doors. They begin to open.

Before you is a great hall with walls that tower upward to a ceiling far above. They seem to be made of pastel-colored lights that change continuously. Music, soft and sweet, can be heard just on the threshold of hearing and a light, fragrant incense adds to the ambience. But all this pales into insignificance when you look ahead. Twenty-two high-backed and elaborately carved chairs set upon a flight of seven marble stairs line the way to a golden throne. There are eleven chairs on either side and before each one is a kneeling stool of red velvet on which is embroidered one of the letters you now know so well.

In each chair sits a presence of power and majesty: the letters of the Aleph-Beth. Row upon row of seats fill the hall, rising up until the highest can hardly be seen. All are filled with inhabitants of the higher realms. You are overwhelmed by what is before you, and you look behind you to see if some important person is due to arrive. But there is only the person who helped you bathe and change and four others dressed in white who are carrying on trays of sandalwood the lamens and chains you designed.

A ripple of sound and movement runs through the hall. The atmosphere changes and all eyes look to the throne. It is now occupied by something that is hard to look at; it changes form, color, levels of power and light continuously. Gradually it settles into a stable pattern and a being that appears to be multilayered sits there. It radiates a power that is just bearable for you. Everyone in the hall rises, turns to the throne, and bows. Whatever or whoever it is acknowledges the greeting. You bow, or rather kneel, for your legs are disconcertingly weak. A voice—deep, resonant, powerful—fills the hall.

"Greetings, child of Earth, welcome to the hall of the Aleph-Beth. I am Metatron and once I too was a child of Earth, then my name was Henoch. But I was called by the Most High and obeyed. Do you know why you have been summoned?"

You manage to find your voice. "Not exactly, but I hope I have done nothing wrong."

Soft silvery laughter ripples through the hall, and Aleph stands up, brilliant and shining. Love spills out of its aura like sunlight.

"No, Life, you have done nothing wrong. You have completed the tasks you took on and we have called you here to honor you. Come and kneel before me."

You walk to the first chair on the right and kneel before the Aleph. You look up into the Light above you and see a miniature Aleph א descending toward you. It gleams gold in the light of the Aleph's countenance, then there is a sharp stab of pain as the miniature letter sinks into your head. Aleph soothes the spot and you feel the pressure of its hand upon you.

"Life, be blessed in the possession of the power of Aleph, use it well." You are lifted and directed across to the chair of Beth, who rises to greet you as you kneel. The Beth ב is placed in your head beside the other letter.

"Life, be blessed in the possession of the power of Beth, use it well," again the pressure on the head. You rise and cross to Gimel and kneel before it to receive the miniature Gimel ג and the blessing.

"Life, be blessed in the possession of the power of Gimel, use it well."

And so it goes on, each letter placing a miniature of itself into your head center and blessing you with its power. As you receive the last letter, the hall erupts with shouts of joy. You stand before the steps leading to the throne of Metatron, who rises and descends to you. You kneel before this servant of the Lord and feel the gentle pressure of hands on your shoulders.

"You have done well, child of Earth, you have shown love, patience, and courage in this task. Now the Aleph-Beth lives within you and will be there to lend their substance and their powers. Be careful how you use them in words, thoughts, and deeds."

You answer: "Metatron, servant of the Most High, I have brought gifts for the letters. May I give them now?" The Brightness shows surprise, racing through many changes of color, then speaks with a gentle laugh. "Yes, you may give them now."

You bow and turn to the double row of letters; your heart is full to overflowing. "I have met and touched each one of you, mind to mind and heart to heart;

you have been and will always be my dear friends and companions. You have made me aware of the power of words in a way that I never knew existed. I will try to use them as you have taught me, though I know that, being human, it will be difficult and I will sometimes fail, but I will keep on trying. You have honored me with the gift of yourselves in miniature and now I would honor you. These lamens are created by my thoughts and represent my love, my respect, and my reverence for you all. Please accept them as they are given, with love." You pass down the lines and offer a lamen to each letter; they are put on and they gleam against the light body of the letter. Each bows as they receive their gift.

Then the letters come forward and stand in a semicircle before the throne, drawing you into their midst. Metatron descends, holding in his hands a chalice of wine. He offers it to each one in turn. The wine tastes sweet, then warm and mellow, and lastly, fiery. It fills you with new energy. When all have drunk, the audience bursts into a paean of triumph and the letters circle you and begin to dance. Round and round they go, their voices blending with the others. You stand and watch as the letters grow more and more brilliant until you cannot see them. You close your eyes against the light and when you open them again you are back in your own world, a little bemused, a little lonely, a little sad, but also filled with strength and new knowledge.

Aleph-Beth Ritual

Place your altar with a white cloth in the center of the temple and cover it with flowers. In the center put a bowl containing the altar light and a chalice of wine, plus a bowl with twenty-two polished stones of any kind in it. Use the semiprecious stones you find in shops selling occult ephemera, or craft shops, and put this on the altar. Lastly, prepare a basket of flower petals. This is a simple ritual, but it symbolizes the circling of the stars, galaxies, and planets around the central sun of the universe, that sun being the Creator. When you reach this point in the work of the Mysteries you will find rituals and workings become more simple, less involved, and less full of pomp. The closer one gets to the God within or without, the more simple life becomes. Enter your temple, seal the door, and at the altar pick up the basket of petals and go to the east. Draw a pentagram and throw a handful of petals through it.

"In the name of Adonai, I open the east. Be welcome, Raphael and all the elements of air." *Move to the south, make a pentagram, and throw some flower petals through it.*

"In the name of Adonai, I open the south. Be welcome, Michael and all the elements of fire." *Go to the west, draw a pentagram, and throw some petals through it.*

"In the name of Adonai, I open the west. Be welcome, Gabriel and all the elements of water." *Go to the north, make a pentagram, and throw some petals through it.*

"In the name of Adonai, I open the north. Be welcome, Uriel and all the elements of earth." *Take the bowl of stones and place the stones in a circle around the altar, naming them as you go.*

"Aleph, the ox, the first letter and, like Adonai, a unity.

"Beth, the house, the second letter, the one that opens the Torah.

"Gimel, the camel, the third letter, the giver of kindness and help.

"Daleth, the door, the fourth letter, the humble door that is open to the stranger.

"Heh, the window, the fifth letter, through which comes illumination and knowledge.

"Vav, the nail, the sixth letter, joining things together and making them stronger.

"Zayin, the sword, the seventh letter, a defender and an avenger of the weak.

"Cheth, the fence, the eighth letter, enclosing sacred space.

"Teth, the serpent, and the ninth letter. Do not judge by appearances, give to charity.

"Yod, the hand, the tenth letter, the smallest letter but big in spirit.

"Kaph, the palm of the hand, the eleventh letter, the open hand of friendship.

"Lamed, the ox goad, the twelfth letter, who watches over us from on high.

"Mem, water, the thirteenth letter. The great ocean from which all life emerges.

"Nun, the fish, the fourteenth letter. The faithful who live and are supported by the ocean.

"Samech, the staff, the fifteenth letter, the support we all need from time to time.

"Ayin, the eye, the sixteenth letter. Look for the good in all things.

"Peh, the mouth, the seventeenth letter. Praise God every day for what is given to you.

"Tzaddi, the fish hook, the eighteenth letter. The righteous who looks up to heaven.

"Qoph, the back of the head, the nineteenth letter, the giver of blessings.

"Resh, the head, the twentieth letter. The repentant achieves forgiveness.

"Shin, the tooth, the twenty-first letter. Discrimination between good and evil.

"Tau, the cross, the twenty-second letter. Achievement of goals."

Scatter the rest of the petals over the stones and bless them.

"Holy Ones, I stand before you as one who has completed a long journey full of delights and fears, joys and sorrows, discoveries and realizations. You have opened my eyes to a new way of thinking, seeing, and behaving. I am just one part of Life, what have I to offer in thanks? Only myself, my knowledge of you as beings of power and love, and my hope that in some way I can make you visible to others in the way I speak, write, and in my actions. I offer to you now a plan for the future, a future I pray will include your presence in my life.

"I will aspire in my intents.

"I will bless those who share my life every day.

"I will give to those who are in need, secretly.

"I will deal fairly with others in my home and in the world.

"I will help where I can and as much as I can.

"I will value my friends and my family.

"I will choose my words carefully for I now understand their power.

"I will test myself often to make sure I keep improving.

"I will yield up vanity and self-deception.

"I will keep faith with the Creator to the best of my ability.

"I will learn something new each day.

"I will maintain my self-respect and self-discipline.

"I will nourish my faith each day with a prayer.

"I will speak with understanding and use the Aleph-Beth with love.

"I will ask that I may receive.

"I will persevere in my work.

"I will zealously pursue my obligations in life.

"I will question my motives more closely.

"I will remember to give thanks for all that I receive.

"I will share what I have with those who have not.

"I will teach what I learn to others and be happy to be of use.

"This is my offering. May we all be blessed by the One Creator."

Start the music and either dance or walk in a spiral pattern in and out of the stones. Make several circles of this. All the time chant the names of the letters, their numbers and symbols, values and definitions. The sound of their names is actually a call sign for the Aleph-Beth. They are sounds, intelligent sounds, sentient vibrations. Vibrations are the basic building matter of the universe. After some ten minutes, stop, bless the quarters and dismiss. Unseal the door and leave.

318

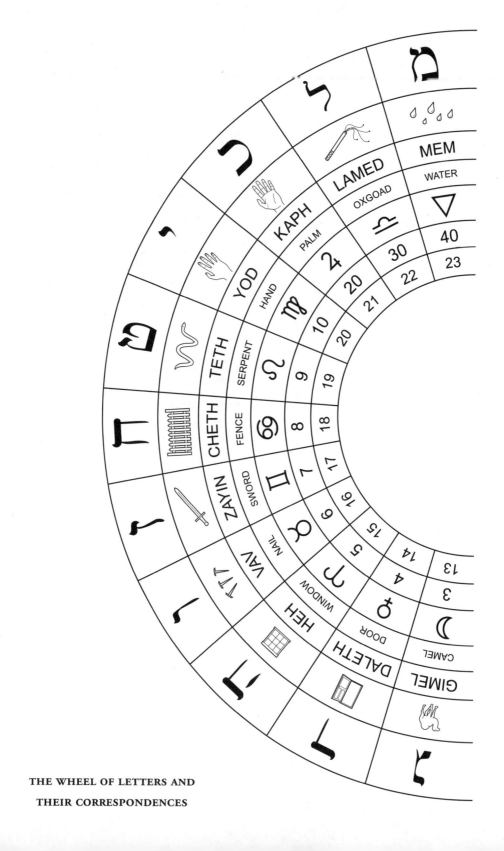

THE WHEEL OF LETTERS AND

THEIR CORRESPONDENCES

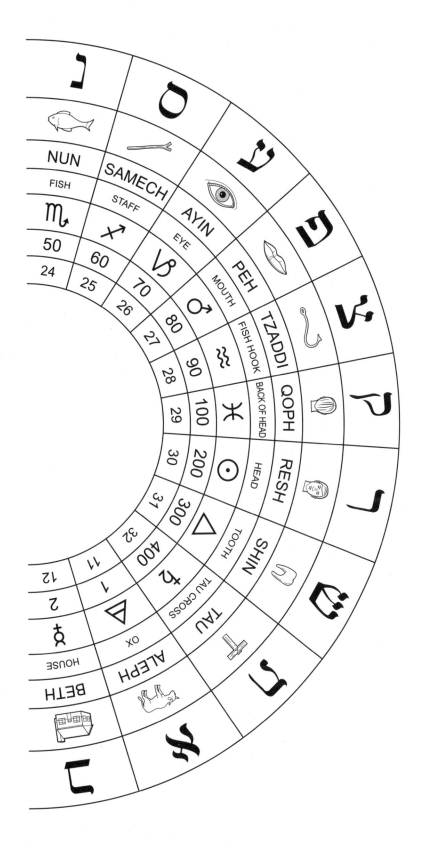

Epilogue

This has been a wonderful book to write. Demanding, time consuming, at times difficult and painful, but wonderful. It has been a healing task for me and I hope that it will strike a chord with others who read it.

We all have times when we feel at odds with the world and very much alone. I certainly did, but I found a way through the darkness and, having done so, felt it was important to share it with others. Perhaps the most important realization I have made during this time is this: "We are stronger than we know; we can win through self-doubt and loss of confidence so long as we keep within the Light."

I have been blessed in having friends and advisors in the Jewish faith who have helped, advised, and encouraged me, for my main concern throughout has been not to give offense. I hope my love and respect for the Aleph-Beth has been made apparent, for the letters themselves have been my teachers.

Toward the end of the book, as time ran short, my deadline had already come and gone and I was putting in a fourteen-hour-day and hardly noticing the fact. Thank you, Llewellyn, Carl Weschcke, and Nancy Mostad, for being so understanding.

May the blessing of the Creator,

He of the many names and forms,

be with us all as we move

into the Age of Aquarius.

Paths on the Tree of Life

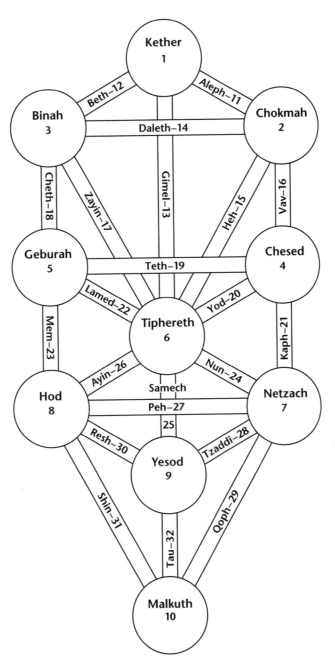

Note: See Dion Fortune's *The Mystical Qabbalah*, Israel Regardie's *Art of True Healing*, and Gareth Knight's *Practical Guide to Qabbalistic Symbolism* for more on the Spheres.

Tarot Cards on the Tree of Life

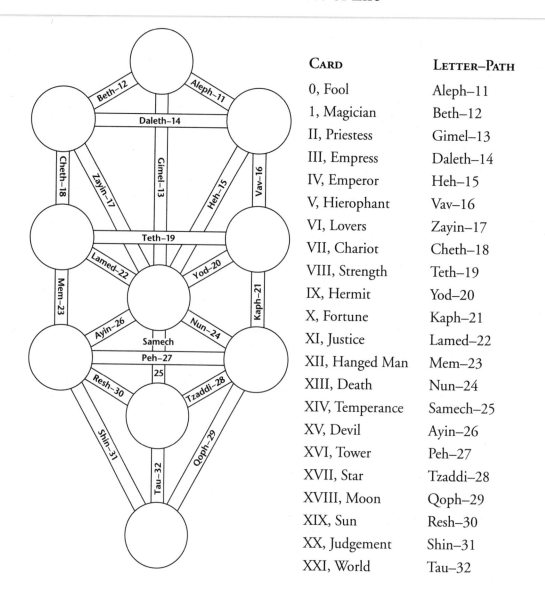

CARD	LETTER–PATH
0, Fool	Aleph–11
1, Magician	Beth–12
II, Priestess	Gimel–13
III, Empress	Daleth–14
IV, Emperor	Heh–15
V, Hierophant	Vav–16
VI, Lovers	Zayin–17
VII, Chariot	Cheth–18
VIII, Strength	Teth–19
IX, Hermit	Yod–20
X, Fortune	Kaph–21
XI, Justice	Lamed–22
XII, Hanged Man	Mem–23
XIII, Death	Nun–24
XIV, Temperance	Samech–25
XV, Devil	Ayin–26
XVI, Tower	Peh–27
XVII, Star	Tzaddi–28
XVIII, Moon	Qoph–29
XIX, Sun	Resh–30
XX, Judgement	Shin–31
XXI, World	Tau–32

The Work of Wisdom and Understanding

BY SALOMO BAAL-SHEM

The power of the Hebrew letters has often been used for magical purposes. In the following ritual the letters are consumed by the practitioner of the ritual in order to absorb the power of the magical names. The intention of this ritual is to become wise and understanding in order to be able to study all kinds of religious or mystical texts and understand their deeper and sometimes hidden meaning and not forget the text or its interpretation. This ritual will be very helpful in your work, not only with traditional religious texts but with all kinds of Cabbalistic writings, including this book.

The ritual should be done on Atzeret, which is the sixth day of the month called Sivan, when the Shavuot festival is celebrated. Sivan corresponds with the time of the astrological sign Gemini, but since the Jewish calendar is based on the moon it will always begin on the day of the new moon. (For the exact day, look into a Jewish calendar or ask your local Jewish community.) Thus this ritual is performed during the waxing moon, which is helpful to increase your wisdom. Gemini is connected with studies and learning. Tradition teaches that Moses received the Torah on Shavuot and therefore this is the time when you can increase your ability to understand the scriptures.

The original manuscript for this was written in the late fourteenth or early fifteenth century. It was in a very corrupt state and I had to put the pieces together in order to turn them into a ritual that will work. The original does not include an opening. I have added this small opening to increase the power of the ritual. (There are some passages that could be interpreted in such a way as to suggest the ritual was to be done on more than one day. But I have decided to write it down in such a way that it can be performed on one single day, since this is easier and there is no need to make things unnecessarily complicated. The preparation will be hard enough.)

To perform this ritual you will need a fig leaf, three olive leaves, a silver cup, red wine, and the egg of a hen. Fig and olive trees can be found in a good market garden. You may be able to get a few leaves without having to buy the whole tree. To write the letters I advise you to use food coloring used for cakes, rather than ink, for it is often based on sugar and will easily dissolve in wine—and it will taste much better.

The Holy Names

Some of the names used in this ritual are permutations of traditional Names of God. For example: MAPATZ (Mem Peh Tzaddi מפץ = Yod Vav Heh יוה). This method of permutation is called "at-bash" because Aleph will turn into Tau and Beth into Shin, etc. For better understanding, look at the list below:

א ב ג ד ה ו ז ח ט י כ ל מ נ ס ע פ צ ק ר ש ת

ת ש ר ק צ פ ע ס נ מ ל כ י ט ח ז ו ה ד ג ב א

Preparation

To prepare for this ritual, fast from the new moon of Sivan until the sixth day of Sivan, when the ritual is performed. (This does not mean you may not eat at all, but not before sunset.) During this time purify yourself every morning, every evening, before you bake your bread or prepare your meal, and after baking and before eating. After eating it is not needed. (Isn't that nice?) Before you eat you should drink some wine and before drinking the wine you should purify yourself. Before drinking the wine count nine times. The manuscript does not say clearly what to count, but it seems to be the first invocation: In the Name of YAH YAH YAH, YAHU YAHU YAHU, YAHEY YAHEY YAHEY, HEY HEY HEY, HU HU HU, AHU AHU AHU, EHEYEH EHEYEH EHEYEH, BARUCH BARUCH BARUCH, QADOSH QADOSH QADOSH, SHADDAY SHAD-DAY SHADDAY, YAHUTZ YAHUTZ YAHUTZ, PATZ PATZ PATZ, RACHUM RACHUM RACHUM, CHANUN CHANUN CHANUN. His Name is elaborated in forty-two letters. He who performs it is wise and filled with wisdom. "This is my Name forever, this is my remembrance from generation to generation." (Exodus 3:15) AMEN AMEN SELAH. The manuscript says immerse in a river in order to purify yourself, but a short shower in the morning and in the evening (and maybe another one before eating) will purify you as well. I advise you to have a bath before the ritual itself. This will be enough, since most readers will neither have access to a Jewish ritual bath nor to a river. Sexual abstinence is not needed (God thanks!) and intercourse seems even to be encouraged; as the manuscript says, *He should not sleep alone, so he will not be harmed!*

The Opening

Before me is SANDALPHON,

Behind me is MICHAEL,

On my right is METATRON,

On my left is AGAMTAYA,

And YAHOEL is above my head.

The Intention

This is the work of Wisdom (Chokmah) and Understanding (Binah),

all who practice it become wise and understanding.

In the Name of

YAH YAH YAH

YAHU YAHU YAHU

YAHEY YAHEY YAHEY

HEY HEY HEY

HU HU HU

AHU AHU AHU

EHEYEH EHEYEH EHEYEH

BARUCH BARUCH BARUCH

QADOSH QADOSH QADOSH

SHADDAY SHADDAY SHADDAY
YAHUTZ YAHUTZ YAHUTZ
PATZ PATZ PATZ
RACHUM RACHUM RACHUM
CHANUN CHANUN CHANUN

His Name is elaborated in forty-two letters.
He, who performs it is wise and filled with wisdom.
"This is my Name forever, this is my remembrance
from generation to generation." (Exodus 3:15)

AMEN AMEN SELAH

The Fig Leaf

I invoke thee, SANDALPHON,
the angel who ties a crown for his Master,
to go up and say to Him:
"Two angels, Metatron and Agamtaya,
may they give wisdom in the heart of (magical name)."
And may he (she) know and may he (she) be wise and understanding
and study and not forget and learn and not neglect,
what comes before him (her) and what comes after him (her).
In the name of בשוס
PATZ MAPATZ MAPATZ פץ מפץ מפץ
TZEAH TZEYEAH SHAQ BAQAQ צאה ציאה שק בקק
AH YAH אה יה
WE-AZAMER ואזמר
KEGON HU GAMAR כגון הוא גמר
KEGON AKRACHEY-NIYAH כגון אכרכיניה

In the name of בשום
AH VE-AH BE-AH אה ואה באה
YAHU YAHU YUHA יהו יהו יוה
YA-EH HE-AY יאה האי
from now and forever. מעתה ועד עולם

Write these divine names on the fig leaf, erase them in wine, and eat the fig leaf and drink from the wine.

Olive Leaf

ME-SUMSANAN BE-MUSAMA KE-MUQAMA
AIYN SAMAIN GE-AH QAMEA
AGIFIEL MESAFO
YAH WE-AY YE

These are the princes who split the firmament
and gave the Torah to Moses by the power of
YAHU YAHU WE-HEH
יהו יהו והה

I invoke thee, in the name of the great dwellers,
to keep the Torah in my heart.

Write the holy names on three olive leaves, erase them in wine, and drink.

Silver Cup

I invoke thee, MICHAEL,
great Prince of Israel,
give me the study of the teachings in my heart.
AMEN AMEN SELAH

Write the Name "Michael" inside the silver cup, erase it in wine, and drink.

MICHAEL מיכאל

Say the following prayer twenty-four times. To count you may use a meditation cord with twenty-four beads or with a mark after twenty-four beads. The prayer belongs to the "Shmoneh Essreh," which consists of eighteen benedictions. Try to give the words a melody, almost like singing. Jewish readers will know what I mean, and non-Jewish readers may get some inspiration from traditional Yiddish music or they might even find Jewish prayers on CDs. Try to use the melody in order to get into an almost trance-like rhythm. It does not have to be loud. Look at this as a Western equivalent of a mantra-meditation.

Shema qolenu,

(Hear our voice)

IHVH *(speak: Adonai)* ELOHEYNU,

(IHVH our God)

chus we-rachem aleynu

(spare us and have mercy upon us)

we-qabel berachamim u-we-ratzon et tefilatenu,

(and accept our prayer with mercy and with goodwill)

ki EL shomea tefilot we-tachanunim Atah.

(for Thou art God, who hears prayers and petitions)

U-milfanecha MALKENU reqam al teshiwenu.

(and do not reject us, our King empty from thy Face.)

After you have said the prayer twenty-four times, end with the following words:

Ki Atah shomea tefilat amcha Yisrael be-rachamim.

(For Thou hear the prayer of thy Folk of Israel with mercy.)

Baruch Atah IHVH *(speak: Adonai)*, shomea tefilah.

(Blessed art Thou IHVH, who hears prayers.)

Wine

Say this forty-one times over the wine. To count you can use the same meditation cord you were using before, if you add another mark after forty-one beads. Again get into a melody as described above. Feel the vibration of the sound filling the wine.

Cast into me Scriptures, Mishnah and Talmud, and enlighten my heart with words of the Torah, and let me not stumble with my tongue in all I learn.

Be-Shem YAHOEL VE-EL,

(In the name of Yahoel ve-El)

U-be-Shem HA-EL HA-GADOL,

(and in the name of the great God)

YAH YAHU YAH YAH ELI EL,

(Yah Yahu Yah Yah, my God, God)

U-be-Shem HA-EL HA-GADOL

(and in the name of the great God)

YAH YAHU YAH YAH

(Yah Yahu Yah Yah)

EL HA-ELOHIM,

(God of the Gods)

SHEM HA-MEFORASH VE-HA-NICHBAD

(the unspeakable and honored name)

AMEN AMEN SELAH.

(Amen Amen Selah.)

After you have said it forty-one times, drink the wine.

The Egg

לאיגנסם בפסה פר אנה

LE-IGNESAM BEPASAH PAR ANAH
the great Sar ha-Torah, Prince of the Law,
who was with Moses at Mount Sinai and crowned him with a wreath,
all that he learned and all that his ears heard.
So may thou crown, and come to me,
and remove the stone from my heart,
speedily, and do not delay.

AMEN AMEN SELAH

Write the magical name on a roasted and peeled egg. Eat the egg.

The Closing

I have invoked all ye Angels that have assisted me in this ritual
I bless ye and release ye.
Depart in peace,
and go peacefully to your abodes,
and do not harm me.

The rite is ended.

Fast for the rest of the day, and do not drink. The instructions say further: ". . . and sit in a box." If you wish to do so, get a big box used for moving. Spend the rest of the day in meditation.

Further Reading

Ashcroft-Nowicki, D. *The Shining Paths*, 2nd ed. (Thoth Publications, 1997).

Caravella, M. B. *The Holy Name* (Radha Soami Satsang Beas, 1988).

Forms of Prayer for Jewish Worship, 7th ed. (The Reform Synagogue of Great Britain, Spernberg Centre for Judaism, 1977).

Fortune, Dion. *The Mystical Qabbalah* (Williams and Norgate, 1935).

Franck, A. *The Kabbalah* (University Books, 1967).

Ginburg, L. *On Jewish Lore and Law* (Athenaeum, 1970).

Ginsburg, C. D. *The Kabbalah and Its Doctrines* (Routledge, 1970).

Halevi, Shimon Ben. *The School of Kabbalah* (Rider, 1986).

———. *Adam and the Kabbalistic Tree* (Gateway Books, 1990).

———. *The Tree of Life* (Rider, 1982).

———. *The World of the Kabbalist* (Gateway Books, 1984).

Knight, G. *Practical Guide to Qabbalistic Symbolism* (Helios, 1969).

Levertoff, P., trans. *The Zohar* (Bennett, 1959).

Luzzatto, Rabbi M. *General Principles of Kabbalah* (Research Center, 1970).

Munk, Rabbi M. *The Wisdom in the Hebrew Alphabet* (Mesorah Ltd., 1983).

Parfitt, W. *The Living Qabbalah* (Element, 1988).

Saunders, Dale. *Mudra: Study of Symbolic Gestures* (Bollingen/Princeton, 1985).

Scholem, G. *On the Qabbalah & Its Symbolism* (Shocken, 1965).

Seiger, I., ed. *Jewish Encyclopedia* (12 vols.) (KTAV, 1964).

Suarez, C. *The Qabbalah Triology* (Shambhala, 1985).

Waite, A. E. *The Holy Kabbalah* (University Press, 1965).

Index

Aaron, 9
Abraham, 9, 21, 39, 61, 86, 104, 145, 220, 235, 248
Abulafia, Abram, 48
Adam, 9, 74–75, 86–87, 96, 119–120, 200, 229, 249, 262
Adonai, 9, 239–240, 313–314, 328–329
after-image, 12
Aleph, 1–13, 18–19, 23, 36–37, 61, 65, 75, 103, 132, 172, 191, 193, 197, 208, 213, 266, 290, 302–303, 312, 314, 324
Aleph-Beth, xiii–xx, 11, 63, 93, 147, 150, 158–159, 163, 167, 176, 193, 197–199, 204, 206, 208, 221, 230, 249, 267–268, 295, 302–303, 310–313, 315–316, 320
Amalekites, 290
Anubis, 159, 236
Archangel, 3, 18, 55, 102, 150, 200, 255, 267, 269
Arizal, 100
Ark of the Covenant, 97, 199
"as above, so below", 5, 73–74, 173
Asclepius, 119
Ashim, 23
Atum, 130–131
Ayin, 209, 211–226, 233, 314

Baal Shem Tov, 144
Baruch, 23–24, 324–325, 329
Berachah, 19
Beth, 15–27, 36, 60, 65, 144, 208, 230, 266, 276, 312, 314, 324

Binah, xiv, 19, 32–33, 36, 46–47, 49, 89, 93, 102–103, 127, 133, 172–173, 186, 215, 219, 231, 263, 321, 325
Black Isis, 217
Black Pillar, 5, 187
Blackwood, A., 264
Blessing, 10, 13, 18, 27, 40, 65–66, 68–70, 74, 96, 106, 136, 140–141, 144–147, 150–153, 163, 167, 176, 193, 208, 238, 243, 248, 253, 257, 262, 286–287, 293, 312, 315, 320
Boaz, 86
breathing pattern, 4-2-4-2, 35
Brennan, J. H., 22, 201
Bruno, Giordano, 235, 294
Butler, W. E., xi, 59, 74

Cabbalistic, 323
Calvary cross, 6, 89
camel, 31–33, 35–37, 208, 314
Cancer, 108
Castor, 86
Cerridwen, 277
Chaldean, 220
Chasmal, 47
Chayah, 60
Chesed, 46, 117, 131, 146, 172, 186, 214, 230, 304, 321
Cheth, 97–111, 208, 314
Chokmah, 7, 33, 47, 49, 63, 89, 93, 127, 133, 172, 215, 231, 263, 321, 325
Chronus, 303
Cohen, Stanley, ix

Creative Word, 5, 235. *See also* the Word.
Creator, 4, 9, 13, 37, 41, 50–51, 53, 55, 64, 66, 71, 73–74, 76–77, 82, 91, 99, 101–102, 122, 125–126, 131, 134, 136, 139, 146, 150, 153, 162, 166–167, 186, 201, 207, 216, 224–225, 227, 245, 248–249, 251, 279, 284, 286–287, 289, 296–297, 310, 313, 315, 320
Crown, 9, 19, 39, 51, 66, 77, 88, 127, 144, 148–150, 152–154, 159, 176, 187, 220, 231, 248, 250, 277, 289, 306, 326, 330
crown of the good name, 148, 159, 187, 231, 248, 277

Daa'th, 46, 60, 89
Daleth, xv, 18, 43–56, 60, 63, 65, 208, 266, 302, 314
dark night of the soul, xi, 4, 11, 17, 73, 86, 199, 229
death, 3–4, 38, 43, 50, 74, 87, 102, 107, 122, 160, 178, 183, 208, 219, 233, 241, 243, 245, 247, 259, 262, 278, 298
Dionysius, 248
Djed, xv, 195, 197
Djinn, 80–81, 153, 179, 181, 238, 243, 269, 285, 293, 296
Duat, 187

Echud, 5
Eden, 87, 102, 121–122, 146, 303

Elgar, Edward, 8
Elijah, 26, 150, 200, 267, 291
Epona, 277

Footprints in the Sand (poem), 143
Fortune, Dion, 321
Four Holy Creatures, 187, 226, 255, 269

Gabriel, 18, 26–27, 53–54, 56, 69, 80, 95, 109–111, 153, 224, 226, 235, 238, 243, 255–257, 267, 269, 285–286, 296, 298, 314
Gaia, 153, 225, 242
Geburah, 32, 102, 117, 160, 172–174, 187, 230, 321
gematria, 186, 198, 230
Gemini, 86, 323
Gentile, 3, 276
Gevurah. *See* Geburah.
Ghob, 80–81, 153, 180–181, 238, 243, 270, 285, 296
Gimel, 29–41, 46, 208, 266, 290, 312, 314
God, 1, 3–4, 9–10, 12–13, 15, 17, 19, 22, 24, 26–27, 37, 39, 43, 46, 53–55, 61–66, 68–70, 74, 76, 78–79, 81–82, 88, 91, 95–97, 100–101, 107, 116, 119, 124–125, 127, 129–132, 140–141, 143, 145–146, 148, 153, 157, 172, 178, 188, 192–193, 195, 197–200, 204, 207–208, 211, 216–217, 219, 222, 224–226, 230, 232, 234–235, 238–240, 247–249, 253–254, 257, 262–263, 267, 276–279, 286–287, 289, 293, 295–297, 299, 301–303, 307, 311–314, 324–325, 328–329
Godform, 6, 130, 264
Godhead, 4, 47, 124, 140, 250, 254, 290

Golgotha, 248
Govannon, 291
Grail, 39, 88, 131, 138, 264
Graves, Robert, 302
Great Plan, 33, 40, 65
Gurdjieff, 20

Hand of Fatima, 130, 133
Hashem, 9, 65–66, 101, 136, 144, 186, 219, 232, 248, 267, 282
Hathor, 86
heaven, 25–26, 82, 88, 91, 94–95, 164, 192, 195, 197–198, 200, 234, 254, 290–291, 295, 302, 314
Hebe, 264–265
Hebrew, 4, 19, 46, 49, 131, 149, 174, 199–200, 216, 290, 302, 323
Heh, 57–70, 74, 100–101, 103, 197, 202, 208, 217, 266–267, 314, 324
Heliopolis, 131
Henoch, 311
Hephasteus, 291, 302, 306
Hermes, 18, 248, 250
Higher self, 11, 20, 85, 90–92, 109–110, 125–126, 173, 187, 199, 207, 222
Hod, 172–174, 216, 230, 279, 290–291, 321
Horus, 89, 215

Isis, 89, 211, 217, 235, 242, 259

Jesus, xiii, 48, 99, 173, 302
Jew, 65, 145, 186, 198, 230
Jewish, 32, 46, 48, 88, 107, 144, 158–159, 186, 198, 276, 320, 323, 325, 328
Job, xv
justice, 6, 54, 90, 102–103, 117, 129, 136, 166, 187, 208, 231, 279

Kaph, 116, 141–154, 158, 161, 172, 187, 197, 208, 230, 261, 277, 290, 314
Kedushah, 263, 265
Kether, xviii, 7, 31, 33–34, 75, 89, 93, 127, 133, 144, 215, 263, 321
Khayyam, Omar, 45
Knight, Gareth, x, 146, 173, 187, 264, 303, 321
kundalini, 90, 117, 119, 124

Lamed, 155–167, 208, 302, 314
Lilith, 264–265
Lishkas Chashaim, 47
Longinus, 88
Lords of Form, 40
Lords of Light, 40
Lords of Mind, 40
Lucifer, 88, 145, 201, 249–250, 263, 277

Maggid, 172
Maid of Orleans, 235
Malech, 172
Malkuth, 32, 34, 75, 89, 172, 186, 263, 290, 303, 321
Maslow, Abraham, 21
Melech, 23–24, 172
Mem, 169–181, 187, 197–198, 209, 245, 247, 252–253, 290, 302, 314, 324
menorah, 26–27, 50, 80–81
Mercury, 18
Merkaba, 200
Mesopotamia, 47
Metatron, 153, 311–313, 325–326
Michael, 26–27, 53–54, 56, 69, 80, 95–96, 109, 111, 138, 152–153, 174, 199, 224, 226, 238, 243, 255–256, 269, 285–286, 292–293, 296, 298, 314, 325, 327–328
Middle Pillar, 5
Mishnah, 158, 329

Morpheus, 261
Moses, 117, 171–172, 174, 230, 232, 236, 290, 323, 327, 330
mudras, 132–133, 150
Munk, Rabbi M., 46, 102, 144, 158, 174, 186, 199, 302
Mysteries, xiii, xix, 4, 7, 18, 31–33, 47–49, 70, 74, 102–103, 115, 125, 130, 157, 211, 255, 264, 284, 286, 313

Narada, 259, 261
Nefesh, 60
neocortex, 90, 262
Nephilim, 249
Nephthys, 259, 261
Netzach, 146, 160, 172, 187, 230, 249, 263–264, 321
"Nimrod", 8
Nixsa, 80–81, 153, 180–181, 238, 243, 269, 285, 296
Nun, 130, 183–194, 197, 209, 245, 247–248, 253, 259, 261, 302, 314

Oak King, 48
Orpheus, 48, 235, 277, 306
Osiris, xv, 6, 48, 89, 101, 151, 159, 195, 235, 259, 280, 306

Paralda, 80, 152, 179–180, 238, 243, 269, 284, 296
Path of the Hearth Fire, 18, 74
peak experiences, 21–21, 275
Peh, 209, 227–243, 314, 324
Pentecost, 227, 230, 295
Pisces, 259, 261, 263
Pollux, 86
Poshut, 290
prayer, 3–4, 11–12, 17–18, 26, 31–32, 45, 51, 59–60, 73–74, 85, 91, 99, 106, 115–116, 119, 129, 138,

140, 143, 146–147, 157, 167, 171–172, 185, 194, 197–198, 213, 229–230, 247, 261, 275, 284, 286–287, 289, 295, 301, 315, 328
Prometheus, 48, 277, 279
Psalm, 7, 10, 25, 27, 38, 52, 67, 79, 94, 107, 123, 136, 205, 219, 238, 283
Psychism, 175

Qabalah, xiii, 32, 103, 146, 172–173, 199, 303, 321
Qoph, 209, 259–272, 276, 315

Raphael, 27, 53, 55, 68, 80, 95, 109, 111, 152, 224, 226, 238, 243, 255–256, 269, 284–286, 296–297, 313
Resh, 209, 273–286, 290, 315
Ritual, 11–12, 26–27, 32, 38–39, 53, 68, 80–82, 94, 107–108, 124, 130, 133, 137, 152, 158, 165, 173, 179, 191, 193, 206–207, 223, 238, 255, 269, 284, 296, 308, 313, 323–325, 330
Rosh Hashanah, 158
Ruach, 60

Samech, 107, 195–209, 252–253, 290, 305, 314
Sandalphon, 26–27, 150, 200, 325–326
Satan, 119, 201, 277
Scorpio, 187
Seneschal, 69
Sephira, 7, 19, 32, 36, 186
Sephiroth, 151
Servants of the Light School (SOL), ii, 159, 187, 276
Shekinah, 86, 199, 241, 254, 264, 290
Shema, 186, 328

Shin, 201, 209, 220, 230, 287–298, 315, 324
Shofar, 158
Silver Pillar, 5, 187
Solar Logos, 65, 153, 224, 239
Son(s) of the Morning, 40, 53–55, 88, 95, 109–111, 113, 117, 121–122, 249, 296
Sphere, 32, 46, 102, 173–174, 186, 199, 225, 230, 263, 277, 279, 291, 304
St. Christopher, 248
Supernals, 18, 32, 89, 133, 173, 186, 211, 213–214
Synagogue, 20, 199, 248, 265

Talmud, 46, 50, 148, 198, 329
Tarot, xiii, 5, 7, 20, 31, 34, 47, 49, 60, 62, 73, 75, 86, 99, 102, 119, 131, 146, 159, 173, 187, 198–199, 216–217, 231, 249, 263–264, 277, 279, 291, 303, 322
Tarot Trumps
    The Chariot, 99, 102–104, 106, 153, 200
    Death, 187, 231, 322
    The Devil, 73, 216–217, 219, 231
    The Emperor, 60, 249–250
    The Empress, 47, 49
    The Fool, 5, 7, 303
    The Hanged Man, 173–175
    The Hermit, 131, 163
    The Hierophant, 75
    The High Priest, 9, 75, 141
    The High Priestess, 31–35, 290, 302
    Judgement, 291
    Justice, 159
    The Lovers, 86, 263

The Magician, 20
The Moon, 35, 38, 54, 63, 89, 94, 108, 199, 204, 263, 296, 307, 323
The Star, 60, 63, 80, 152, 163, 223, 263
Strength, 3–4, 11–13, 95, 104, 121, 132, 139, 148, 163, 185, 199, 207, 222, 230–231, 252, 271, 294, 297
The Sun, 23, 57, 94–96, 105, 122, 127, 129, 153, 162, 167, 176, 190, 199, 202–203, 217, 222, 233, 269–270, 273, 277, 279, 281, 296, 298, 304–305
Temperance, 199
The Tower, 231, 277
The Wheel, 59, 146, 318
The World, 7, 9–10, 12–13, 19, 22, 31, 47–48, 57, 59, 74, 77, 110, 119, 126, 159, 165, 171, 177, 185–186, 195, 213, 216–217, 219–220, 222, 224, 229, 231, 243, 247–249, 253, 264, 284–286, 290, 303, 315, 320

Tau, 1, 3–4, 103, 117, 209, 299–317, 324
Tefnut, 131
Teth, 113–126, 187, 208, 314
Tetragrammaton, 4, 46, 62, 77, 230
Thanatos, 261
Tiphereth, 31, 33, 63, 89, 131, 160, 187, 199, 216, 226, 277, 321
Torah, 19, 50, 144, 198, 216, 314, 323, 327, 329
Tubal Cain, 249, 291
Tzaddi, 209, 245–257, 302, 314, 324
Tzaddikim, 248
Tzadoka, 116

Uriel, 3, 53, 55–56, 69–70, 80, 95–96, 110–111, 153, 225–226, 238, 243, 255, 257, 269, 285–286, 296, 298, 314

Vav, xv, 4–6, 18, 46, 71–82, 87–88, 100–101, 132, 144, 158, 161, 172, 186, 197, 208, 230, 299, 302, 314, 324
Virgo, 131

Wayland the Smith, 291
Weigher of Hearts, 119, 159
Western Mystery Tradition, xiii, xv, 4, 7, 18, 31–33, 47–49, 70, 74, 100, 102–103, 115–116, 125, 130, 133, 141, 151, 157, 160, 188, 211, 216, 225, 232, 243, 249, 255, 264, 284, 286, 313
Wilson, Colin, 20–21, 275
The Wisdom in the Hebrew Alphabet, v, 46, 174, 199
The Word, xiv–xv, xix, xx, 3, 5, 19, 46, 62, 65, 74, 91–92, 95, 103, 116–117, 131, 152, 158–159, 189, 197, 201, 204, 208, 214, 216, 230, 243, 248, 263–264, 268, 271, 290, 303–304

Yeshua, 33, 73–74, 85, 88, 186, 198–199, 233, 235, 291, 301
Yesod, 89, 132, 185, 199, 249, 279, 303, 321
Yggdrasil, 197
Yod, xv, xvii, 4–5, 32, 34, 60, 63, 65, 127–140, 159, 197, 208, 214, 216, 248, 253, 267, 293, 314, 324

Zayin, xv, 32–34, 83–96, 100–101, 103, 116, 186, 208, 214, 216, 314

To Write to the Author

If you wish to contact the author or would like more information about this book, please write to the author in care of Llewellyn Worldwide and we will forward your request. The author and publisher appreciate hearing from you and learning of your enjoyment of this book and how it has helped you. Llewellyn Worldwide cannot guarantee that every letter written to the author can be answered, but all will be forwarded. Please write to:

Dolores Ashcroft-Nowicki
℅ Llewellyn Worldwide
P.O. Box 64383, Dept. 0-7387-0186-6
St. Paul, MN 55164-0383, U.S.A.

Please enclose a self-addressed stamped envelope for reply, or $1.00 to cover costs.
If outside U.S.A., enclose international postal reply coupon.

Many of Llewellyn's authors have websites with additional information and resources. For more information, please visit our website at
http://www.llewellyn.com

To Order Llewellyn Books

Online: Visit our website at www.llewellyn.com, select your books, and order them on our secure server.

By Phone: Call toll-free within the U.S. at 1-877-NEW-WRLD (1-877-639-9753). Call toll-free within Canada at 1-866-NEW-WRLD (1-866-639-9753). We accept VISA, MasterCard, and American Express.